Praise for
The Trusted Advisor Fieldbook

"The groundbreaking book *The Trusted Advisor* has been hugely influential. Now, Charles Green and Andrea Howe have taken the ideas further and fleshed them out with a wealth of practical advice. For anyone whose business is based upon trust (and what business isn't) this book is essential reading."

—Neil Rackham, author of
SPIN Selling

"Trust will always be an important part of business (and life!), but Charles Green and Andrea Howe have put this book in your hands at the most important time. Get into this book, absorb the lessons, then live them. Your business might depend on it."

—Chris Brogan, president, Human Business
Works, coauthor of *Trust Agents*

"There are few who dispute the value of increasing trust. The question always comes down to 'how?' This book offers practical, hands-on advice on how to build trust with others. It's clear the authors have years of experience on the topic. They provide tremendous insight into an increasingly important attribute of the twenty-first century workplace."

—Ross Smith, Director of Test,
Microsoft Office Lync

"Charles and Andrea have dramatically changed the way consultants in my unit think about relationships. They have introduced a new vocabulary, mental models, and behaviors. I am confident that their *Trusted Advisor Fieldbook* will further accelerate the growth of our talent with this easy to use and comprehensive set of tools, models, and exercises. I know I too will be referencing the Fieldbook on a regular basis to reflect and hone my consulting skills."

—Leif Ulstrup, CSC, President,
Federal Consulting Practice

"Charles Green has spent much of his business career applying his considerable intellect to the science and discipline of trust. This understanding is combined with practical methods in *The Trusted Advisor Fieldbook*. These ideas and techniques have transformed the way I and our company approach prospects, clients, and work."

—Michael Colacino,
President, Studley

"Charles and Andrea cut to the chase on trust—the one thing you can't lead without. They have provided us with a hands-on, state-of-the-art look at building trust, which is the essential component for becoming valued leaders to our teams and true business partners with our clients."

—Gary S. Jones, Chief Human Resources Officer,
Grizzard Communications Group

The Trusted Advisor Fieldbook

A Comprehensive Toolkit for Leading with Trust

Charles H. Green
Andrea P. Howe

WILEY

JOHN WILEY & SONS, INC.

Published by John Wiley & Sons, Inc., Hoboken, New Jersey. Published simultaneously in Canada.

No part of this publication may be reproduced, stored in a retrieval system, or transmitted in any form or by any means, electronic, mechanical, photocopying, recording, scanning, or otherwise, except as permitted under Section 107 or 108 of the 1976 United States Copyright Act, without either the prior written permission of the Publisher, or authorization through payment of the appropriate per-copy fee to the Copyright Clearance Center, Inc., 222 Rosewood Drive, Danvers, MA 01923, (978) 750-8400, fax (978) 646-8600, or on the web at www.copyright.com. Requests to the Publisher for permission should be addressed to the Permissions Department, John Wiley & Sons, Inc., 111 River Street, Hoboken, NJ 07030, (201) 748-6011, fax (201) 748-6008, or online at http://www.wiley.com/go/permissions.

Limit of Liability/Disclaimer of Warranty: While the publisher and author have used their best efforts in preparing this book, they make no representations or warranties with respect to the accuracy or completeness of the contents of this book and specifically disclaim any implied warranties of merchantability or fitness for a particular purpose. No warranty may be created or extended by sales representatives or written sales materials. The advice and strategies contained herein may not be suitable for your situation. You should consult with a professional where appropriate. Neither the publisher nor author shall be liable for any loss of profit or any other commercial damages, including but not limited to special, incidental, consequential, or other damages.

For general information on our other products and services or for technical support, please contact our Customer Care Department within the United States at (800) 762-2974, outside the United States at (317) 572-3993 or fax (317) 572-4002.

Wiley publishes in a variety of print and electronic formats and by print-on-demand. Some material included with standard print versions of this book may not be included in e-books or in print-on-demand. If this book refers to media such as a CD or DVD that is not included in the version you purchased, you may download this material at http://booksupport.wiley.com. For more information about Wiley products, visit www.wiley.com.

Library of Congress Cataloging-in-Publication Data:

Green, Charles H., 1950–
　　The trusted advisor fieldbook : a comprehensive toolkit for leading with trust / Charles H. Green and Andrea P. Howe.
　　　p. cm.
　　Includes index.
　　　ISBN 978-1-118-08564-6 (pbk.); ISBN 978-1-118-16366-5 (ebk);
　　　978-1-118-16365-8 (ebk); ISBN 978-1-118-16364-1 (ebk)
1. Business ethics. 2. Trust. 3. Leadership—Psychological aspects.
　4. Interpersonal Relations. I. Howe, Andrea P. II. Title.
　　HF5387.G719 2011
　　658.4'092--dc23

　　　　　　　　　　2011028239

Printed in the United States of America.

V10017795_022520

To our wonderful significant others,
Judy and Alan, without whom
the book could not have been written.

Contents

List of Lists

Acknowledgments

This book clearly draws on *The Trusted Advisor*, which I (Charlie) coauthored with David Maister and Rob Galford. David was also greatly helpful in providing guidance early on.

We were helped immensely by a remarkable team of Trusted Revisors: Barry Edwards, Chris Brown, Ellen Lohsen, Gary Jones, Julian Powe, Linda O'Connor, Marisa Sanchez, Matt Swayhoover, Rich Sternhell, Sandy Styer, Scott Parker, Shawn Westfall, and Stewart Hirsch. The book also benefited editorially from the good people at John Wiley & Sons.

Our gratitude goes to those who contributed the stories and insights that make the pages come to life: Andy Lechter, Anthony Iannarino, Ava J. Abramowitz, Bill Green, Cary Paul, Cate Gregory, Chip Grizzard, Craig Leach, Gary Celli, Greg Pellegrino, Hazel Thompson, Ian Brodie, Jane Malin, Jim McCurry, John Edwards, L. J. Rittenhouse, Larry Friedman, Loreen Babcock, Lynn P., Mahan Khalsa, Neil Rackham, Pat Pannone, Paulo Novaes, Robert Porter Lynch, Ross Smith, Russell Feingold, Sally Foley Lewis, Sarah Agan, Shawn Westfall, and Sriram.

Special thanks to our Book Angel, Shaula Evans, and to Sandy, a.k.a. Attila the Honey, along with Kristin Abele and Tracey DelCamp for their unparalleled organization and encouragement, Justin Evans and the good people at Stress Limit Design for their dedication, Ian Welsh for his unsolicited generosity in a time of need, Patty Orsini for early thought development help, and Erik Hansen for his partnership in book promotion.

With appreciation to Andrea's stepfather, Tom Wolf, for the many hours spent at the kitchen table working on English papers; and to Charlie's dad, Thomas Green, who infected Charlie and others with curiosity.

Above all, thanks to our extraordinary clients, from whom we have learned all that we have managed to pass along.

Introduction

Why a Fieldbook

When my first book *The Trusted Advisor* was published in 2000, I (Charlie), along with my coauthors David Maister and Rob Galford, had no idea how many lives it would touch. To our delight, it has proven to be a perennial favorite for people in professional services. *The Trusted Advisor* is routinely recommended to and read by people at the middle manager, prepartner, and partner level in law firms, consulting firms, and accounting firms around the world. Much the same is true for industries like financial services, health care, architecture, and project management. In the decade since the book's release, tens of thousands of readers on every continent have gained insight into developing and maintaining trust-based relationships that are prosperous and rewarding. Yet, at the time we wrote it, none of us envisioned the impact the ensuing decade would have on the importance of trust in business and society at large. The case for trust is even more compelling than we had imagined.

The Trusted Advisor, for all its virtues, did not address how to apply the principles, models, and practices to sales—which I subsequently wrote about in *Trust-Based Selling*. What was now needed, I felt, was a more detailed how-to guide for people in *any* professional role. This latter need is met by this fieldbook, a hands-on addition to *The Trusted Advisor* and *Trust-Based Selling*.

> Your success as a leader will always be based on the degree to which you are trusted by your stakeholders.

Andrea P. Howe joins me to bring you *The Trusted Advisor Fieldbook*. It is the culmination of what Andrea and I have learned from working specifically on the subject of trust, with national and global leaders. Andrea brings the expertise she has gained in her 20 years in consulting, including five years working with me at Trusted Advisor Associates. Together, we speak in concrete terms about how to dramatically improve your results in sales, relationship management, and organizational performance.

Who Should Read this Book

The Trusted Advisor Fieldbook is a practical guide to being a trusted advisor for leaders in any industry. Being trusted is a leadership quality that is neither cyclical nor faddish nor role-bound. Whether you are a business developer, account manager, salesperson, project manager, program manager, unit leader, team leader, client relationship manager, C-level executive, consultant, or manager, your success as a leader will always be based on the degree to which you are trusted by your stakeholders.

In this book, you will find answers to pervasive questions about trust and leadership—such as how to develop business with trust, nurture trust-based relationships, build and run a trustworthy organization, and develop your trust skill set. Put the knowledge and practices in this fieldbook to work, and you will become someone who earns trust quickly, consistently, and sustainably—in business and in life.

How to Use this Book

This pragmatic workbook is one you will want to reference again and again. The term *fieldbook* connotes a practical, dog-eared manual that you can keep in your laptop bag as an instant helper. It delivers everyday tools, approaches, exercises, resources, and actionable to-do lists for the wide range of situations that you will inevitably encounter. Each chapter offers specific ways to train your thinking and change your habits in order to earn the trust that is necessary to be influential, successful, and known as someone who makes a difference.

The book is meant to be applied to the myriad stakeholder relationships in your life. As such, we've deliberately used the word "partner" as a term for anyone with whom you endeavor to build trust: clients, customers, buyers, prospects, colleagues, vendors, and more.

Throughout the book, you will find the following aids:

> The best way to use this book is to get messy with it. Highlight your favorite passages. Fill out the worksheets. Complete the quizzes. Bend the corners of the pages you want to come back to. Wear it out!

- *Self-administered worksheets* and *coaching questions* that provide immediate insights into your current business challenges.
- *Real-life examples* that demonstrate proven ways to walk the talk.
- *Action plans* that bridge the gap between insights and outcomes.

The best way to use this book is to get messy with it. Highlight your favorite passages. Fill out the worksheets. Complete the quizzes. Bend the corners of the pages you want to come back to. Wear it out!

Where to Begin

While *The Trusted Advisor Fieldbook* is not meant to be read in any particular order, you may find it helpful to peruse the first two sections before flipping to pertinent sections that speak to your situation today. If you have any doubts about the business case for trust, start with Chapter 28, "Making the Case for Trust."

- *Read Section I, "A Trust Primer," to get grounded in the fundamental truths of trust and trustworthiness.* You will learn the fundamental attitudes of trust and trustworthiness, the dynamics of influence, and the essential frameworks and skills for building trust.
- *Study Section II, "Developing Your Trust Skill Set," to increase your self-awareness and self-efficacy in the five essential trust skills.* It provides practical details and helpful exercises to help you pinpoint where you need to grow.
- *Use Section III, "Developing Business with Trust," when you want to up-end the traditionally adversarial relationship between buyer and seller, client and consultant, influencer and influencee.* Using real-life examples in a "Dear Abby" format, this section explores a full range of business development challenges, from before the first client meeting all the way to expanding the sale once the deal is done.
- *Turn to Section IV, "Managing Relationships with Trust," to find out how to overcome your ego.* It's true what the cartoon character Pogo famously said: "We have found the enemy and it is us." This section delves into the ins and outs of relationships—from better navigating organizational politics to building trust remotely to dealing with difficult partners who present themselves as aloof, disorganized, inappropriate, or simply untrustworthy.
- *Consult Section V, "Building and Running a Trustworthy Organization," to discover the four shared beliefs that contribute to every organization's success.* This section addresses major questions of implementation that arise, including how to create a culture of trust, build trust in teams, ease the tension between the long-term nature of

trustworthiness and the urgency of quarterly measures, and how to train for trustworthiness.

If we have erred in any way, it is on the side of giving you too much, rather than too little. There is a lot to digest, so zero in on what resonates most for you today. Leave the rest for now—it will be here when you need it later.

Cheers!

Charles H. Green
Andrea P. Howe

A Trust Primer

U.S. Supreme Court Justice Potter Stewart once despaired of defining obscenity, but noted pointedly, "I know it when I see it." Trust is much the same. People know when it exists and when it doesn't, but cannot explain why or how it exists. And the concept of building trust seems even harder to describe, let alone implement.

We have made it our life's work to better understand trust. Before we can discuss trust, however, we begin by putting it in context—without context, there is just theory and no practical implications. We could have simply suggested you do this or do that to build trust. That would only get you so far.

So we begin with a primer. This first section defines the key terms and concepts of our trust framework. We walk you through the difference between trusting and being trustworthy, along with other fundamental truths about trust. We also explore the dynamics of influence, which are important to grasp if you wish to consistently lead with trust.

Three frameworks will help you create personal and organizational trust:

- Attitudes—mind-sets or beliefs that provide fertile soil for trust.
- Models—three simple structures for understanding and applying trust.
- Essential Skills—the indispensable abilities and capacities of trust building.

With this solid foundation, you will be well equipped to put the practical tips, strategies, and best practices of later sections to work.

Fundamental Truths

Building trust can be a surprisingly simple thing—yet it is anything but easy. Trust is a complex concept in human relationships. It is often misunderstood, even though it is something practiced somewhat unconsciously all the time. We intend this book to do double duty: to give you practical, commonsense advice, while at the same time allowing you to think critically and speak fluently about trust.

In this chapter we take aim at the complexities of trust, breaking it down so that it can be managed and more readily increased. We take a critical look at the paradoxes, dynamics, and language of trust. We explore maxims, such as "Trust is personal," "Trust takes time," and "There is no trust without risk." We also describe the relationship between trust and influence and reveal the key that unlocks the mystery to being influential.

Fundamental Truth 1: Trust Requires Trusting and Being Trusted

Too often people use the word *trust* when what they mean is something else. In plain language, people talk about trust*ing*—being willing to take a risk. People also talk about being trust*ed*, or being trust*worthy*. When one person trusts and another is trustworthy, there is trust.

It is important to remember the distinction between trusting and being trustworthy. Usually, leading with trust requires you to focus on being trust*worthy*. However you cannot avoid occasionally having to do the trust*ing*.

Fundamental Truth 2: Trust Is Personal

When trust is discussed, it usually refers to people. Yes, you can trust a company, but when you do, you are typically focusing on just one part of trust—dependability. It makes perfect sense to say a company or organization is dependable or reliable. It does not make much sense to say that a corporate entity has your best interests at heart or is sensitive to your needs, or is discreet. Those are things you would usually say about people.

Even when it does make sense to say an organization is credible or careful or focused on your interests, the reference is usually to the people in it. At root, trust is personal.

From the Front Lines: Trusting the Taxi Driver[1]

During a trip to Denmark, I (Charlie) took a taxi from my hotel to the local train station. The fare was 70 kroner (about 15 U.S. dollars). I gave the driver a 200-kroner note. He gave me back 30 kroner change. Clearly something was wrong.

I realized I had three options for dealing with this little unpleasantness:

1. I could assume the taxi driver made a mental slip, and politely point with a smile at the note that was still in his hand, so he would notice his error.
2. I could assume he was trying to cheat me—but since he still had the 200-kroner note in his hand, I could just sternly point to it, and let him pretend it was an honest mistake.
3. I could assume he was trying to swindle a foreigner, and respond in anger: "You're short, buddy; give me the other 100, and you can forget about a tip."

I went with option one. I noted my suspicions, but chose not to act from them. The driver quickly gave me the extra 100 kroner back with a smile as if to indicate, "Oops, my mistake," and I chose to believe him.

The thing about trusting is that it's catching. The way you behave toward others influences the way they respond back to you. Whether you expect the best or the worst of people, you'll almost always be right.

—Charles H. Green

Fundamental Truth 3: Trust Is about Relationships

That trust is about relationships seems an obvious point. Yet many people in business slip all too easily into self-absorption by focusing in ways that take their attention away from the person whose trust they are looking to gain. There is no such thing as a *solitary* trusted advisor—the term itself implies a relationship.

A major factor affecting trustworthiness is the issue of whether you are self-focused or other-focused. A great phrase to remember is this: "It's not about you." If you can remember that, then you will always remember trust is about relationships.

Fundamental Truth 4: Trust Is Created in Interactions

You will not become a trusted advisor through great marketing programs, great presentations, or even great blogs or tweets. Trust is created in your exchanges with others—especially one-on-one. That requires mastering the art of conversation, which you will learn to do using the Trust Creation Process: Engage, Listen, Frame, Envision, and Commit.

Fundamental Truth 5: There Is No Trust without Risk

Ronald Reagan, the fortieth president of the United States, was known to quote a Russian proverb, "Trust, but verify." For our purposes, the opposite is true. Real trust does not need verification; if you have to verify, it is not trust.

Insight: The Three Ps of Trust

The Three Ps represent the core of our thinking on trust. This mnemonic device is designed to help you remember them:

1. Trust is Personal.
2. Trust is Paradoxical.
3. Trust is Positively correlated to risk.

Ready to start your new trust-based mind-set? Mind your Ps.

Sometimes businesspeople forget this and try to ameliorate or mitigate all risks. This is particularly true in professions like law, finance, or banking. But the essence of trust contains risk. A trust relationship cannot exist without someone taking a chance—and it is your job to lead the way. If you think, *I can't take that kind of risk yet because there's not enough trust in the relationship*, check your thinking. It is the very *taking of risks* that creates trust in the relationship.

Fundamental Truth 6: Trust Is Paradoxical

Over and over again, you will discover that the things that create trust are the opposite of what you may think. That is why we say trust is paradoxical—in other words, it appears to defy logic. The best way to sell, it turns out, is to *stop trying to sell*. The best way to influence people is to *stop trying to influence them*. The best way to gain credibility is to *admit what you do not know*.

The paradoxical qualities of trust arise because trust is a higher-level relationship. The trust-creating thing to do is often the opposite of what your baser passions tell you to do. Fight or flight, self-preservation, the instinct to win—these are not the motives that drive trust. The ultimate paradox is that, by rising above such instincts, you end up getting better results than if you had striven for them in the first place.

Fundamental Truth 7: Listening Drives Trust and Influence

One of the most important drivers of influence, says Robert Cialdini,[2] is reciprocity—the tendency to return a favor. If you do X for me, I will do Y for you. The inverse is true as well: If you do not do X for me, I will not do Y for you.

Reciprocity in trust-based relationships begins with listening. Listening is the skill that drives trust and influence. If you listen to me, I will listen to you. If you do not listen to me, I will not listen to you.

Fundamental Truth 8: Trust Does Not Take Time

Contrary to popular wisdom, people make serious judgments of trust very quickly. Trust is a mix of the rational and the emotional and snap emotional judgments are commonplace. People decide almost instantaneously whether they trust you—without much proof.

The one exception is trust-as-reliability. Since reliability requires the passage of time to assess, that kind of trust necessarily takes time: others—not so much.

CASE STUDY

From the Front Lines: The Power of Personal Connection

Larry Friedman, former Executive Vice-President at Gallagher Benefit Services, one of the largest employee benefit agencies in the northeast United States, tells a story of going beyond professional boundaries to make a difference for someone in a very personal way.

"My client, Harold, and I happened to have a meeting several years ago in the January time frame. Harold and I had known each other professionally for over 20 years. During that time, he had progressed from bookkeeper to controller to CFO. My guess is that during these years he had also maintained a steady weight of 270 pounds—a lot for his 6-foot frame.

"It was a new year and I was focused on my own goal-setting for the year. It suddenly occurred to me to ask Harold about his goals. He said he wanted to take the weight off in a healthy way, once and for all.

"We created a structure, right then and there, to help him meet that goal. We wrote it down and reviewed his progress monthly. He joined a weight loss program, discovered he liked going to the gym, got a personal trainer, and worked out regularly.

"Then he mentioned that he had been running regularly on a treadmill. I had been a runner for many years. I found a five-kilometer race near Harold's home, and said, 'If you sign up, I'll not only help you train for it, I'll run it with you.' He had never run that far in his life.

"I suppose it would have been easy to say, 'I'll be rooting for you. Call me and tell me how it went.' But I really wanted to do it with him. It was risky for both of us: risky for me to offer, and risky for him to accept.

"He did accept my offer. When the race day arrived, he was determined to run it, not walk it. I ran next to him the whole way, and we finished the race together.

"To this day, Harold still runs, takes long walks with his wife, and has maintained a healthy weight for more than three years. In fact, this year he ran a 5K race on his own while raising money for a cause that he believed in. He's a client for life as a result of our experience together. More importantly, he's a friend for life.

"I have always believed that if I could help someone get more of what's important to him as a person, then everything else will take care of itself. I don't know *how* that happens—I'm not that scientific about it—but I believe it. I always taught people at Gallagher that when they build a personal relationship, it affects their business relationship, too. New or sustained business is a nice byproduct. The ultimate 'win' is making a difference for people."

—*Larry Friedman (former Executive Vice-President, Gallagher Benefit Services)*

Fundamental Truth 9: Trust Is Strong and Durable, Not Fragile

It's often said that trust takes a long time to build, but only a moment to destroy. This is something of a myth. The propensity to trust others is a character trait derived from our upbringings, and it changes very slowly. When people lose trust in other people or institutions, it is roughly at the same level and pace that trust was built. Where trust is lost quickly, it often wasn't deep trust to begin with. And when we deeply trust people, we are slow and loath to give up on them.

Fundamental Truth 10: You Get What You Give

Trust is a relationship characterized by reciprocity. If Person A trusts Person B, the odds are that Person B will behave in a more trustworthy manner than if Person A is suspicious of her. Leaders who are willing to trust their followers produce more trustworthy teams. Followers who are willing to trust their leaders invite them to live by a more trustworthy standard.

In the realms of buyers and sellers, clients and professionals, bosses and subordinates, this reciprocal relationship is particularly clear. If you listen to others, they are more likely to listen to you. If you take a risk, you increase the odds of a risk being taken in return. If you share personal information, chances are your partner will share in kind. While it may sound like a New Age mantra of some kind, "you get what you give" is an accurate description of human nature—and of successful business relationships.

These 10 fundamental truths are embedded in this book. They foundationally describe how we have come to think about trust.

Worksheet: Your Truths about Trust

What's true for *you* about trust?

_____

_____

_____

_____

What trust maxims do you live by?

_____

_____

_____

_____

Which maxims serve you well? In what ways?

_____

_____

_____

_____

Which maxims are limiting? In what ways?

_____

_____

_____

_____

Fundamental Attitudes

This chapter explores five attitudes that provide the foundation for building trust. These attitudes arise from the fundamental truths about trust explored in Chapter 1, and in turn inform the specific trust skills we will explore in Chapter 5. Understanding and adopting these attitudes will increase your success in your efforts to build trust and lead with trust.

Being trustworthy requires more than following a behavioral checklist—it demands getting right the underlying attitudes, mind-sets, outlooks, and ways of thinking. Adopt them, and you will find the behaviors come far more naturally and with less difficulty. In contrast, if you jump ahead to skills, tips, and tricks, you will be working the hard way. Get the attitudes right, and the actions will follow.

Fundamental Attitude 1: Principles over Processes

Processes are important to business life—without them, wheels would constantly be reinvented. Leaders do not want a client-facing consultant to stare off into space when asked what his firm does, nor a receptionist to improvise when answering a phone call. Processes are a form of routine that foster consistency, scale, and a host of other benefits.

Insight: Trust-Building Is Learnable[1]

"You can communicate your intent without even saying a word. When people can sense that your intent serves their best interests, they are willing to open the trust valve at least a little. If that little bit is rewarded, they can risk a little more, and so on. If the risk is continually rewarded, trust grows. Of course, as you well know, all the hard earned work can vanish suddenly if the bond is broken. So constant attention to language and behaviors is critical—and learnable, and improvable."

—*Mahan Khalsa (author of Let's Get Real or Let's Not Play, and partner, ninety five 5)*

The limitation of processes is they do not give you much guidance when *new* situations arise. Your firm may have a sales process that says, "Don't mention price until you've discussed value." But what do you do when a potential client says, "Will you please just tell me the price?" before you have had an opportunity to talk about value?

A process rarely contains the metacode to determine when to ignore the process. Yet that is the sort of judgment required by trusted advisors. When do you deviate from the agenda? Do you or do you not continue a conversation that turns personal? How do you respond to anger? How firmly do you stick to a point of negotiation in the face of resistance? How important is it to hold that first transcontinental meeting in person?

There are a near-infinite number of such situations—certainly more than one can write processes for. And the more exceptions that must be made, the more processes must be written to deal with the exceptions, up to a point of diminishing returns of complexity at which point someone has to resort to principles.

Trust-based relationships cry out for principles. A role that can be completed largely or wholly from processes alone is not a role that requires much trust. By contrast, a role that is defined by gaps, questions, and risks is a role that requires flexibility. Principles are tools of maximum flexibility—the Swiss Army knife of your toolkit.

The key to making principles work is to *remember to use them*—to be constantly conscious of them and apply them in all situations, large and small. Bring them to bear in staffing, pricing, interviewing, negotiating, deal-making, networking, marketing, planning, business development, and more—in other words, *live* the principles in all your interactions.

CASE STUDY

From the Front Lines: A Dropped Connection[2]

Our colleague Hazel Thompson in Australia tells about what happens when you forget to check in.

"Recently I met a CEO from an ASX top 200 company (our Aussie version of DJI or FTSE 100) at a social event. I had gotten to know him through my work with a Big 4 firm. Our conversation turned to the partner who had completed much work for his company—let's call the partner Joe.

"I asked, 'Have you seen Joe recently?'

"He replied to the effect of, 'I haven't heard from Joe for a couple of years. He must be too important to contact me nowadays.'

"Joe had since taken on very senior roles within the firm, and even though the comment was meant in jest, there was a tone of underlying disappointment. I'm sure they had spent many hours together, probably talking not just about work, but about personal issues as well, developing intimacy over time.

"Now in the rearview mirror of time, this CEO may have come to believe that the care shown at the time by Joe was not authentic, and that it was used only as self-interest to gain revenue.

"Because I know Joe, I am confident that his care and engagement was genuine—but that didn't change the CEO's perception or his sense of disappointment.

"This conversation reinforced for me the value of the simple 'checking in' call as a way to maintain long-term connections."

—*Hazel Thompson (Trusted Advisor Associates, Australia)*

Fundamental Attitude 2: You Are More Connected than You Think

The word *relationship* is usually used to refer to a direct connection or association. You have an obvious relationship with your friends and family. You probably also use the word *relationship* to describe the connection between you and your coworkers, and with some of your customers and suppliers.

Most would say you *do not* have a relationship (in the direct sense) with people in a far-off division of your company, or with potential customers, or strangers. Most of you also would not assert this kind of relationship with competitors.

The fundamental attitude of "You are more connected than you think" invites you to redefine your notion of relationship to include *everyone*. Why? Because leading with trust requires an expansive view of relationships. If the number of relationships available to you is infinite, not finite, then there is no reason to operate out of scarcity. If your primary purpose is to support a greater good, then it becomes possible to focus on an agenda larger than your own.

Fundamental Attitude 3: It's Not about You

The concept of self-orientation is so fundamental to being a trusted advisor that it is enshrined as the denominator in the Trust Equation, a tool we share in detail in Chapter 4, "Three Trust Models." For now, let's define self-orientation as our tendency to view events and actions in the world as being about us.

An old *Peanuts* cartoon showed Charlie Brown observing two girls talking at a distance from him. After a while, he approaches and says accusingly, "You girls were talking about me, weren't you!"

The girls reply, "No, we weren't." Charlie Brown returns to his distant post, and the girls go on talking.

After a while, Charlie Brown returns to them and says, "How come you girls never talk about me?"

Charlie Brown was exhibiting a classic case of self-orientation. It is not the same as selfishness—it is more about self-preoccupation, self-obsession, self-absorption. All humans are self-oriented, much of the time. An infant is extremely self-oriented, viewing all that happens around it as a response, or lack of response, to the infant itself. In some ways, growing up is about learning that not everything is about you.

Both being trusted and having your advice accepted require that you recognize that not everything you hear, everything that is said, everything that happens, is about you. Take the example of someone who appears to be angry with you, going so far as to yell at you in your face. Instead of taking it personally, assume that the person is *not* angry with you, but rather is an angry person who happens to be standing in close proximity to you. This mental disassociation makes it possible to spend less time managing your own reaction and more time being present for another.

So the next time you are preparing for a difficult meeting, take a quiet moment and say to yourself, *Let me check my ego at the door, and simply be there to help others as best I can.*

Fundamental Attitude 4: Curiosity Trumps Knowing

A state of curiosity builds relationships. It is intrinsically other-focused—its purpose is discovery. If you are constantly curious about your clients, customers, prospects, peers, leaders,

From the Front Lines: Building Trust by Design[3]

An architect who often gives away his professional expertise as a volunteer on projects, Pat Pannone is sometimes asked by fellow volunteers to do architectural work for them. About a year ago, one of them invited Pat to design a home renovation.

The renovation was a big job: building a master suite. A job this size was something Pat enjoyed doing, and the fees would more than address some expenses that came with his newborn son.

Pat looked at the house and asked to see the attic. It had a large vaulted ceiling and was used for storage. He said he'd be happy to design what they wanted, but perhaps they should consider having the attic converted into the master suite, and save themselves a lot of money. He suggested that they move their bedroom furniture there for a couple of weeks just to test it out.

The result is they loved it. No need for major work. No need for an architect. No fee for Pat.

Pat's response to losing? He felt great about it. He could have done what the client originally asked and designed the addition. Instead, he was creative and thoughtful.

Some people are afraid of losing fees, especially when the fee will put food on the table. Pat had other work, so maybe *fear* is too strong a word. But he definitely wanted that new project. Pat's choice to let go of that desire for the sake of the client is a great example of low self-orientation.

If Pat had been worried about making sure he got that fee, he might not have seen the easy, low-cost solution for his client.

The story doesn't end here. A few months later, that same couple called him again. This time, they were buying a new property, and needed an architect for a job that would not be solved by moving furniture into the attic. And they wanted Pat because they knew he would put them first.

—*Pasqualino "Pat" Pannone (architect), as told to Stewart Hirsch*

suppliers, even your competitors, then you are always poised to learn, to create connection, and to positively influence others. By contrast, being in a state of *already knowing* leads to narrow focus, disconnection, and worst of all, arrogance.

People admire those who are comfortable exhibiting curiosity—who are okay with not knowing certain things, and confident in their ability to phrase questions about those things in socially acceptable ways. For example, "Susanna, maybe you went over this earlier and I missed it—why is it that the average age in the shipping department seems so much higher than in procurement?" Any fear of appearing stupid or unprepared is subordinated by a desire to learn. Any desire to show off what you know or prove your worth is trumped by a genuine interest in another.

Curiosity also requires that you be open and *aware*. If you are walking through a customer's distribution center for the first time, you have a wonderful opportunity to *notice*. You can notice whether things are busy or not, whether workers seem harried or comfortable, whether things look organized or chaotic, how old the technology is, how the center is laid out, what the overall vibe is, and so on.

If you are *incurious*, you may focus on only those things that impact *you*—the sound of your heels clicking on the floor, the temperature, the echo in the room. Or you may be oblivious, immersed in thoughts about the meeting you are coming from or going to, or on what you should have said in the conversation with your significant other last night. Curiosity is fostered by being in the moment, focusing your thinking on the situation at hand.

Being curious is enabled by good planning. To strengthen your curiosity muscles, do some homework. Force yourself to sit down regularly and define a list of questions you wish you knew the answers to—then set about asking them, over time. Planning for curiosity leads you to spend some time simply *wondering* about other people; acting on curiosity allows you to engage with them. That combination of planning for and acting on curiosity dramatically improves your relationships.

Fundamental Attitude 5: Time Works for You

The felt boundaries of time are everywhere: quarterly earnings, quotas, budgets, New Year's resolutions, metrics, return on investment (ROI) calculations, Gantt charts, goals. We will call this time-based thinking. There is nothing wrong with time-based thinking per se. It helps gauge progress, to review and evaluate, to achieve consensus. But all too often it steers you in the wrong direction.

Time-based thinking goes awry when instead of using it to *measure* reality, you use it to *control* reality. A classic example is the quarter's-end push to close more deals, meet the quota, and make your projections. Such pressure is self-focused, not other-focused; it is solitary, not collaborative; and it is quintessentially short-term, not medium- to long-term focused.

If your thoughts and actions are being driven by time in this sense, then time is your master. If time is imposed externally, for some opaque purposes, it is not in service to a trusted relationship.

Changing your relationship to time has many benefits: You will rarely feel panicked, you will remain committed—but not attached—to goals and measures, and you will never feel alone. Instead, you will treat time as another aspect of a shared journey with your customers, colleagues, and other partners.

Worksheet: Attitude Is Everything

For each fundamental attitude, reflect on how this attitude is present (or not) in your day-to-day interactions with others. Jot down examples of how your actions align with each attitude, and examples of how they do not align.

	How Your Actions Align	How Your Actions Do Not Align
Principles over processes		
You are more connected than you think		
It's not about you		
Curiosity trumps knowing		
Time works for you		

What do you notice as a result of answering these questions?

The Dynamics of Influence

The "advisor" aspect of "trusted advisor" serves a critical business function: fulfilling the promise of providing expertise in a way that makes a difference. Effective advice-giving is part art, part science, and mostly nonrational. How we listen to others matters much more than what we say. This paradoxically has the result of making others more likely to listen to us. The act of listening itself creates relationship and trust. This chapter explores three steps to being more influential. It also offers a five-point checklist for influencing meetings.

Have you ever had the experience of not having your advice taken? Let's say you are very confident about your advice—you know the right thing to do on a given issue. Let's even say that you are, in fact, right. You advise your partner to do the right thing, and ... your partner chooses another option.

It may even happen to you on a regular basis (especially if you have teenagers at home). To understand why this happens, we need to look more closely at the interplay of trust and influence.

Trust and influence go hand in hand. The more someone trusts you, the more likely he is to be influenced by you. The less someone trusts you, the less likely he is to be influenced by you. In the business of advice-giving, it is not enough to be right—you have to *earn the right* to be right.

> In the business of advice-giving, it is not enough to be right—you have to earn the right to be right.

Earning the Right to Be Right: Three Steps

The key to getting your advice taken has little to do with the content of the advice you give and everything to do with the context of how you listen to others. Fundamentally, you earn the right to be right by listening first. The *act* of listening itself creates relationship and trust. This sounds straightforward enough in theory; in practice it is more challenging.

Let's look at how this works. Here are three steps to being more influential:

1. Change the way you think about how people think.
2. Understand an important driver of influence: reciprocity.
3. Do a better job of listening, not a better job of making your case.

> ### CASE STUDY
>
> ## From the Front Lines: The Business Value of Empathy[1]
>
> When a Midwestern U.S. office of a global accounting firm was informed by a major client that the audit work would be going out to bid, the partners were shocked. "We hadn't seen it coming," said one partner, "and they were very clear that this was final." They were given the opportunity to bid as a nicety. The client organization clearly intended to change auditors.
>
> "We decided that, if there were ever a time where not to take a risk was too risky, this was it. We decided to do something dramatic."
>
> Instead of using their 90 minutes of presentation time to do a conventional presentation, the four partners decided to act out a play for the four client executives from the finance organization. The roles they assumed: those very client executives having a meeting, deciding to fire their auditor. In other words, the four partners role-played the very clients sitting in front of them deciding their fate.
>
> They said things like, "Well, those audit folks just haven't showed us that they have what it takes." "That's right, they haven't been proactive enough." They articulated the critical thoughts that they imagined the client was thinking—humbly and genuinely.
>
> "We were prepared to get yanked out of there in two minutes," said one partner. "And, in fact, after five minutes, we stopped and asked them if they wanted us to stop. But they were fascinated; they asked us to keep going. And we did, for nearly an hour. We just kept talking—as if we were the client—about the things that we had done wrong and should have done better. And the client listened."
>
> Here's the dramatic ending to the play: the decision to put the work out to bid was rescinded, and the firm got the job back. Why? Because the audit partners had been able to prove they understood their clients' concerns—in a dramatic and effective demonstration of empathy. They showed they had finally been listening. As a result, they won the right to try again.
>
> *—As told to Charles H. Green*

Step 1: Change the Way You Think about How People Think

There is a fundamental error in the way people *think* that people think and make decisions.

Most people believe that decision-making is a rational process of accumulating facts, applying logic, and coming out with some variation of the truth (Figure 3.1). This is an oversimplified description, yet more often than not it is the operating model that gets applied in business and in life. As a result, there is an overreliance on rational methods when trying to be influential: pro-con analyses, appendices with backup data, and lengthy PowerPoint decks.

You may be among those people who pride themselves on their ability to have a ready answer for any objection or concern that their presentation raises: point, counterpoint.

> Human beings make complex decisions all the time in manners that are extremely difficult to model in cold, clear, rational terms.

Figure 3.1

How People Think People Think

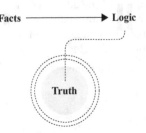

From the Front Lines: Decisions Aren't Just Rational

Russell Feingold, now of Black & Veatch, recalls an early-career sales win.

"The client was a large electric utility in Hong Kong, and the project was complex. My company invested considerable time preparing our proposal, responding to questions, and meeting with the client face to face in Hong Kong. We won the project.

"However, it was during our working lunches that I really won the client's trust—by my proficiency with using chopsticks. Quite simply, my clients appreciated my respect for their tradition, when even their own children were turning to Western ways of eating. To this day I believe my ability to use chopsticks not only ingratiated me with our client for the remainder of the project, but was a deciding factor in our being selected in the first place."

—Russell Feingold (Black & Veatch)

Unfortunately, these efforts are misguided. Human beings make complex decisions all the time in manners that cannot be modeled in cold, clear, rational terms.

This does not mean decisions are made *irrationally*—it simply means that decisions are usually made *nonrationally*. People buy with their hearts, and then rationalize their choice with their minds. The data matter ... secondarily.

> One of the most important drivers of influence is reciprocity. To put it simply, reciprocity is the tendency of human beings to want to return a favor done for them.

Whatever your role is, you are selling *something*: a product, a program, an idea, a recommendation, an opinion—in short, you are trying to influence another to adopt your advice. And to influence effectively, you must redirect your efforts from convincing the other person's intellect to winning the other person's heart.

Step 2: Understand an Important Driver of Influence: Reciprocity

Robert Cialdini is a well-known psychologist who has spent 35 years researching the power of persuasion, including three years going undercover to observe real-life situations. As a result of his lifelong work, Cialdini identified six factors of influence—none of which has anything to do with intellectualizing or logic.[2]

According to Cialdini's research, one of the most important drivers of influence is reciprocity. To put it simply, reciprocity is the tendency of human beings to want to return a favor done for them.

> To influence effectively, you must redirect your efforts from convincing the other person's intellect to winning the other person's heart.

In business, reciprocity plays out in the form of listening. Others will be open to your thoughts, perspectives, and point of view once they feel they have been fully heard and understood by you. Conversely, people will not accept what you are offering if they do not feel understood by you. And the way you give others the experience of being heard and understood is by listening.

So much for thinking that rational argument—which requires a lot of talking—is what really matters.

Step 3: Do a Better Job of Listening, Not a Better Job of Making Your Case

Practically speaking, if others are not taking your advice as often as you would like, it will not help to build a better business case—you probably need to do a better job of listening first. Listening creates reciprocity in the relationship, which naturally leads to a willingness and openness to ideas.

> Your ability to listen with empathy directly drives your ability to be influential.

Furthermore, the *quality* of your listening matters. John Gottman, well known for his work on marital stability, states, "It is not enough for you to listen to another—you have to let your partner know that you fully understand and empathize." Your partner has to have the experience of being listened to. You do not determine whether you have listened well—your partner does.[3]

To be trusted and to have influence require mastery of a skill known as empathetic listening—a kind of listening that leaves people feeling completely understood, comfortable, and safe. Your ability to listen with empathy directly drives your ability to be influential. (For more details on how to listen with empathy, see Chapter 6: "Listen".)

A Five-Point Checklist for Influencing Meetings

Influencing by listening is not easy for most people. Business people in particular are well trained to think in linear terms, to believe in persuasion by PowerPoint, and to count on the power of logic. So when we say, "To influence, you must listen," it may sound like, "In order to do something, don't do anything." This is particularly evident in meetings. How can you redirect your can-do, get-results attitude to one of subtle influence that is gained by sitting back and listening?

Insight: Empathy Is the Life Blood of Influence[4]

Empathetic listening is the key to being influential. It's not enough to be smart and well-researched and just plain right, even (especially) when you have the evidence to prove it. You have to earn the right to be right. Others will listen to you—be open to your advice, to your point of view, to your perspective—once they feel they have been fully heard and understood by you. And they really do have to feel it. Here's another way of saying it: It is not enough for you to get them; they have to *get* that you get them.

This is precisely where empathy gets left out of the usual business conversation, because getting others requires more than taking good notes, or periodically pausing to summarize the content of their communications; it means you have to tune into the music (tone, mood, emotion) as well as the words, and then reflect it all back accurately and frequently enough that you get some kind of cue that you're doing a good job of relating to the entirety of their world.

Thomas Friedman hit the nail on the head when he said, "It's not what you hear by listening that's important; it's what you say by listening that's important." Friedman was talking about empathy.

The answer is this: practice.

Here is a five-point checklist for being more influential in meetings:

1. Before you enter the meeting, take one minute to *prepare your mind*. We recommend you:

    - *Quietly detach from the outcome.* Accept that your partner may not accept your advice. Loosen your grip on the results. You have done all the prep work. As good golfers say, "Trust your swing."
    - *Remind yourself that the ultimate objective of the meeting is to improve your partner's situation, as well as the relationship between you.* Period.
    - *Be willing to be influenced in the process.* Be open to ideas, collaboration, and the learning that results. Allow yourself to be confidently vulnerable.

2. *When you state your point of view during a meeting, state it crisply and simply.* Do not take much time. Do not overstate. Keep it simple and to the point.

3. *Spend the majority of your time listening.* Cultivate an attitude of curiosity about what is being said and what is coming next. Remember that the act of listening requires what may feel like inaction on your part. You will know you have listened well when others naturally turn the conversation back to you ("Bob, what do you think?").

4. *When you get the cue that it is your turn to be listened to, be sure to build on what has been said.* Words like "the problem with that is …" or "the only issue with that approach is …" or "I understand, but …" are negating, not validating. Instead, use the "Yes, and" approach. Lead with what you liked about what you heard, make linkages, expand ideas. (For more about "Yes, and …" see Chapter 8, "Improvise.")

    If you have concerns, express them separately and with curiosity. Use words like, "I think you're on to something important about the performance specs. I wish I knew how to deal with the level of risk implied by raising the specs. Would you share with me your thinking on that?"

5. *When the conversation begins to conclude, summarize the outcome with your partner.* If you are mutually pleased, congratulations—you have done well. If you are dissatisfied, go back to point 2—state your point of view and listen more.

Worksheet: Learning from Role Models

Bring to mind someone whom you consider remarkably influential—someone who succeeds at getting the best result for all parties while cultivating a strong relationship in the process.

My model influencer:

What makes this person so effective? What does she think, say, or do?

_____

In what ways do you consistently apply the same best practices your role model applies?

_____

What opportunities do you see to improve your ability to be influential?

_____

Worksheet: Putting the Dynamics of Influence to Work

Bring to mind an upcoming opportunity to be influential with one or more people. Describe it briefly, and then use the questions below to prepare for your interaction.

Opportunity:

_____

What will help you detach from the outcome and remind yourself that the ultimate objective is to improve your partner's situation, as well as the relationship between you?

_____

What point of view are you bringing to the interaction? State it crisply and simply.

_____

What are you curious about? What questions might you ask to thoroughly understand and appreciate the perspectives of the other(s) with whom you will be in conversation?

_____

In what ways can and will you be open to be influenced in the process? What might you learn? What could you discover that might alter your feelings or your point of view?

_____

As a result of this preparation, how will you approach this opportunity differently from the way you have in the past?

Three Trust Models

The three trust models provide a powerful framework for creating personal and organizational trust. The first model, the trust equation, divides trustworthiness into four components: credibility, reliability, intimacy, and self-orientation. The second model, the trust creation process, describes how trust is built in conversations. The third model, the trust principles, provides a set of values to guide organizational decisions and individual action. This chapter explores these fundamental ideas, which we refer back to throughout the course of this book.

Most people know trust when they see it, but have no idea why trust exists where it does or what happened when trust is lost. Based on our work with professionals around the world, we have distilled our core thinking on trust into three trust models. These three models provide the organizing frameworks for being personally and organizationally trustworthy:

1. *The trust equation* lays out the four components of trustworthiness.
2. *The trust creation process* shows how to build trust in conversations.
3. *The trust principles* provide a set of values to guide organizational decisions and individual actions.

Together, these three trust models, Figure 4.1, provide the theoretical foundation for leading with trust. The rest of this book makes frequent reference to these models.

Model	Description	Sample Uses
Trust equation	An analytical model of the components of trustworthiness	When you know something is missing from a relationship but you're not sure what it is
Trust creation process	A depiction of how trust is built in conversation	When you are preparing for a conversation and your goal is to be influential
Trust principles	A set of values to guide organizational decisions and individual action	When you want to establish a culture of trust in a team or organization

Figure 4.1

Using the Three Trust Models

The Trust Equation

Trust is a two-sided relationship: One person trusts, and the other person is trusted. While trusting and being trustworthy are related, they are not the same thing. The trust equation is about trustworthiness: It provides a model for the person who wants to earn and deserve trust.

In everyday speech, the word *trustworthy* is used in a range of contexts. In reference to your business interactions, your partners may use it to evaluate the quality of what you say. They may also use it to describe what you do. They can use it to describe whether they feel comfortable sharing certain information with you. And they use the same word to indicate whether they feel you are prepared to put their interests above your own.

Those four aspects of trustworthiness can be collated into four variables: credibility, reliability, intimacy, and self-orientation. They cover most of the meanings of trust in everyday business interactions, and they have been combined in the trust equation (see Figure 4.2, The Trust Equation).

To put it simply, when you increase credibility, reliability, and intimacy (the factors in the numerator), your trustworthiness increases. The flipside is that when you increase your level of self-orientation (the denominator), you *decrease* your trustworthiness.

Note that to be exceptionally trustworthy requires good scores on all four variables in the equation. The more consistent your trust variable scores are, the higher your overall trust quotient. An even blend of the four trust variables is the ideal, as high standard variations among the four variables have been found to be correlated with lower trust quotient scores.

> The more consistent your trust variable scores are, the higher your overall trust quotient.

Let's look closely at each variable.

Credibility

Credibility means more than having good credentials. Credibility generally has to do with your *words*. It is derived from what you know, as well as how you communicate. Credibility includes your honesty and your presence. Someone might say about you, "I can trust what she says about intellectual property. She is very credible on the subject." (Figure 4.2.)

The more obvious ways to boost your credibility include:

- Develop deep expertise in your industry.
- Stay current with industry trends and business news.
- Offer your point of view when you have one.

Unexpected ways to increase your credibility include:

- Be willing to say "I don't know," when "I don't know" is the honest answer.
- Express passion for your subject.
- Communicate with self-assurance: a firm handshake, direct eye contact (when culturally appropriate), and a confident (not arrogant) air.

Figure 4.2

The Trust Equation

$$T = \frac{C + R + I}{S}$$

T = Trustworthiness

C = Credibility   I = Intimacy

R = Reliability   S = Self-Orientation

Reliability

By contrast, reliability typically has to do with *actions*. A colleague might say about you, "If he says he'll deliver the product tomorrow, I trust him, because he's someone who does what he says he will." Reliability is rooted in consistency, predictability, and a feeling of familiarity. Reliability brings with it a certainty that people know they won't be surprised by you—they get what they expect from you.

Examples of ways to boost your reliability include:

- State expectations up front and report on them regularly.
- Make lots of small promises and consistently follow through on them.
- Be on time (as culturally appropriate).
- Communicate if you fall behind, and take responsibility for it.
- Use others' language, templates, dress code, and so on, respecting their norms and environment.

Intimacy

Intimacy is a key part of the trust equation, though it can be a shocking word to use in the business world. It refers to the safety that you feel when entrusting someone with something. A colleague might say about you, "I can trust her with that information—she's never violated my confidentiality before, and she would never embarrass me."

Some ways to promote intimacy in a relationship are:

- Listening beyond another's words by tuning in to the music of her communications such as tone, emotion, and mood, and then acknowledging those elements out loud.
- Telling someone what you really appreciate about him, rather than keeping it to yourself.
- Using a person's name.
- Sharing something personal about yourself—it makes you human and far more interesting.

Insight: Impeccability Is the Key to Reliability[1]

Here's the rub of reliability: Consistency matters. But don't let that daunt you. The key to achieving it is aiming for impeccability, not perfection.

What's the difference?

Let's envision Perfection and Impeccability as two characters in a play. Where Perfection is determined with gritted teeth to always get it right, Impeccability is determined to be thorough and complete. Where Perfection endeavors to never make a mess, and experiences distress when the inevitable occurs, Impeccability recognizes that all humans make mistakes and chooses to see the inevitable as an opportunity to build trust. Perfection constantly feeds a need to satisfy something internal and self-oriented. Impeccability, on the other hand, is other-oriented at the core; his motivation is the satisfaction that comes with being of service and making a difference.

Even Perfection agrees that Impeccability is much more pleasant to be around. Impeccability is much easier to relate to. He endeavors to do his best and humbly accepts that he will fail at times. He cleans up his messes with transparency, swiftness, and an appropriate amount of lightheartedness. Impeccability recognizes that all humans make mistakes and chooses to see the inevitable as an opportunity to build trust.

The risk required to build trust in the first place typically shows up in the intimacy variable (see Chapter 9, "Risk").

Self-Orientation

The variable most people identify as a significant opportunity for improvement in the trust equation is self-orientation. For this reason, it is deliberately placed in the denominator position to highlight its ubiquity.

Simply defined, self-orientation is about focus, more specifically, *who* you focus on—yourself or others. If your partner can say, "I trust that she cares about me and how this project will impact my career," then you have a low level of self-orientation. And that's good.

Alternatively, if your partner says, "He cares about his reputation," "He cares about getting the sale," or "He is focused on getting ahead," then you have a high level of self-orientation or Big S. And that's bad.

Take the stereotypical used car salesman as an example. He is misleading, in it for himself, and armed with manipulative tactics to get his customers to do what he wants. He obviously displays classic Big S behavior. Most of us aren't like that. Most of the time, self-orientation sneaks into interactions with others in more subtle, insidious ways. For example:

- Rushing to a solution.
- Hoarding information, resources, and ideas.
- Talking a lot.
- Subtly competing for attention and recognition.

Strategies to lower your self-orientation include:

- Taking the time to find the best solution.
- Sharing time, resources, and ideas.
- Asking lots of questions from a place of curiosity to figure out what success for your partner really looks like.
- Negotiating for a true win-win.
- Listening even when it is uncomfortable to be silent.
- Speaking hard truths, even when it feels awkward to do so.
- Giving your partner the credit.

Paradoxically, what helps the most in lowering self-orientation is self-awareness. The better you know your own quirks and foibles, the more you can work every day to manage them and focus on others. (See Chapter 10 "Know Yourself.")

The Two Biggest Levers: Intimacy and Self-Orientation

People working to increase their trustworthiness generally devote more time and attention to improving their credibility and reliability variables because it is easier to figure out what to

---

Insight: Fear Makes Your S Look Big[2]

Self-orientation, which we like to call your "S," rears its ugly head most often when you feel some sort of fear: fear of looking bad, fear of rejection, fear of loss. All of these fears are perfectly normal. And they are what makes your S look big.

What makes a difference is having the ego strength to see the fear, acknowledge it, "get off your S," and move on. After all, obsessing about Big S mistakes is just more Big S.

do about them. Unfortunately, these efforts are misguided because most professionals are already strong in these areas. On average, the greatest strength for participants taking our Trust Quotient Test is reliability. As of 2010, for 53 percent of respondents, reliability is the highest (or tied for the highest) variable.

> Herein lies your greatest opportunity for distinguishing yourself in the realm of trustworthiness: Increase intimacy and lower self-orientation.

In contrast, intimacy and self-orientation have the lowest overall component scores; only 28 percent of respondents lead with each of these areas. Herein lies your greatest opportunity for distinguishing yourself in the realm of trustworthiness: Increase intimacy and lower self-orientation.

The Trust Creation Process

Trust doesn't just happen—it gets created at the individual level, between people, usually through conversations. The trust creation process is a five-step model that describes how it works: engage, listen, frame, envision, and commit, "ELFEC" for short. (Figure 4.3.)

1. *Engage (E)*—offer something of value in an open discussion about issues key to the other.
2. *Listen (L)*—hear what is important and real to the other and earn the right to offer solutions.
3. *Frame (F)*—state the root issue in terms acceptable to both, using caveats, problem statements, and hypotheses; take personal risks to explore sensitive issues in depth; articulate a point of view.
4. *Envision (E)*—define an alternate reality or to-be state of affairs, including win-win descriptions of outcomes and results along with emotional states.
5. *Commit (C)*—jointly articulate actionable next steps that imply commitment and movement on the part of each party.

The order in which these steps occur in a conversation has as much impact as the steps themselves. That is, you could do a wonderful job of framing the issue or on the commitment to action, but if you do them before you have adequately listened, then the trust process breaks down or freezes.

The importance of the sequence of steps becomes clearer when we translate the trust creation process into a sales context, as follows:

- *Engage:* "I hear X may be an issue for you. Is that right?"
- *Listen:* "Gee, that's interesting. Tell me more: What's behind that?"
- *Frame:* "It sounds like what you may have here is a case of Y."
- *Envision:* "How will things look three years from now if we fix this?"
- *Commit:* "What if we were to do Z?"

By far the most powerful step in the trust creation process (and the least practiced) is the listening step. The two most common errors in practice are inadequate listening and jumping too

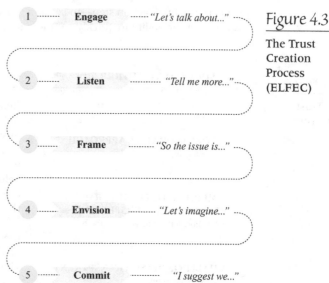

Figure 4.3

The Trust Creation Process (ELFEC)

1 ---- **Engage** ---- "Let's talk about..."

2 ---- **Listen** ---- "Tell me more..."

3 ---- **Frame** ---- "So the issue is..."

4 ---- **Envision** ---- "Let's imagine..."

5 ---- **Commit** ---- "I suggest we..."

CASE STUDY

From the Front Lines: Client Focus and Long-Term Orientation[3]

Ruben Vardanian, Chair and CEO of Troika Dialog Group, the oldest private investment bank in Russia, tells a story of pioneering trust principles in the Russian banking industry in the early nineties:

"We put forward three principles in 1991, which continue today in our business. First, we said we are long-term oriented, which was quite unusual in Russia, especially at that time. The second principle says we are a client-service company. It's unusual to explain in Russia that you are a client-service company, because client service was never a key aspect of our country; industrial production was the key .... Our proprietary position was very small [at that time], and I continued telling my people, 'We are servicing the client.' It's a very important point, which again, in the 1990s, was not so obvious when everything was unstable, and nobody cared about the client. The third principle was this: I said to myself, 'I want to respect myself, and I want to respect my people, my country, my competitors, my clients.' So I want to build this respect, and I want people to enjoy working together. It took us a lot of effort to convince people to trust each other in business, because the level of trust in Russia in the 1990s was very low, when the old system collapsed. Building a partnership in Russia, where nobody believed in partnership, was a challenge.

"I wanted to change that perception: that you can trust a 24-year-old Armenian guy and operate in a professional, international way. I think it was good motivation for all of us to try to convince people this was possible."

Troika Dialog is now the largest private investment bank in Russia, with core lines of business in capital markets, investment banking, asset management, and alternative investments.

—*Ruben Vardanian (Chair and CEO, Troika Dialog Group, Russia)*

quickly to the final, action step—to commit. This can pose a big challenge as most have been rewarded for the ability to quickly get the right answer.

Figure 4.4

The Trust Principles

1 A **FOCUS ON THE OTHER** for the other's sake, not just as a means to your own ends.

2 A **COLLABORATIVE APPROACH** to relationships.

3 A **MEDIUM- TO LONG-TERM RELATIONSHIP PERSPECTIVE,** not a short-term transactional focus.

4 A **HABIT OF BEING TRANSPARENT** in all your dealings.

The Trust Principles

Being or becoming trustworthy cannot be reduced to pure behaviors. Your actions are driven by your beliefs, and your beliefs are driven by your values or principles. Trustworthy behavior is far too complex to fake without beliefs and values behind it. If your values don't drive you to behave in a trustworthy manner all the time, you will be found out quickly.

Hence, the trust equation and the way you use the trust creation process are really just outcomes of the principles you hold, the trust principles. The way to become trusted is to act consistently from those principles. (See Figure 4.4.)

We have found it useful to focus on four specific principles governing trustworthy behavior:

> If your values don't drive you to behave in a trustworthy manner all the time, you will be found out quickly.

1. *A focus on the other*[4] *for the other's sake, not just as a means to your own ends.* In business, the terms *client-focus* or *customer-centric* are commonplace. But these terms are all too often self-serving—they intend to be of economic benefit to the seller. Ultimately all successful relationships must be equally valuable for both parties, which will happen when you *start* with the interests of the other party. Lead with other-focus, not self-focus. Bona fide other-focus requires mindfulness, compassion, patience, and generosity.
2. *A collaborative approach to relationships.* Collaboration here means a willingness to work together to create both joint goals and joint approaches to getting there. Think of your interests as intertwined with others' interests. Don't wonder what others are thinking— ask them. Keith Ferrazzi's brilliantly titled book, *Never Eat Alone*,[6] is a good reminder to be continually aware of opportunities to collaborate.
3. *A medium- to long-term relationship perspective*, not a short-term transactional focus. Focusing on relationships nurtures transactions, whereas focusing on transactions chokes off relationships. Never make one sale, one deal, one transaction in isolation—always make them in a broader context, acting and thinking that this is but one moment in an ongoing relationship. The most profitable and rewarding relationships for both parties are usually those where multiple transactions over time are assumed in the approach to each transaction.
4. *A habit of being transparent in all your dealings.* Instead of implicitly treating information on a need-to-know basis, start with the assumption that all information should be shared. Make exceptions to this rule only if sharing the information would be illegal or injurious. Transparency increases credibility and lowers self-orientation by its insistence on keeping no secrets.

Applying these principles to all of your actions will develop the most trusting relationship possible. Of course, it is easy to nod your head in agreement with these right-sounding principles, while actually acting on them consistently is tough for most of us. There is often a vast difference between espoused principles and lived principles.

> Focusing on relationships nurtures transactions, whereas focusing on transactions chokes off relationships.

Here are some examples:

You claim you are customer-focused and yet you …

*   Define problem statements that overtly or covertly blame the other party for the problem.
*   Get tentative about suggesting additional work you could do.

Insight: Thinking about Others[5]

"'Other side' implies the people are *opponents*. 'Other' implies they are *just not us*. It is hard to build common ground with opponents, but a bit exciting, invariably challenging, and sometimes even fun to build common ground with people who, although they want a solution to a shared problem as much as we do, view that problem differently because they have different sets of eyes and experiences. A small change in mind-set, but it's an important and useful one to use and remember. Not a friend. Not an enemy. Just an Other."

—*Ava J. Abramowitz (lawyer, mediator, and author of Architect's Essentials of Negotiation)*

- Set a goal to double revenue in an account. (Imagine sitting down with a client and leading with: "We want to double what you're paying us!")

You claim you are collaborative and yet you ...

- Don't present your ideas until they are fully formed and polished.
- Secretly love to win arguments.
- Practice sales techniques like "Always Be Closing."

You claim you think in the long term and yet you ...

- Set up projects and relationships in ways that are not sustainable. (Litmus test: Ask yourself if you would do it the way you've done it another 100 times.)
- Make a bad first deal just to get in the door. ("We'll fix it later.")
- Hoard work for yourself when, if you were really honest, you would admit that a competitor could do a better job.

You claim you are transparent and yet you ...

- Say things to yourself or to each other that you don't/won't say to your clients.
- Avoid delivering bad news.
- Cover up or downplay mistakes so as not to make others uneasy.

Of course, you are not alone—we all fall short of these principles with some regularity. The key is to continually strive to make progress toward these principles.

CASE STUDY

From the Front Lines: Living the Principles

Ian Brodie, who specializes in marketing and sales advice for consultants, coaches, and other professionals, tells a story that illustrates the difference between intentions and impact.

"Back in '98, I was working in the Netherlands; part of my role was to lead a series of workshops with the executive team to develop their strategy. My colleague was a real expert but badly organized. And to be frank, that's not one of my strong points either.

"We ended up doing the prep very late. For one workshop in particular we were brainstorming in the bar at 2:00 A.M. The next day the client's executive team was excited about the possibilities we'd discussed. Great result. With one exception.

"I had a partner on the client side I was supposed to be working with to develop the strategy and prepare the workshops. The next day in the workshop he'd been quietly embarrassed that he didn't know what we'd prepared.

"He was quite blunt with me afterward: 'We were supposed to prepare that workshop together. You said when we started this project that you weren't like other consultants—you'd work in partnership with us. But you're just like all the others.'

"It didn't matter that we'd had a great result, or that there was no malicious intent. We'd promised we'd work together and we didn't. We'd let him down. He no longer shared his opinions or his insights and we suffered because of that.

"Others can't see your intentions—they can only see your actions. My intention was to be a great collaborative partner. My actions excluded him and told him I was working in my own interests.

"Here's the bottom line of what I learned that day: It's important to *live* the principles all the time."

—Ian Brodie (Ianbrodie.com, United Kingdom)

Worksheet: Use the Trust Equation to Transform
Your Relationships

Bring to mind a key stakeholder (e.g., client, prospect, colleague, staff member) with whom you'd like to have an improved—or even transformed—relationship.

My stakeholder:

Now score yourself in that relationship, using a scale of one 1 to 5, on each of the four variables of the Trust Equation. How credible does your stakeholder perceive you to be? How reliable? Intimate? Focused on him or her?

In the numerator, 5 is your highest score and 1 is lowest; in the denominator, 1 is your highest score and 5 is lowest.

$$\frac{C + \quad R + \quad I}{S}$$

Next, do the math: What is your Trust Quotient for this relationship? Plot it on the spectrum below. (Note that the median is skewed left. So of a possible .6 – 15, if you score a 7, that's actually very good.)

<------------------------->
.6 lowest   highest 15

For each variable where your score is relatively high (4 or 5 for credibility, reliability, and intimacy, or 1 or 2 for self-orientation), what contributes to your success?

_____

_____

_____

_____

For each variable where your score is relatively low (1 or 2 for credibility, reliability, and intimacy, or 4 or 5 for self-orientation), in what ways might you close the gaps?

_____

_____

_____

_____

_____

Tip: Share your assessment with your stakeholder and get her feedback.

Worksheet: ELFEC in Action

Reflecting on and studying the conversations you are having is a great way to increase your awareness about trust. Begin by thinking of a recent conversation with a key stakeholder.

My stakeholder: _____

Engage. How did you begin the conversation?

_____

_____

Did you offer something of value?	☐Y ☐N
Did you set a tone of openness for the conversation?	☐Y ☐N

In hindsight, what could you have said that might have been more engaging?

_____

_____

Listen. What kinds of questions did you ask to elicit information?

_____

_____

Looking back, were your questions open (as opposed to leading)?	☐Y ☐N
Did your questions elicit information about the rational *and* emotional reality of your stakeholder?	☐Y ☐N
Did you regularly summarize or paraphrase what you heard?	☐Y ☐N
Did you acknowledge out loud what you heard in the music of your stakeholder's communication (tone, emotion, mood)?	☐Y ☐N

In hindsight, what could you have asked or said that might have demonstrated that you were listening more deeply?

_____

_____

Frame. What did you say to frame the issue?

_____

_____

_____

If risks were required to frame the issue honestly and accurately, did you take them?

☐Y ☐N

Did you articulate a point of view?   ☐Y ☐N

Did you get confirmation that you had framed the issue appropriately?   ☐Y ☐N

In hindsight, what could you have said that might have framed the issue more effectively?

_____

_____

Envision. What did you say to move the conversation to the Envision stage?

_____

_____

Did you vividly describe the to-be state of affairs?   ☐Y ☐N

Did you include both emotional and rational aspects of the to-be state? ☐Y ☐N

In hindsight, what could you have said that might have been more effective at this stage?

_____

_____

Commit. What did you say to invite a commitment to take action?

_____

_____

Did you get a commitment to move forward, in some way?   ☐Y ☐N

Were the next steps clear and agreed-to?   ☐Y ☐N

Did they require movement for both parties?   ☐Y ☐N

In hindsight, what could you have said that might have elicited more satisfying results?

_____

_____

Tip: Solicit feedback from a colleague who was present for the conversation—or even better, from the actual stakeholder—to test the accuracy of your self-assessment.

Tip: Video or audio-record an actual conversation, or a mock conversation. Use this worksheet to debrief it.

Worksheet: Living the Principles

For each trust principle, reflect on how you live by this principle (or not) in your day-to-day interactions with others. Jot down examples of how your attitudes and actions align with each principle, and examples of how they do not align. Use the examples in this chapter to guide your reflection.

Trust Principle	How Your Attitudes and Actions Align	How Your Attitudes and Actions Do Not Align
A focus on the other for the other's sake, not just as a means to your own ends.		
A collaborative approach to relationships.		
A medium- to long-term relationship perspective.		
A habit of being transparent in all your dealings.		

Five Trust Skills

There are five skills of trustworthiness that underpin everyday actions: the abilities to listen, partner, improvise, risk, and know yourself. They improve with focus and practice, and yield greater rewards as you get better at them; over time, they become natural and instinctive behaviors. We refer back to these skills in the specific strategies and best practices for leading with trust throughout the rest of this book.

Aristotle suggested that excellence is but a habit. He meant that excellence is not something we are born with, or inherit, or are given. Excellence consists in doing the excellent thing time after time, until it becomes ingrained in your behavior. And then people call you excellent.

Trust skills, likewise, are not fixed at birth, though your upbringing may have had some influence. And they are not fixed later in life: you can improve at them—or choose not to. Leading with trust is largely a matter of doing the trustworthy thing time after time, until it becomes ingrained in your behavior, at which point people consider you a trusted advisor. See Figure 5.1.

The five trust skills share several characteristics:

- *They can appear elementary.* You might dismiss them as being too apparent to merit your attention. ("I've been in sales for twenty years—I know how to listen by now!") Breathing is basic too, but we shouldn't take it for granted.
- *You can practice them,* and you should, over and over. They are what scales are to a concert pianist.
- *They are linked.* Improvisation requires risk, partnering requires listening, and all of them require knowing yourself well enough to be effective.
- *Their effect increases when combined with attitudes.* How much deeper is your listening when you are motivated by curiosity, rather than by self-interest? How much richer is your collaboration when based on service rather than ego?

Listen

Almost everyone in sales, consulting, or general business knows the importance of listening. And most (certainly us) still have room to improve. Here's a bold assertion: The kind of listening that

> Here's a bold assertion: The kind of listening that most people consider to be high order listening or active listening is insufficient when it comes to building trust.

Figure 5.1

Five Trust Skills

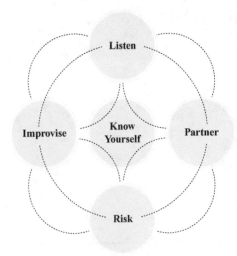

most people consider to be high order listening or active listening is insufficient when it comes to building trust.

The kind of listening that engenders deep trust is not listening to identify needs or to mine for data to justify your pitch, recommendation, or opinion. What we are talking about is empathetic listening, where the focus is actually on the act of listening itself. When you are fully engaged in the act of listening itself, your partner experiences it as an act of respect.

Empathetic listening matters because empathy is the foundation of influence. It is not enough to be smart and well-researched, or to be right—even when you have the evidence to prove it. You have to earn the right to be right. Others will listen to you and be open to your advice, your point of view, and your perspective once they feel they have been fully heard and understood by you.

> When you are fully engaged in the act of listening itself, your partner experiences it as an act of respect.

Partner

The metaphor of dancing partners is perfect for trust-based relationships. It conjures up images of give and take, synchronization, graceful movement, and being in step and in tune with one another.

CASE STUDY

From the Front Lines: *Apollo 13*: Heroes in Action[1]

Our colleague Sandy Styer recounts an incredible story of high-stakes collaboration.

"'Houston, we've had a problem' are the famous words uttered by Jim Lovell in the *Apollo 13* space mission, when both the flight's oxygen tanks failed, stranding the crew 200,000 miles from Earth with dwindling supplies of electricity, light, and water.

"The 1995 movie based on the event features a powerful scene where Flight Director Gene Kranz, played by Ed Harris, assigns teams to create emergency scrubbers to save the astronauts from dying of carbon monoxide—using only the gear the astronauts had on board.

"The backroom experts at Mission Control weren't worried about career-limiting moves, one-upmanship, or even being on the winning team that engineered the solution. They were focused on just one thing: How do we bring these guys home?

"In their moment of truth, they listened, they improvised, and they partnered to solve the problem under incredible duress and brought the *Apollo 13* crew home safely, transforming the likelihood of the worst disaster NASA had ever faced into its finest hour."

—Sandy Styer (Trusted Advisor Associates)

Someone who partners well:

- Maintains a mind-set of collaboration, not competition.
- Works from a position of equal status.
- Is willing and able to both lead and follow.
- Balances assertiveness and cooperation.
- Deals with disagreements and missteps productively and gracefully.
- Demonstrates a commitment to sharing responsibility for achieving a goal.
- Takes responsibility for her role in the partnership's successes and failures.

Partnering, like nearly everything that relates to being a trusted advisor, is simple but not easy. There are specific personal traits, habits, and mind-sets that make the act of partnering difficult from the outset. Fortunately, there are also ways to improve your ability to partner.

Improvise

The business world is rife with the unexpected, including uncomfortable, awkward moments that inevitably occur at the worst possible times in your business relationships. We call these moments of truth—when something happens and suddenly it feels as though you are alone on a sinking ship with no life preserver.

The skill of improvising is what will get you out of a difficult spot and turn a crunch or a crisis into an opportunity. Moments of truth are inevitable, and how you handle them says a lot about what you are made of. Being effective in a moment of truth demands a new way of thinking and being.

You can get better at improvising by practicing improvisation—practicing being quick to respond, offering "yes, and" responses, subordinating your ego in the interest of collaboration, and giving up looking good in exchange for being real.

Risk

There is no deep trust without risk. Yet most of us worry about doing something that feels risky, like speaking a hard truth or sharing something personal, because we don't think we have enough trust in the relationship for that risk to be tolerated. The irony is that it is the very act of taking those risks that creates trust. And trust, in turn, is a fabulous risk-mitigation strategy. Think about the risks associated with a project gone wrong and how those risks are diminished when there are solid relationships to fall back on.

When you take risks you:

- Act proactively to reduce ambiguity.
- Acknowledge uncomfortable situations out loud.
- Deliver hard news promptly and concisely.
- Take responsibility for mistakes.
- Are willing to express emotions.
- Share something personal.

All these actions will go a long way in building trust-based relationships.

Know Yourself

Introspection is a distinguishing trait of a trusted advisor. Introspection does not imply narcissism or self-obsession. In fact, the more self-aware you are, the lower your self-orientation tends to be.

> There is no deep trust without risk.

Blind spots interfere with your ability to be true to yourself in your everyday life. What keeps you from being your best self? Examples might include:

- You don't realize the full extent of your need to be liked, which interferes with your willingness to say something unpopular, which, in turn, lowers your credibility.
- You are unaware of your strong internal drive to achieve, moving too quickly from listening to commitment, thus rushing the process of trust-building.
- You don't grasp your fear of appearing unprepared, which prevents you from engaging in the messiness that the best collaborations usually require.

To know yourself is to have a full and complete inventory of your weaknesses, triggers, and hot buttons, as well as your strengths, interests, and sources of passion and purpose. Knowing yourself is not meant to serve the goal of being perfect, or even striving to be. It is about achieving a level of self-awareness that is required for good self-management. Armed with this knowledge, you can make choices that align with your positive traits and devise strategies for dealing with your weaknesses, such as surrounding yourself with people who compensate for your shortcomings. In the next five chapters, we explore each of these trust skills in greater detail, and provide you with specific strategies to develop them and put them into action.

Insight: The Key to Skill Mastery[2]

"Deliberate practice, while not a particularly sexy phrase, is the term commonly used in the science of expert performance to describe the single most common and powerful attribute of top-flight performance in almost any field. It contends that the *quality* and *quantity* of mindful practice and application is what separates star performers from the decent, average, and poor performers. (Geoff Colvin's *Talent is Overrated* is a good read on this topic.)

"Deliberate practice is not ordinary practice. As Edward Deming once said, 'It is not enough to do your best. You need to *know what* to do and then do your best.' So the quality of the practice and application is as important as the quantity of practice—and the quantity is essential.

"What I find liberating and motivating about the research is that everything, repeat *everything*, we need to do in order to get really good at sales is learnable—if we are willing to practice. It doesn't have to do with our DNA, our native IQ, our personality type or social style, our years of experience. If we are willing to engage in a high number of repetitions of quality practice we can become as great as we want to be. That's powerful."

—*Mahan Khalsa (author of Let's Get Real or Let's Not Play, and partner, ninety five 5)*

Worksheet: Your Trust Skills: A Self-Assessment

Knowing your own strengths and weaknesses is the first stop on the road to improving your trust skills. Try rating yourself on each of the five trust skills presented in this chapter.
- Score yourself toward the right side of the scale if you identify the trust skill as a natural or developed strength that you consistently bring to your relationships.
- Score yourself toward the left side of the scale if you are less developed or inconsistent in that area.

I bring this skill to my relationships:				
	Seldom	Occasionally	To a Considerable Degree	Almost Always
	1	2	3	4
Listen. An ability to listen with empathy, with a focus on the act of listening itself.	☐	☐	☐	☐
Partner. The ability to give and take, be in sync, move gracefully, and be in step and in tune with another.	☐	☐	☐	☐
Improvise. The ability to be quick to respond, offer "yes, and" responses, subordinate your ego in the interest of collaboration, and give up looking good in exchange for being real.	☐	☐	☐	☐
Risk. The willingness and ability to tolerate ambiguity and exposure.	☐	☐	☐	☐
Know Yourself. The ability to be introspective about weaknesses and strengths, and maintain a level of self-awareness that is required for good self-management.	☐	☐	☐	☐

Choose one skill where you gave yourself a 3 or 4. In what ways do you demonstrate this strength? What contributes to your success?

_____

Choose one skill where you gave yourself a 1 or 2. What makes it challenging for you to apply this skill?

_____

What did you learn about yourself as a result of this exercise?

_____

Tip: Share your assessment with a trusted colleague to get her perspective and feedback.

Developing Your Trust Skill Set

When it comes to trustworthiness, both mind-sets and skill sets matter. On the one hand, the right attitude without the right skills makes for great intentions with unpredictable results. On the other hand, skill mastery without the right mind-sets leads to superficial finesse at best, and manipulation at worst.

This section defines five skills that complement the mind-sets discussed in *Section I: A Trust Primer:* the abilities to listen, collaborate, improvise, risk, and know yourself. This section provides practical details and exercises to help you practice and master these skills. Throughout the rest of this book we refer back to these skills in the specific strategies and best practices for leading with trust.

Listen

Listening serves a far greater purpose than gathering information—it paves the way for you to be more influential. Listening requires adeptness at tuning in to others as well as expressing yourself on multiple levels. The payoff is a far greater likelihood of the other person listening to you.

This chapter explores empathetic listening in depth and introduces a tool—three-level listening—for putting it into practice. We also offer practical advice on how to listen masterfully in a variety of business settings, including one-on-one and group interactions.

In the business of advice-giving, recommendation-making, idea-offering, or selling, it is not enough to be right—you have to *earn the right* to be right. Others will listen to you, and be open to your advice, point of view, and perspective once they feel they have been fully heard and understood by you. Conversely, people will not accept what you are offering if they do not feel understood by you. You give others the experience of being heard and understood by listening. (See Chapter 3, "The Dynamics of Influence.")

> In the business of advice-giving, recommendation-making, idea-offering, and selling, it is not enough to be right: You have to earn the right to be right.

Here's the problem, though: Most of the listening done in business today leaves a lot of room for improvement. What most of us have been taught about listening is far from sufficient when it comes to making a connection. By applying the techniques in this chapter, you will be able to listen and connect to partners in ways that build trust (Figure 6.1).

The Listening Differentiator: Empathy

What most leadership development and sales training programs teach is listening for a purpose. And usually that purpose is subtly self-oriented: to sell, to convince, to buy time until it is your turn to talk.

The kind of listening that engenders trust—deep trust—is about paying attention. Really paying attention. It is empathetic, through and through. The focus is not on what you hear, but on *the act of listening* itself. Thomas Friedman hit the nail on the head when he said,

Figure 6.1

**Five Trust
Skills: Listen**

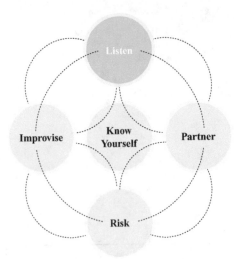

"It's not what you hear by listening that's important; it's what you say by listening that's important."[1]

Here's another way of putting it: It is not enough for you to understand your partner—he has to *feel* understood and experience that your sole purpose is to understand him because you care. This requires more than taking good notes or periodically pausing to summarize the content of a conversation. It means tuning into the music, the tone, mood, and emotion as well as the words of his communication. It requires reflecting it all back accurately and frequently enough that you get some kind of cue that you are relating to the entirety of his world.

It's easier said than done.

> The kind of listening that engenders trust—deep trust—is about paying attention. Really paying attention.

Four Barriers to Paying Attention

You cannot be empathetic if you are not tuned in. There are many reasons we humans do a bad job of giving others our undivided attention.

Here are four barriers to paying attention:

1. *A habit of talking.* Most of what passes for listening is not really listening at all. Let's be honest, it consists of waiting for the other person to stop talking so that you can talk some more. The habit of talking is especially pervasive in consulting and other professional

---

CASE STUDY

From the Front Lines: Earning the Right[2]

Unit7, a direct marketing/CRM agency that is part of the Omnicom family, figured out an ingenious way to give heart to a CRM campaign for a Type 2 diabetes medication. Before beginning work on the campaign, 80 Unit7 staffers signed up to live the life of a diabetic patient. Finger-pricking, careful eating, regular exercise: The staff was asked to do exactly what a patient, someone in their ultimate audience, does every day—for a 14-week period. Only then were they ready to create an ad campaign that spoke to the people being served.

One of the fundamental principles of trust is that we trust those who we believe understand us. In fact, if we don't believe they understand us, we don't trust them. Call this "empathy" if you like. You can also find it in the old sales line, "People don't care what you know until they know that you care."

—*Loreen Babcock (CEO, Unit7), as told to Charles H. Green*

services where people are paid by the hour to deliver insight and wisdom, which leads inappropriately to a perceived need to talk and look really smart doing it.

2. *Everyday distractions.* The human brain has limited bandwidth and a finite ability to process information. Furthermore, most research suggests that we get less efficient as we attempt to multitask. Today's business environment is rife with distractions that challenge our ability to focus and be present: Computers ping when a new message is received; Twitter accounts entice you to share trivialities on an ongoing basis; smart phones place your office in your pocket. In the same way you can sense when others are distracted—when they instant-message during a conference call—others can sense when *you* are not really there.

3. *A fear of intimacy.* If you really listen to people so they feel truly at ease with you, you may be fearful they might really open up—and *then* what? What if your client tells you something personal that you would rather not know? What if your boss expresses how she really feels about something? What if your colleague cries? If you are not completely confident in your ability to handle what could come out of an interpersonal exchange, you will unconsciously keep things at arm's length.

4. *The little internal voice.* The little internal voice is the constant companion that clogs your brain with incessant chatter. Think you don't have a little voice in your head? Your little voice is the one that says, "What little voice? I don't have a little voice." Here's a brief snippet from a typical internal dialogue:

Partner: [says something work-related]

Your little voice: *Uh oh. I should have spent more time preparing for this meeting. You know, I'm not sure I like this guy.*

Partner: [says something work-related]

Your little voice: *I do like his tie. The suit, not so much.*

Your little voice: *Did I remember to take my black suit to the dry cleaners?*

Partner: [says something work-related]

Your little voice: *I wish he'd hurry up and finish so I can re-focus this conversation. He has taken us way off course.*

And so it goes. Like static on a radio station, the little voice interferes with your ability to tune in.

Three-Level Listening

Great listening happens in two arenas—the rational and the nonrational, as shown in Figure 6.2. In each arena, the same three things must happen: You get some data, you understand its context, and you do a form of acknowledgment. In the rational arena, data include facts, processes, and metrics. On the nonrational side, data include emotions, culture, politics, and history.

Great listening happens in two arenas—the rational and the nonrational.

Let's walk through the simple example in Figure 6.2: Assume you are working on a process redesign and you are speaking with someone for the first time to understand the existing business processes.

Listening for Data

While there is no prescribed order when listening for trust, most of us begin with what is rational:

- *Listening for data.* You ask a question to get rational data—the upper left of Figure 6.2. You say, "How many transactions go through this process in a month?" And the answer is "3,000."
- *Putting it in context.* Then, you will probably want a sense of scope and scale, so you dig for rational context—see the middle left of Figure 6.2. You ask, "How big is 3,000?" And the answer is: "The most we ever had—up 50 percent from the prior period."
- *Offering acknowledgment.* And if you have been trained in active listening, you will probably acknowledge what you have heard by paraphrasing—see the bottom left of Figure 6.2. You say, "3,000 per month, the most you ever had—do I have that right?" And the answer is "Yes."

These are great first steps: You have gotten some data, asked questions to put it in context, and confirmed that you got it right. The result? Your partner knows you've understood the rational side.

There's much more.

Figure 6.2

Three-Level Listening

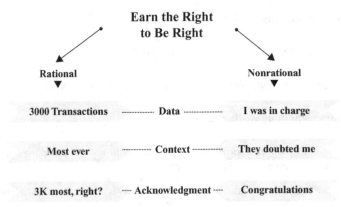

Listening to Build Intimacy

Listening to build intimacy goes beyond the rational and data-based. When you move into the nonrational realm, you get to the heart of the matter and build intimacy in the process, which is more personal and more risky—see the right-hand column in Figure 6.2.

- *Listening for nonrational data.* You might be curious about your partner's role. You say, "Hmmmm ... where were you during this tumultuous time?" And the answer is: "I was in charge."

- *Putting it in context.* Putting that into context, you follow-up saying, "Well, interesting—what was that like for you?" And the answer is: "Upper management doubted me."

Now things are getting interesting. Your partner has just revealed the following: 3,000 per month, the most they have ever had, it was his operation, and his superiors didn't think he could handle it. This is a moment where your partner is opening up. And if you meet him in intimacy—*with empathy*—then you will have increased trust.

- *Offering nonrational acknowledgement.* You acknowledge with empathy—see the bottom right of Figure 6.2. You say, "Sounds like you got the job done. Congratulations." Or "Good for you, I guess you showed them." Or "Ugh—that must have been challenging."

You may be tempted to revert back to the rational side instead *without even realizing it* ("Oh really? Why did they doubt you?"). Beware the consequences: You have now closed the door on trust. If you respond to an increasingly personal and emotional line of discussion with a purely rational question, you send a message that you either don't get it or you are not interested in his emotional reality. Either way, the effect is the same: At best, the conversation narrows and at worst, it shuts down.

Earning the Right to Be Right

> If you do not validate your partner when he risks sharing something personal, then you haven't earned the right to anything beyond politeness, and you certainly haven't earned the right to be right.

The biggest errors in good listening come from short-changing acknowledgment in the Three-Level Listening framework and, in particular, the nonrational side. If you do not validate your partner when he risks sharing something personal, then you have not earned the right to anything beyond politeness, and you certainly have not earned the right to be right.

Note that empathy might look and sound a lot of different ways. In the southern United States, it might sound like, "Aw, shucks." On a surfboard in Australia, it might sound like,

---

CASE STUDY

From the Front Lines: Listening to Recover Trust

Catherine Gregory, Senior Principal at SRA International in its Touchstone Consulting Group in Washington, DC, tells a story of the business value of listening.

"I had a team of four working on a long-term project with an important client who especially valued seeing the same faces year after year. In the course of three months, the entire team turned over. I had to deliver the bad news as each team member departed.

"After several turnovers, my client vented to me his frustration. I listened, and then listened some more, as he expressed his concerns and aggravation. He concluded with, 'I know you are doing all you can. I just had to get that out.' He was still unhappy *and* we were able to move forward together.

"Once things were stable with the team, I brought up the possibility of phasing out our support and letting him phase in a contractor who he felt would be more reliable. He didn't want anyone else; he wanted our team.

"This experience proved to me without a doubt that listening is a critical business skill, and a way to recover trust in the face of challenging circumstances."

—*Catherine Gregory (Senior Principal, SRA International, Touchstone Consulting Group, Washington, DC)*

"Way to ace it, mate!" In Southeast Asia, it might look like a glancing smile, a nod, and a quiet laugh. In the end, empathy is translatable into any language and culture. And as with languages, the particulars may vary, but the underlying humanity is the same.

Empathy as Statements, not Questions

Asking questions is an important skill—just do not confuse it with empathy. Spoken empathy[3] most often comes in the form of statements, as seen in Figure 6.3, that demonstrate that you have heard and understood the world of another. Genuinely insert an empathetic turn of phrase before asking your next great question, and you will be amazed at the difference it makes.

Here are some examples:

Figure 6.3

Empathetic Statements Followed by Great Questions

What Your Partner Says	Empathetic Statement	Your Next Great Question
"I was in charge, and they doubted me."	"Sounds like you got the job done. Congratulations."	"What was that like for you?"
"You people have still not given me an answer to my original question."	"Ouch, I can hear your anger on this subject; I get that you're frustrated."	"Can we address right now how we go about getting that answer for you?"
"I don't see value in that."	"Sounds like we haven't done a good job making the case!'	"What's missing for you?"
"We're just not sure which way to go."	"That's a tough spot to be in."	"What options are you considering?"
"I'm disappointed by your team's results."	"I'm very sorry to hear that. We've clearly missed the mark from your perspective."	"Would you share some specifics about your disappointment?"

One cautionary note: When offering an empathetic statement, be careful not to say variations of "Yes, but ..." or "I understand." A "Yes, but" does not reflect any time spent in the world of another, and the word "but" has the effect of negating everything that came before it. "I understand" is a generalized assertion that you cannot prove. It is actually a demonstration of your misunderstanding and has the potential to annoy your partner ("Really? How could you possibly understand?").

How to Acknowledge Another When You Don't Agree

It is entirely possible to validate other people's perspective and feelings without agreeing. The key is to understand how things might make sense from their perspective—and then say so. Things *do* make sense over there, and there *is* a way to see it, if you take the time to look at it.

Try saying the words "That makes sense." When said from the heart, "That makes sense" is a powerful expression of validation. It is also particularly disarming in response to an opposing viewpoint, or to something you don't really want to hear. Some examples:

- "I see you're concerned about investing a lot of money and time without being sure of the return. That makes sense."
- "Sounds like it's imperative for you to have the right executive sponsor in place before we move forward. That makes sense."
- "It makes sense to consider all the options before you decide which firm you want to hire."

Listening to Groups

Great facilitators are great listeners. When they work with groups, they empathize all the time—so gracefully, in fact, that it is hardly noticeable. Listening well to multiple people requires an ability to first analyze and synthesize what you are hearing, and then reflect back the facts *and* emotions of the group. For example:

- "It sounds like we're 95 percent there in terms of agreeing on XYZ."
- "I'm hearing real concern expressed by at least half the group about ABC."

Skilled facilitators are also adept at constantly scanning the group to ensure inclusion. They say things like "Jan, you're shaking your head, so I'm thinking we don't have the whole story here. What do you think?"

Insight: Nine Ways to Express Empathy

1. "That makes sense."
2. "That's a valid concern/problem."
3. "It sounds like [restate what you heard—words and music]."
4. "If I understand you correctly, _____."
5. "In other words, _____."
6. "So from your perspective, _____."
7. "I can appreciate how [challenging/frustrating/disappointing/unnerving/irritating/lonely/exciting/motivating] that would be."
8. "If I were in your shoes, I would probably be [concerned/upset/angry/disappointed/disheartened/ready to throw in the towel/happy/relieved/encouraged/psyched], too."
9. "I'm [disappointed/concerned/disheartened/sorry/happy/excited/relieved/encouraged] to hear that."

Seven Listening Best Practices

Here's a list of seven ways to become a masterful listener:

1. *Really care.* Techniques are no substitute for caring and paying attention. Mind your intentions. If you truly don't care, replace yourself with someone who does.

It is entirely possible to validate another person's perspective and feelings without agreeing.

2. *Tune in.* You cannot multitask undiscovered—not for long. Eschew the distractions: close the door, face away from the computer, turn the smart phone over, decline to Instant Message with others. In short, *give your undivided attention.*

3. *Acknowledge early and often.* Paraphrase rational data and empathize with emotions—even the ones you sense but don't overtly hear. Do this ten times more than you think you should. Check for cues that you are on track and acknowledge more if you are not.

4. *Express yourself nonverbally.* Lean toward the person who is speaking—even when you are on the phone. Smile, use facial expressions, and express yourself naturally with your hands and arms. Vary your pitch and tone to convey your own emotions. Don't suppress yourself. Make listening a whole-person endeavor.

5. *Keep it about them—not you.* Ask open-ended questions, both rational and nonrational. Let them tell their own story in the way they want to—don't use them as foils for your hypotheses.

6. *Get a little Zen.* When the little voice pipes up, notice and observe it; raise your consciousness about it in the moment. Gently yet swiftly return your focus to the real conversation at hand. This is similar to the practice that experienced meditators use of refocusing on the breath when distracted.

7. *Think out loud.* Get the chatter out of your head and into the conversation. This is especially valuable when your little voice is expressing a concern. See Figure 6.4 for some examples.

Figure 6.4

Thinking Out Loud

What Your Little Voice Says	What You Might Say Out Loud
"He seems distracted."	"Let's take a time out to be sure we're going in the right direction with this conversation."
"I'm not sure she understands what I'm getting at."	"At the risk of being overly assertive here, may I be blunt?
"I am doing a lot of talking; someone shut me up!"	"I'm hearing myself doing a lot of the talking here. What haven't I asked that's important for you?"

You will notice a lot of these best practices require some risk-taking. As does all trust.

Your Everyday Empathy Workout: Low Weights, High Reps

Clunky empathy trumps no empathy every time—you will get credit for your efforts, your intentions, and your willingness to take a risk.

Learning to listen with empathy takes practice. If it feels too risky to try this with customers or colleagues, or if you want to practice more, take empathy baby steps with people you interact with every day.

Empathize with the grocery store clerk. And the dry cleaner. And the newspaper vendor. And the babysitter. Why?

There are several good reasons to use empathy in your daily encounters.

1. *The stakes are low.* You will worry less about getting it wrong and you are less likely to be reactive. Empathy gets a lot harder when your senior leader has just informed you that she's disappointed in your team's results.

2. *The environment is target-rich.* Most of us interact with service providers on a daily basis. And we need daily practice to build muscle memory. When the stakes are high we especially need those strong muscles to counteract our natural tendency to fight or flee.

3. *You will make a big difference for someone.* People in service roles are used to dealing with complaints, not empathy.

CASE STUDY

> ## From the Front Lines: The Fascinating Wife
>
> A colleague of mine (Charlie's) and his wife were invited to an important company affair, a dinner party. His wife was seated next to one of the key people at the dinner. She later said to her husband: "What a bore! I didn't say two words all night; all he did was talk about himself."
>
> The next day the colleague ran into the bore, who told him: "Your wife is an absolutely fascinating woman."
>
> Ah, the power of listening!
>
> *—Charles H. Green*

Here are some examples of what "everyday empathy" sounds like:

To the grocery store clerk who has a strained look on her face: *"Looks like maybe you've had a rough day."*

To the cab driver who's stuck in traffic and horn-happy: *"I'm sure there's nothing more frustrating than dealing with this mess all the time."*

To the mail carrier whose brow is moist in the midday sun: *"I'll bet there are days like today when you wish you had an indoor job!"*

To the waitress who drops a tray full of dishes: *"Bummer."*

To the Facebook friend whose status message says, "Hit a home run today!": *"Congrats! You must be psyched!"* (Empathy is called for in happy situations, too.)

Use your own words, of course. And use emotion words whenever you can like "frustrating" or "psyched." While it is true you might not get the emotion right, the risk you take to be in their world matters more. Plus even if you get corrected, it provides another opportunity to practice. Clunky empathy trumps no empathy every time—you will get credit for your efforts, your intentions, and your willingness to take a risk.

With daily practice, you will be poised and ready the next time you are given an opportunity to recover from a project failure, help an executive team see the value of your recommendation, or demonstrate to a client the value they would gain if they hired you.

Worksheet: Listening for Trust

In general, what do you find most challenging when it comes to paying attention? Use the Four Barriers to Paying Attention list in this chapter as a guide.

_____

_____

_____

Bring to mind an upcoming opportunity to listen to one or more people. Describe it briefly, and then use the questions below to prepare for your interaction. Use the description of Three-Level Listening in this chapter as your guide.

Opportunity:

_____

_____

_____

What questions might you ask to elicit _rational_ data and rational context?

- _____
- _____
- _____
- _____

What questions might you ask to elicit _nonrational_ data and nonrational context?

- _____
- _____
- _____
- _____

Imagine what your partner might say in response to your nonrational questions. What will you say to demonstrate empathy? And what question might you ask next to be curious and further build intimacy? An example is in the first row.

What Your Partner Says	Empathetic Statement	Your Next Great Question
"I was in charge, and they doubted me."	"Sounds like you got the job done. Congratulations."	"What was that like for you?"

What did you learn as a result of this exercise?

Partner

In our increasingly connected world, the ability to partner is essential. It is a foundational skill that advances collaboration, synergy, and expanded results. You know the benefits of having good partnering skills, yet you may not apply them as consistently as you would like. This chapter explores partnering traits and the most common barriers to making them part of daily life. It also provides practical suggestions for strengthening your partnering muscle.

7

Chapter

The word *partner* has several definitions, including either of two persons dancing together. The dancing metaphor conjures up images of give and take, synchronization, graceful movement, and being in tune and in step with one another. It is very apt for trust-based relationships, where you have to both lead and follow, interchangeably.

In this chapter, we use the word *partner* as a verb—it is an act, not a person or thing. Dancing together well is the ultimate goal.

Partnering Traits

When you partner well (see Figure 7.1), you:

- *Maintain a mind-set of collaboration, not competition.* This means thinking about your interests as intertwined with others' and staying focused on reaching a solution that works for all concerned.
- *Work from a position of equal status.* You are appropriately respectful of hierarchy but not distracted by it. You are committed to a sense of fairness and balance in the relationship.
- *Lead and follow.* You are willing and able to switch between the two, depending on what would be of greatest service in the moment. You lead when your own strengths are called for; you follow when another's strengths are called for.
- *Balance assertiveness and cooperation in the face of conflict.*[1] You combine ideas and real points of view with a willingness to make things work for all involved.
- *Deal with disagreements and missteps productively and gracefully.* You view creative tension and mistakes as opportunities to learn and improve. You address things and move on.

Figure 7.1

**Five Trust
Skills: Partner**

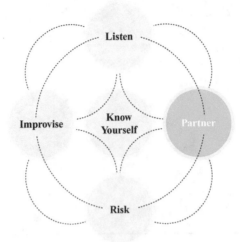

- *Demonstrate a commitment to sharing responsibility for achieving a goal.* You see the entirety of the problem, opportunity, task, or project as "ours." You don't hoard, dominate, or control; neither do you abdicate, give up, or give in.
- *Take responsibility for your part in the partnership's successes and failures.* You don't see roles as 50-50, but instead 100-100.

Ten Common Partnering Barriers

Partnering, like nearly everything that relates to being a trusted advisor, is simple but not easy.

We have encountered 10 personal traits, habits, and mind-sets that make the act of partnering difficult from the outset:

> Effective partnering demands that you think beyond traditional relationship

1. *A narrow view of relationships.* Effective partnering demands that you think beyond traditional relationship boundaries. When you grasp the fundamental attitude that "you are more connected than you think," you expand your view of relationships, in both number and nature. You set your sights on supporting the greater good. (See Chapter 2, "Fundamental Attitudes.") It is actually much easier to partner when your primary focus is on an agenda larger than your own. When you redefine your notion of relationship to include *everyone* (even competitors), partnering becomes second nature.

2. *A win/lose mind-set.* A win/lose mind-set dictates that only one person can come out on top—and the winner should be you. Usually what is underneath a win/lose mind-set are fears all humans deal with. Ask yourself: Am I afraid of losing control? What if I'm taken advantage of? Will I lose my place in the spotlight? Am I afraid of being overpowered? What if I make a bad choice? Without awareness, the fear prevails, even when you rationally know the benefits of partnership.

3. *Undermanaged self-orientation.* All humans are self-oriented, much of the time. Yet, not everything you hear, everything that is done, or everything that happens revolves around you. If you can mentally disassociate yourself, you will be able to spend less time managing your own reactions and more time being a good partner.

4. *Lack of confidence.* Insecurity is a form of excessive self-orientation. It interferes with important partnering skills like offering a point of view, leading tasks, and taking responsibility for mistakes.

5. *An overdeveloped ability to criticize.* Being well-trained to see what is missing or what could be wrong can be a great asset in a partnership. However, being perceived as picky, judgmental, and wanting perfection does not advance solutions.

6. *A tendency to either lead* or *follow.* Partnerships work best when you are able to lead *and* follow, interchangeably, depending on what is called for in the moment. A good partner is an agile partner.

> Good partners have high tolerance levels for not knowing and not being in control.

7. *A need for immediate gratification.* A drive for action and results can be a good thing for a partnership. But the more you *want it right now*—whether "it" is the answer, the plan, or the results—the more likely you are to choose actions that are in service of you, rather than the partnership.

8. *Intolerance of ambiguity.* When you are working with others, sometimes things are not always as clear as they would be if you were working solo. Good partners have high tolerance levels for not knowing and not being in control.

9. *Discomfort with conflict.* The word *conflict* has a strong negative connotation for most people—it implies struggle, opposition, and discord. Conflict, which usually arises out of differences, is a natural outcome of interacting with others. Partnering is much easier when you are able to celebrate it and direct its energy toward the good of the partnership. (See "At the Corner of Assertiveness and Cooperation: Collaboration.")

10. *A limited view of problems and opportunities.* It is human nature to see and define the world from your own vantage point. Unfortunately, this narrow view limits the range of creative options available to the partnership. Reframing problems and opportunities in an inclusive and expansive way is an important partnering skill.

CASE STUDY

From the Front Lines: The Power of Unqualified Commitment[2]

Robert Porter Lynch, a long-time thought leader in strategic alliances, and author of several books on collaboration and innovation, explains how trust drives championship performance.

"Arguably the greatest worst-to-first performance of all time was the 1980 American hockey team that won Olympic Gold against all odds, culminating in a win over the monstrously dominant Finland team.

"Coach Herb Brooks considered adding a player to the team who had more talent and better credentials than probably any other player on the team.

"The player was asked to practice with the team. And the team confronted the coach unanimously, saying 'You can't hire him.'

"'Why not?' asked the coach.

"'Because he doesn't give 100 percent,' the team said.

"'But even at less-than-full effort, he's arguably the best player on the ice,' Brooks countered.

"'But coach,' the players said, 'if you never know what effort he's going to give, you can't trust what he'll do. You never know how much game he's bringing. You can't depend on him to be reliable. He wasn't a collaborative kind of guy; he'd rather try to score himself than pass the puck to someone better positioned.'

"The super player wasn't hired, and the team went on to win the gold.

"This sense permeates all great teams. They trust each other to give the utmost to the team. Which means everyone can rely on everyone else's motives, and everyone can trust the results. Unqualified commitment by each member of the team drives trust, and trust enables high performance."

—*Robert Porter Lynch (author and founding Chairman of the Association of Strategic Alliance Professionals)*

Insight: At the Corner of Assertiveness and Cooperation: Collaboration[3]

What do you meet at the corner of Assertiveness and Cooperation? The work of Kenneth W. Thomas and Ralph H. Kilmann, creators of the Thomas-Kilmann Conflict Mode Instrument, suggest the answer is Collaboration.

Collaboration combines the energy of Assertiveness, ideas and real points of view championed by people who care, with the energy of Cooperation, a willingness to make things work for all involved. The idea or solution which is fashioned from everyone's input is better than what any one person could have come up with on her or his own. Collaboration leads to the best result for everyone.

Self-Assessment: Are You Primed for Partnership?

Knowing your own strengths and weaknesses is the first stop on the road to improving your partnering skills. Try rating yourself on each of the factors in Figure 7.2.

- Score yourself toward the right-hand side of the scale if you identify the factor as a natural or developed strength that you consistently bring to your partnerships.
- Score yourself toward the left-hand side of the scale if you are less developed or inconsistent in that area.

The middle point on the five-point scale is the neutral point. It represents neither strength nor weakness.

CASE STUDY

From the Front Lines: Partnering in the Supply Chain[4]

Steve Peplin is CEO of Talan Products, a Cleveland-based metal-stamping company that embraces the partner concept. A cornerstone of the firm's philosophy is to develop relationships in which it becomes an integral part of its customers' success.

Peplin can quickly present the benefits his firm brings to a partnership: quality, integrity, and a problem-solving nature, among them. "We do things right, and we're always getting better. We're a top performer. That's part of being a partner," Peplin says.

In return, Talan Products boasts a cadre of key customers who bring loyalty and long-term relationships on their side of the equation, and they pay their bills on time. Relationships with several key customers date back 20 years or more.

Talan Products' embrace of partnering paid dividends during the recent recession, when in 2008 soaring steel prices preceded a fourth-quarter price dive and a suddenly tanking economy. The abrupt change in fortunes left many companies, including Talan Products, with pipelines clogged with high-cost material and customers that weren't taking any product.

A bad situation could have been worse if Talan Products' partners along the supply chain hadn't worked together to mitigate the hurt. "We developed a creative way to deal with a unique problem," Peplin says.

—*Steve Peplin (CEO, Talan Products, Cleveland, Ohio)*

	1	2	3	4	5	
A narrow view of relationship	☐	☐	☐	☐	☐	An expanded view of relationship
A win/lose mind-set	☐	☐	☐	☐	☐	An all-for-one mind-set
Undermanaged self-orientation	☐	☐	☐	☐	☐	Well-managed self-orientation
Lack of confidence	☐	☐	☐	☐	☐	Confidence
An overdeveloped ability to criticize	☐	☐	☐	☐	☐	A balanced perspective of positive and negative
A tendency to either lead *or* follow	☐	☐	☐	☐	☐	The ability to lead and follow interchangeably
A need for immediate gratification	☐	☐	☐	☐	☐	The ability to delay gratification
Intolerance of ambiguity	☐	☐	☐	☐	☐	Tolerance for not knowing or being in control
Discomfort with conflict	☐	☐	☐	☐	☐	Comfort with conflict
A limited view of problems and opportunities	☐	☐	☐	☐	☐	A "we"-oriented view of problems and opportunities

Figure 7.2

Rating Your Partnering Strengths and Weaknesses

Specific Ways to Build Your Partnering Muscle

Here's a starter list of ways to improve your ability to partner (Figure 7.3). Identify two areas where you could improve. Then choose one practice for each (or develop your own) to build your muscle.

Try mentally restating all of your problems as "we" problems for one week, where the "we" includes both you and your partner(s).

Figure 7.3

Partnering Practices

Partnering Muscle	Partnering Practices
1. An expanded view of relationships	• Notice that when it's raining on you, it's raining on everyone else, too. Make it a point to ponder this all week. • For two minutes each day, consciously envision the other person in the relationship as a partner—not an adversary, or a role, or a means to an end.
2. An all-for-one mind-set	• Re-define what winning is within a particular partnership. Set your sights on a different target—one that is more service-oriented and reflective of a bigger picture. • Notice any fear-based reactions you have. Name what you are afraid of. Then practice responses based in curiosity. ("That could be interesting. Let's talk more.") It might take you seconds, days, or weeks to trump fear with curiosity. That's okay, try it anyway.
3. Well-managed self-orientation	• Identify a situation or interaction when your mental energy was consumed with "it's about me" thinking: for example, when a partner seemed withdrawn and you spent several days wondering what you had done wrong. Then, practice mental dissociation. Make a list of all the possibilities outside of you that could be at play.
4. Confidence	• Keep a running list of all the things you bring to a relationship—personal traits, experience, resources, and more. • Spend time thinking about your point of view on a matter that is relevant to a relationship you are in. Make notes about what led you to that point of view and what experience or evidence you have to back it up. Then make a plan to share your point of view. • The next time you feel the urge to blame someone for something that went awry, sit down and make note of how *you* contributed. It takes a lot of self-confidence to admit when you are wrong or see where you could be responsible.

Partnering Muscle	Partnering Practices
5. A balanced perspective of positive and negative	• Use the improve technique "Yes, and!" to build on ideas. (For more details, see Chapter 8: "Improvise.") • When you give feedback, start a list of what is positive and what works. Do not move to the "what's negative/what doesn't work" list until you are certain your partner really heard the good things. And when you do transition, do not use the words "but" or "however"—they have the effect of negating everything you said prior. • Expand your own capacity to receive positive feedback. When someone compliments you or acknowledges you for something, really hear it and say thank you. Do not deflect or deny.
6. The ability to lead and follow interchangeably	• Note which you tend to do more—lead or follow. Make a point to do the opposite for one day. Create your own experiment, then reflect on it: What was easy? What was hard? What surprised you about the experience? Did you get different results? What makes sense to carry forward into another experiment?

7. The ability to delay gratification	• Use the 'Stoplight' technique that some schools use to teach social/emotional skills. The next time you feel upset or impulsive:
	  • Red light: Stop, calm down, and think before you act
	  • Yellow light: Identify the range of things you should do beyond your first impulse
	  • Green light: Choose the best one and try it out.
	• When your resolve gets shaky, distract yourself with another task.
	• Find a way to reward yourself when you successfully delay gratification.

8. Tolerance for not knowing or being in control	• Adopt an attitude of "Isn't this interesting! I wonder what will happen next." Repeat this over and over to yourself whenever you feel frightened by ambiguity or lack of control.

Partnering Muscle	Partnering Practices
9. Comfort with conflict	• Use the Thomas-Kilmann Conflict Mode Instrument, which measures your behavior in conflict situations along two basic dimensions: (1) assertiveness, the extent to which you attempt to satisfy your own concerns; and (2) cooperativeness, the extent to which you attempt to satisfy another's concerns. (At the time of this writing, a free version is available on-line.) • When a conflict or disagreement arises, celebrate it. Practice saying, "Oh good! We see that differently!"
10. A "we"-oriented view of problems and opportunities	• Try mentally restating all of your problems as "we" problems for one week, where the "we" includes both you and your partner(s).

Worksheet: Working Side by Side

Bring to mind two current relationships: one that is working well and one that isn't. Describe them briefly below, then answer the questions that follow.

Case 1: A Relationship That Is Working Well
Description:

_____

Case 2: A Relationship That Is Not Working Well
Description:

_____

Using the partnering traits at the beginning of this chapter, how would you rate each relationship?

Case 1: A Relationship That Is Working Well

You maintain a mind-set of collaboration.	☐Y	☐N	☐Sometimes
You work from a position of equal status.	☐Y	☐N	☐Sometimes
You are willing and able to both lead and follow.	☐Y	☐N	☐Sometimes
You balance assertiveness and cooperation.	☐Y	☐N	☐Sometimes
You deal with disagreements and missteps productively and gracefully.	☐Y	☐N	☐Sometimes
You demonstrate a commitment to sharing responsibility for achieving a goal.	☐Y	☐N	☐Sometimes
You take responsibility for your part in the partnership's successes and failures.	☐Y	☐N	☐Sometimes

Case 2: A Relationship That Is Not Working Well

You maintain a mind-set of collaboration.	☐Y	☐N	☐Sometimes
You work from a position of equal status.	☐Y	☐N	☐Sometimes
You are willing and able to both lead and follow.	☐Y	☐N	☐Sometimes
You balance assertiveness and cooperation.	☐Y	☐N	☐Sometimes
You deal with disagreements and missteps productively and gracefully.	☐Y	☐N	☐Sometimes
You demonstrate a commitment to sharing responsibility for achieving a goal.	☐Y	☐N	☐Sometimes
You take responsibility for whatever part you play in the partnership's successes and failures.	☐Y	☐N	☐Sometimes

For the traits present in the working-well relationship, what aids and sustains those?

_____

_____

_____

_____

_____

For the traits not present in the not-working relationship, what is in the way?

_____

_____

_____

_____

_____

What opportunities do you now see to close the gaps?

_____

_____

_____

_____

_____

What actions will you take as a result? Be specific.

What	By When	With Whom	Support I Will Ask For

Improvise

8

Things do not always go as planned. There is no escaping those moments of truth that we all face when the unexpected occurs. Ironically, these unpredictable and stressful moments are some of your best opportunities to dramatically increase your trustworthiness—provided you are adept at thinking on your feet and allowing your best self to shine through. This chapter explains the science behind a moment of truth. It also describes "thinking out loud" and "Yes, and … ," two improvisational practices that improve your ability to be powerful and authentic in the moment.

Anyone in business has encountered numerous unexpected and tricky situations. Those uncomfortable, awkward moments seem to occur at the worst possible times.

> Q: Faced with a moment of truth, what do you do?
> A: Improvise.

Examples of the unexpected moments:

- A prospective client asks you point blank, "What experience do you have in XYZ industry?" Even though you saw that question coming, you did not think it would be quite so direct. The honest answer is none—only you are afraid to say so because you think it would be a deal-breaker. How do you let them know about your other relevant experience that they will surely want to hear about before summarily dismissing you?
- You thought the draft report you turned in yesterday was pretty good until you got an e-mail from your supervisor saying she is disappointed in the product and is seriously reconsidering your participation in the next and biggest phase of the project. How do you respond?
- You walk into a client meeting with a very senior leader, to discuss how to expand the successful work you are doing together. But an hour earlier you accidentally overheard him in the lunchroom speaking with colleagues about dumping your organization and hiring a competitor instead. Now what do you do?

We call these moments of truth—when something happens, and suddenly it feels like you are alone on a sinking ship with no life preserver in sight, and you would rather be *anywhere* but where you are.

Q. Faced with a moment of truth, what do you do?

A. Improvise.

The Science behind Moments of Truth

Daniel Goleman, author of the best-seller *Emotional Intelligence: Why It Can Matter More Than IQ*, helps us understand the science behind our reaction in a moment of truth. He used the phrase "amygdala hijack" to describe how the well-functioning thinking brain (the neocortex) gets completely overruled by the reptilian brain—the part that manages your survival. Then your amygdala-threatened self does something untrustworthy like spin a great story of how you don't exactly have direct experience in XYZ industry *but* blah blah blah. Or subtly (and maybe overtly) you blame your colleague for the subpar work product. Or you completely sidestep an awkward interaction in favor of maintaining the pretense that everything is okay.

> Being effective in a moment of truth requires more than mastering a few behavioral tricks—it demands a new way of thinking and being.

In other words: You are in fight or flight mode, and often both at once. The result? A moment of truth can lead you to tell something less than the truth. You improvise, think on your feet—only not with a positive result. Improvisation doesn't have to go that way.

How Moments of Truth Become Moments of Mastery

Being effective in a moment of truth requires more than mastering a few behavioral tricks—it demands a new way of thinking and being.

One approach we have found that works is experiential learning that deals on the spot with your own real-life situations. In other words, we recommend what most people (including us) universally dislike: role-playing to practice improvisation so when the real-life moment of truth arises you will be ready.

The Practice of Improvisation

Improvising means to invent, compose, or perform with little or no preparation. Improvisation (Figure 8.1) is exactly what is called for in a moment of truth: the ability to deal immediately with something unexpected.

Figure 8.1

Five Trust Skills: Improvise

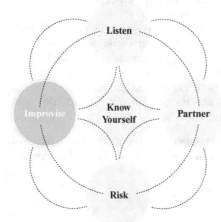

Practicing improvisation may sound like an oxymoron—how do you rehearse something that is supposed to be spontaneous? While it sounds odd, practice is exactly how professional improvisational comedy performers become so skilled at their craft. There are many techniques you can learn from improv performers, such as:

- Being quick to respond instead of overthinking.
- Providing "Yes, and …" responses to build on what has already been said, instead of contradicting or denying what someone else has offered.

- Subordinating your own ego to support what the collective is creating instead of stealing a scene by hogging the spotlight.
- Giving up being clever and witty and funny and instead getting *real*.

> While it sounds odd, practice is exactly how professional improvisational comedy performers become so skilled at their craft.

CASE STUDY

From the Front Lines: Doing Right in a Moment of Truth

Chip Grizzard, CEO of Grizzard Communications Group in Atlanta, Georgia, reminds us that mistakes happen; it's how you handle them in the moment that makes or breaks a relationship.

"We made a big mistake once. Our client had a big media plan that coincided with our direct mail drop. Because of our mistake, the mail arrived in homes before the big media push. In the client's mind, this hurt results. He called and said, 'This is very disappointing. We've done all this planning and you've let us down.' I asked him what would make him feel like we addressed the situation to his satisfaction. He said, 'I don't think we should pay for this mailing.'

"There was a fair amount of money at stake. Right away, I said, 'No problem, done.' As painful as it was, it was the right thing to do.

"Ten years later, he's still a client, despite having moved around to different organizations and locations. And every time I see him—every time—he says, 'Do you remember when we had the problem with that mail drop and you took care of it?' It had a huge impact on him, and he became a lifelong client as a result."

—*Chip Grizzard (CEO, Grizzard Communications Group, Atlanta)*

Improvisational performers make up scenes over and over, always with new scenarios and relationships that are completely invented on the spot. And then when it's show time and the curtain goes up, they still have no idea what they are going to create together because every new scene is based on audience suggestions. What they do know is that they are fully rehearsed at being responsive, collaborative, and authentic. In other words, they may not have rehearsed lines, but they have rehearsed principles. And they are able to lead with trust as a result.

Insight: Four Key Skills of Improv[2]

1. *Being open to new ideas.* Developing comfort with accepting ideas of others, building on them, and taking them to the next level.
2. *Listening.* Being attentive, sensitive, tuned in.
3. *Being in the moment.* Dealing masterfully with the unexpected. Demonstrating agility and flexibility.
4. *Underthinking.* Walt Disney said it best: "The way to get started is to quit talking and begin doing."

Role-Play Your Way to Mastery

In a business setting, role-playing with prewritten cases sometimes feels uncomfortable and contrived. A common refrain during debriefs in our programs is this: "If only I'd known more about the situation I could have handled it better."

Consider this: How many times have you prepped for hours, even days for a meeting, only to learn just as the meeting begins that your senior leader just returned from *another* meeting in which a major decision was made that completely alters (1) your agenda for this meeting and (2) your entire set of recommendations for the engagement?

In a moment of truth, having background, history, and facts does not matter because your reptilian brain does not care—it is focused exclusively on the immediate emotions. Your amygdala has been hijacked. It has neither the time nor the inclination to process anything else. Role-playing helps tremendously by making it possible for you to interrupt or, at the very least, redirect the amygdala hijack.

Role-Play Workouts Anyone Can Do

Try this: Get together with a colleague or two. Brainstorm a list of things your partners have said or could say that are likely to put your reptilian brain on alert. Here are some examples to get you started:

- "I'm very disappointed in your work product."
- "We'd like to find someone else to lead the workshop for us. There are concerns about your style."
- "What experience do you have in XYZ industry?"
- "Why are you so much more expensive?"
- "I'm not sure I really see the point; this is all just common sense."
- "We're giving the account to someone else."

Practice identifying your immediate response in these moments of truth. What is the first thing that comes out of your mouth without thinking? Is it defensive? Explanatory? That would make sense—that is a survival tactic. Or is your response authentic in a positive and productive way? That would be your thinking brain at work.

Practice until you can reliably respond with your thinking brain. Use your colleagues as objective observers and ask them to be tough with their feedback—it is the best way to improve quickly.

Think Out Loud with Your Thinking Brain

The practice of "Thinking out loud," first introduced in "Trust-Based Selling," achieves two things:

1. *Frees you up to be a better listener.* If you listen first, then think out loud, it is possible to separate the two activities, which makes it possible for you to really focus on listening. (For specific ways to improve your listening skills, see Chapter 6, "Listen.")
2. *Trains you to be collaborative.* When you share the very formation of your thoughts in a transparent way, you are demonstrating your partnering skills. (For specific ways to improve your partnering skills, see Chapter 7, "Partner.")

Thinking out loud is a great way to hone your improvisational skills. The key is to get good at thinking out loud with your thinking brain, rather than your reptilian brain. We are not suggesting you unleash your uncensored self on your colleagues—that would be your reptilian brain talking. We *are* suggesting you bring a little more candor, vulnerability, and humility to your interactions.

Of course the words have to be your own, reflecting your own style and personality. The examples in Figure 8.2 are meant to give you general ideas about retraining your brain—and your mouth—to be more effective in a moment of truth.

> Humor is optional, and highly recommended. Those who don't take themselves too seriously seem to know how to bring levity to awkward conversations.

You will note there is a little humor included in our examples. Humor is optional, and highly recommended. Those who don't take themselves too seriously are the ones who seem to know how to bring levity to awkward conversations.

When someone says:	You might be thinking:	Avoid saying:	Instead, think out loud by saying:
1. "What experience do you have in XYZ industry?"	"Uh oh."	"Only a few years in the industry, but I do have blah blah blah …"	"I have two years in the industry. Is that a concern?"
2. "Why are you so much more expensive?"	"Because we're worth it! The other guys are cons!"	"Our prices are higher because blah blah blah …"	"I hear you on 'too expensive.' There could be a number of reasons for a disconnect here. Would you help me understand what you mean by that?"
3. "I'm very disappointed in your product."	"What? Huh? How can that be?"	"We feel it's a quality product and stand behind it."	"I'm not sure what to say—that's not at all what I was expecting to hear. It's certainly not what I want to hear. Can you tell me more?"
4. "We're giving the account to someone else."	"%@#*!"	"Well, I guess we're finished here. Thanks for your time."	"Well, shoot. That's a real disappointment. I'm sorry to hear it. I'd like to hear more about what's behind that, if you're willing to share it."
5. "Do you have any other people who could lead the workshop for us? There are concerns about your style."	"Ummmm… what's wrong with *me*?"	"We have many global clients who like my style."	"Oh, no, ouch! I may need a moment to pick my ego up off the floor. In all seriousness, we do have others, and I'd be glad to work with you to find the best fit. Can you tell me more about what qualities are important to you? I won't take it personally—well, only a little!"

Figure 8.2

Five Ways to Think Out Loud in a Moment of Truth

The Power of "Yes, and …"

The options for thinking out loud in Figure 8.3 all have something in common: they are "Yes, and …" responses, figuratively speaking. "Yes, and …" is a core technique used by professional improvisers to foster collaboration and teamwork. By responding with words that imply "yes," you accept what is happening in the moment and acknowledge what your partner has said. By then adding words that imply "and," you build on that acknowledgment and advance the relationship or the action. Figure 8.3 parses out the "Yes, and …" elements of these statements.

Figure 8.3

Using "Yes,
and ..." to
Think Out
Loud

"Yes"	"and ..."
"I have two years in the industry."	"Is that a concern?"
"I hear you on 'too expensive.'"	"There could be a number of reasons for a disconnect here. Would you help me understand what you mean by that?"
"I'm not sure what to say—that's not at all what I was expecting to hear."	"It's certainly not what I want to hear. Can you tell me more?"
"Well, shoot. That's a real disappointment. I'm sorry to hear it."	"I'd like to hear more about what's behind that, if you're willing to share it."
"Oh, no, ouch! I may need a moment to pick my ego up off the floor!"	"In all seriousness, we do have others, and I'd be I glad to work with you to find the best fit. Can you tell me more about what qualities are important to you? I won't take it personally—well, only a little!"

The next time you are in a meeting, notice how many times your replies embody the spirit of "Yes, and ..." and how many times your contribution is more of a "Yes, but ...." Make a concerted effort to bring more "Yes, and ..." to the conversation and you will notice a marked improvement in your results.

CASE STUDY

From the Front Lines: The Team that Laughs Together Lasts Together[3]

Shawn Westfall, lead instructor at the DC Improv Comedy Club and founder of Improv Comedy Delivered in Washington, DC, shares his perspectives on improv and building trust.

"Improv lays bare the trustworthiness of those involved. Since my students quickly come to understand that they succeed or fail together onstage, they rapidly discern who's going to support their choices, and make them look good on stage—and who isn't. The fellow actor making selfish choices is easy to locate: first, by how often he or she compromises a scene by refusing to either engage with others or share the focus and attention and second, by how reticent others in class are to get on stage with that person. Conversely, the more generous and trustworthy one of my students is, the more readily others are to hop on stage with him or her. They trust that student to make them look good, often with hilarious results.

"It's a lesson I learned long ago: It's really, really difficult to dislike someone who's making you laugh. In fact, when we say we 'miss' someone, what we're actually saying is that we miss laughing with that person, the shared jokes or stories or experiences that result or resulted in laughter. Not only do my students eventually come to like one another, they have, more importantly, come to *trust* one another, which is a necessary component of any successful improv scene."

Worksheet: Transform Moments of Truth into Moments of Mastery

Use this worksheet to script your responses to questions or comments that trigger a fight or flight response. Transform your need to survive into the willingness to be authentic in a positive and productive way.

List moments of truth you either have faced or will likely face in the next week. What was said, or what will likely be said, that will put your reptilian brain on high alert?

Complete the following table. For each trigger, identify what you might be thinking, what you would be tempted to say as a defense or explanation, and what thinking out loud with your thinking brain might sound like.

1	2	3	4
If someone says:	What you might be thinking:	What not to say as a defense or explanation:	Thinking out loud in an authentic, positive, and productive way say this:
"What experience do you have in XYZ industry?"	"Uh oh."	"Only a few years in the industry, but I do have blah blah blah …"	"I have two years in the industry. Is that a concern?"

Tip: Share your assessment with a colleague to get reactions and suggestions.
Tip: Practice saying out loud what you have written in Column 4.

Risk

There is no trust without risk. The ability to build intimacy depends upon willingness and efficacy with risk-taking. Those who tend to avoid risk lose priceless trust-building opportunities, while those who master risk-taking as a skill learn to employ what is paradoxically the greatest risk-mitigation strategy. This chapter provides you with further insight into the relationship between trust and risk, along with a list of practices that expand your comfort and agility with risk-taking. You also get two tools for your risk toolkit: the three-question transparency test and Name It and Claim It.

A client of ours we'll call Jared describes being in a sales meeting. At a key point during the meeting, Jared's potential clients grew silent, in a way that made Jared feel uncomfortable. The awkward moment passed, and the meeting proceeded. During the debriefing, Jared and his colleagues discovered they had all been uncomfortable with the silence. They had no idea how to interpret it. Jared recounted, "We couldn't tell if they were quiet because they were turned off, or because they were really impressed!"

Jared and his colleagues wanted very much to be seen as trusted advisors to their prospective client. Here's the coaching question for them: *Why did you choose not to inquire what was behind the silence at the time?* Choosing not to comment on the silence led to a missed opportunity for trust-building and new business.

More often than not, the simple reason Jared (and others) don't comment is fear. Fear of expressing something awkwardly. Fear of some kind of backlash. Fear of hearing an unpleasant answer. Jared allowed fear to suppress his natural curiosity.

And therein lies the trust opportunity, because it is the very act of taking risks (Figure 9.1) that builds trust. Taking risks means having the courage to respond with curiosity and authenticity in a moment of truth. Risk-taking requires that you go outside your own comfort zone for the benefit of the relationship.

To be a better risk-taker means you expand your willingness and ability to tolerate ambiguity and exposure. In doing so, you become someone who is experienced as a "safe haven" for others. People know where they stand with you and have a real sense of who you are as a professional and as a person.

If you never feel uncomfortable and even scared sometimes, you are not being a trusted advisor. Part of the job description is getting comfortable being uncomfortable.

The Relationship between Trust and Risk

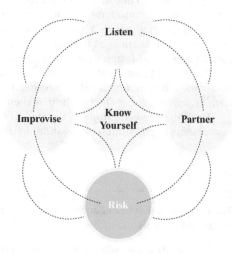

Figure 9.1

Five Trust
Skills: Risk

A lot of what we propose in this book may cause you to think or say, "But that's risky!" True. That's exactly the point.

We would highlight four dynamics about the relationship between trust and risk (see Figure 9.1):

1. *Trust and risk go hand-in-hand.* A trust relationship exists because someone has taken a chance. While levels of risk may vary by relationship or by situation, risk is always present. And if you think or say, "There isn't enough trust in the relationship yet to tolerate that kind of risk," check your thinking. It is the very *taking of risks* that creates trust in the first place. If you never feel uncomfortable, even scared sometimes, you are not being a trusted advisor. Part of the job description is getting comfortable being uncomfortable. And that includes cultivating a habit of going first.

2. *The relationship between trust and risk is paradoxical.* A "safe haven" implies the absence of risk when in fact it is just the opposite—an environment where risks that serve the relationship can be taken any time and are taken often. Risk-taking naturally increases intimacy, which increases trust. And more trust ultimately leads to less risk for all parties. Risk is to trust as inoculation is to immunity. Small doses of risk taken early mitigate much larger risks later. The best way to reduce risk in a relationship is—paradoxically—to take risks in a relationship. (See Chapter 1, "Fundamental Truths.")

3. *Reasons not to risk are usually personal.* The rationalizations behind why *not* to risk in a relationship are usually personal, fear-based motives masquerading as business justifications. Figure 9.2 provides three examples of this.

   If you find yourself advocating for lesser risk, check for personal motives behind the business justifications and deal with those first.

4. *Risk-taking is transformative.* For most people, an uncomfortable moment—like a long period of unexpected silence during a meeting—generates fear and indecision. In that moment of truth, many people overestimate the emotional risk of saying the wrong thing and underestimate the business benefits of having the right conversation for the long-term.

Stated Reasons Not to Risk	Business Justification	Underlying Personal Motive
"I can't say I don't know ..."	"... because they expect subject mastery"	Fear of appearing incompetent
"I can't get too personal ..."	"... because they want an arms-length, 'professional relationship'"	Fear of being rejected
"I can't listen too long ..."	"... because they want answers"	Discomfort with ambiguity

Figure 9.2

The Real
Reasons We
Don't Take
Risks

By choosing to decline the opportunity for intimacy, you avoid the short-term emotional exposure at the considerable cost of forgoing future gains. By choosing to take the risk, you open yourself up to a range of possibilities, including a genuine resolution (not just the cessation of silence) as well as a new foundation for every discussion that follows. Your partner sees you through new lenses. The context of the relationship fundamentally changes.

Recall Jared and his team. By not immediately acknowledging their clients' silence, they overvalued the emotional risk of causing an awkward moment and undervalued the longer-term benefit of getting clear with their clients about what was needed and where they stood.

This situation is not unique to Jared. It is the template of every dilemma that faces us all in moments of potential trust creation: to dive or not to dive into the deep end?

Six Ways to Practice Risk-Taking

The best way to get better at risk-taking is to practice risk-taking. Here are six specific practices to expand your risk-taking aptitude:

1. *Be proactive about reducing ambiguity.* Jared, the salesperson mentioned earlier, could have done this by saying something like: "Hmmmm ... I'm not sure how to interpret the silence in the room." Or he could have used a little humor: "Gee, that silence is getting pretty loud—it's got my collar feeling a little tight (gesture to his collar). Any advice on how we should interpret it?"

> The best way to get better at risk-taking is to practice risk-taking.

The second example seems the riskiest, because it both reveals discomfort and invites others to open up. But it is also likely to build the most trust and lead to the most productive outcome. More often than not, your willingness to address things will be met with gratitude.

2. *Acknowledge uncomfortable situations out loud.* Caveats are conversational jewels. Examples include:
   - "Wow, this is awkward ..."
   - "I wish I had better news ..."
   - "The timing with this is embarrassing ..."

3. *Deliver hard news promptly and concisely.* Practice doing it in 10 words or less. Examples include:
   - "We're not going to make the deadline."
   - "We just don't have the executive sponsorship we need."
   - "Jim is leaving the team."

   The direct approach works especially well in combination with caveats. "A Tool for Truth-Telling: Name It and Claim It" further on provides more detail on applying tips 2 and 3.

> Risk is to trust as inoculation is to immunity. Small doses of risk taken early mitigate much larger risks later.

4. *Take responsibility for mistakes.* No one likes to call attention to the things that have not been done well. It is also human to make mistakes and refreshingly real to be candid about them. "Janet, part of the problem here is that I failed to meet my commitments."

5. *Be willing to express your own emotions.* A partnership, by definition, includes you. Your thoughts and feelings are legitimate too. Examples are:
   - "Gee, Johannes, I must confess to feeling pretty frustrated by what you just said."
   - "You have no idea how happy I am to hear that."

6. *Share something personal.* The next time you are doing the Monday morning "how-was-your-weekend-fine-thanks-yours?" exchange, don't stop at the superficial. "My weekend

was great, Surita, thanks for asking. My parents were in town, and Sam and I really enjoyed the babysitting they offered. We got a much-needed break." Reciprocity applies to risk-taking as well as to listening. You never know what might open up out of your willingness to share.

From the Front Lines: An Unexpected Result

I (Andrea) was at lunch with Wayne Simmons, then the Managing Partner of ICOR Partners, a very successful boutique firm in Washington, DC. My colleague and I had just kicked off a pretty significant project involving the top 17 people in his company. Halfway through the meal we discovered a big disconnect in expectations. We were collecting 360-degree feedback on all of his leaders, and we learned that Wayne expected to have access to each person's detailed feedback report. He was counting on the data to help make some critical staffing decisions.

This is taboo in the world of 360-degree feedback where confidentiality is paramount—something we thought we had communicated clearly, but apparently hadn't. Wayne was angry when I told him we couldn't deliver what he was expecting. I told him as respectfully as I could that we would regretfully abort the project—which was well underway and had been paid for in advance—rather than compromise confidentiality. He reluctantly agreed to continue the project on those terms, and we completed the work in a few months. While I felt the project as a whole was moderately successful, on a relationship level I felt it was a failure.

Six months later, Wayne invited me to lunch, much to my surprise. There was no particular agenda; he just wanted to reconnect. I asked him, with some hesitancy, how things were going in the organization since our work together. He said things were going well and then said something that took me by surprise: "You know, Andrea, I'll never forget how you stood your ground that day when I told you I needed to see all the 360 data. I didn't like hearing what you had to say. You were right not to give in. And I knew right then and there you were someone I could count on."

My key takeaways from this experience: Stand for what you believe in, despite how it might feel in the moment. And don't rely on your own assessment to judge the quality of your relationship with someone.

—Andrea P. Howe

The Three-Question Transparency Test

Most of us probably agree in theory with the principle of transparency—being honest, open, and candid (except when illegal or injurious to others). There are situations where it might feel best to say nothing. On the surface, it is easy to say, "Honesty is the best policy!" Dig a little deeper and it is not so clear.

The principle of transparency is hard to live by. It takes courage. It takes a commitment to removing yourself from the equation. And it takes a certain level of discernment to figure out when sidestepping the truth is hurtful versus helpful.

> ## Insight: Where People Go Wrong with Risk Assessment[1]
>
> When analyzing the pros and cons of taking a risk on telling the truth, people tend to:
> - *Underestimate the value of forthrightness* even when the truth being told is unpleasant to hear. A willingness to face facts is quickly perceived by others as a virtue and usually outweighs an uncomfortable message.
> - *Overestimate the cost of disapproval.* Partners who face an uncomfortable reality usually see it as something to be dealt with and to move beyond. They are not the ones caught up in concerns about disapproval.
> - *Overestimate the probability of a situation righting itself.* It's easy to rationalize that somehow you will be saved from ever having to face the truth, or having to face it as boldly as you know a trusted advisor would. This is the TAMO phenomenon of project management: "Then, A Miracle Occurs."
>
>   In short, lying only seems to make sense if you underestimate the risks and overestimate the benefits. But lying is the most corrosive antitrust action you can take.

Let's look at some business examples to make this real—cases where you know something that your partner does not (or might not), and you wonder, "To tell or not to tell?"

- *Imagine you've discovered a mistake in your work.* The impact is relatively minor. Does it help or hurt your relationship with your boss to call attention to it?
- *What if you discover a mistake in your client's work*? The impact is significant. So is the likelihood of embarrassment (or worse) for them. Are you honoring or dishonoring the relationship by saying nothing?
- *You learn something unfavorable about a competitor—one your customer is currently engaged with.* Are you the hero or the jerk if you bring it up?

Sometimes a lie by omission seems like a very reasonable option.

The next time you are debating to tell or not to tell, use the three-question transparency test to help you decide.

1. *Is your reason for not telling for your benefit, or for theirs?* Look for a personal motive behind the business justification. Consider whether it is truly in your partner's best interest to say nothing or whether your desire to avoid your own discomfort is creating a platform for rationalization.
2. *If you don't tell and he finds out later, will he feel misled?* This question invites you to see the situation from your partner's vantage point, which is always a good practice when it comes to relationship-building. And, if you are banking on the fact that he won't find out later, check your probabilities … and your motives.
3. *Would you tell her if she were your friend?* This question cuts to the chase and invites you to set aside the arm's length decorum that defines most business relationships.

   If at any point your answer is yes, stop and find a way to say what needs to be said with compassion and diplomacy.

A Tool for Truth-Telling: Name It and Claim It

Relationships of any kind are rife with difficult conversations that could be had or should be had. And difficult conversations are inherently risky—it is natural to be afraid of how they will go and what impact they will have on the other person, on you, and on the relationship.

Imagine a long-term personal relationship, like a marriage, where difficult conversations are absent. Such a relationship is probably not sustainable. Concerns pile up over time, and if left unspoken, the relationship can't benefit from the shared experience of intimacy that comes from working through them. Trust-based business relationships are no different. A trusted advisor must take the leap and initiate difficult conversations for the benefit of the relationship. This takes courage *and* skill.

> Unspoken issues have a corrosive effect on relationships, sometimes in an obvious way and sometimes more subtly. Name It and Claim It restores power to the relationship.

Name It and Claim It is a tool for making difficult conversations easier. Use it for elephant-in-the-room issues, to speak about the unspeakable in socially acceptable terms. We call it Name It and Claim It because when you "name it" you claim your power—not as in power over someone, but as in power with another. Unspoken issues have a corrosive effect on relationships, sometimes in an obvious way, sometimes more subtly. Name It and Claim It restores power to the relationship.

When to Name It and Claim It

There are two signs that Name It and Claim It may be called for: (1) when you want to raise a topic that you might otherwise be tempted to avoid and (2) situations that require a metaconversation to break an ineffective pattern.

There are some topics you may be tempted to avoid:

- *Staffing/team issues.* You are worried about a confrontation, so you delay the discussion. Elapsed time usually makes things worse, not better.
- *Pricing.* Price is an awkward topic, one that most people avoid bringing up too soon. Name It and Claim It helps you bring it up earlier rather than later. (See also Chapter 15, "Talking Price.")
- *Scope creep.* When tasks expand outside their original scope and the overall project is at risk. Name It and Claim It makes it possible address issues before they get out of hand.
- *Sensitive behavioral topics.* When a partner's behavior needs to be addressed—say a colleague has hygiene issues or a client says inappropriate things—having a way to address the delicate subject makes a big difference.
- *Wrong project or client.* Sometimes you realize the project you have undertaken is not what you thought it was, or that you are in a relationship with the wrong client. In these cases, hoping for the best is not your best risk mitigation strategy.

There are some situations that require a metaconversation, such as:

- *Aloofness.* When your colleague seems quiet or withdrawn, it is tempting to keep talking. Name It and Claim It gives you a way to address the real issue by raising your concern about his lack of response.
- *Resistance or combativeness.* When you are locked in disagreement or when a teammate is prone to outbursts, Name It and Claim It helps you break the cycle.
- *No communication.* When your client does not return your messages, Name It and Claim It makes it possible to acknowledge that your communications are not getting answered and get to the root of the issue.

How to Name It and Claim It

Use this four-step process to find socially acceptable ways to put hard truths on the table.

1. *Define the issue.* Get clear about the message you have to deliver. Articulate the issue simply and clearly, preferably in 10 words or less.

2. *List all your concerns about speaking the issue.* These are the worries and fears that leave you reluctant to have the difficult conversation. For example, you might not be 100 percent confident in your assessment about executive sponsorship. You might also be concerned that you might offend someone by saying it.

3. *Turn your concerns into one or more caveats.* A caveat is a short phrase that you will use as a warning or cautionary detail. For example, "I may be completely missing the mark here" and "I sure don't want to step on any toes."

4. *Put it all together.* Combine your brief description of the issue (Step 1) with your caveats (Step 3) and deliver the news. For example, "I may be completely missing the mark here, and I sure don't want to step on any toes. I'm concerned we don't have the executive sponsorship we need."

The Power of Caveats

Caveats are not intended to stall or sidestep an issue. They are meant to make it easier for both the giver and the receiver to initiate a conversation about a difficult topic.

Linking back to the Trust Equation, a well-crafted caveat delivered with authenticity increases intimacy in four specific ways (see Figure 9.3). A caveat:

1. Warns your partner that something is coming.
2. Demonstrates humility.
3. Expresses your own emotion and vulnerability, which evokes empathy from another.
4. Preemptively defuses a conflict. If they are thinking it and you are stating it, the conflict loses power and the relationship gains power.

Figure 9.3

Four Steps to Name It and Claim It

Step 1: Define the issue.	We don't have the executive sponsorship we need.	We're not going to make the deadline.	I've lost sight of what we're really trying to accomplish.
Step 2: List all your concerns about speaking the issue.	• I might be wrong. • I'll step on someone's toes.	• I hate being the messenger. • It should have been dealt with sooner.	• It's embarrassing to admit. • I might look stupid.
Step 3: Turn your concerns into a caveat.	I may be completely missing the mark here, and I sure don't want to step on any toes.	I hate being the bearer of bad news, especially at this late juncture.	At the risk of embarrassing myself ...
Step 4: Put it all together.	"I may be completely missing the mark here, and I sure don't want to step on any toes. I'm concerned we don't have the executive sponsorship we need."	"I hate being the bearer of bad news, especially at this late juncture. We're not going to make the deadline."	"At the risk of embarrassing myself, I've lost sight of what we're really trying to accomplish."

From the Front Lines: A Little Levity

I (Andrea) have from time to time been faced with a crashing web browser. Every time, in spite of my temporary frustration, I have had to smile at the power of Mozilla Firefox's very disarming error message, which displays on the screen in big, bold letters: "Well, this is embarrassing."

—Andrea P. Howe

Caveats also reduce your self-orientation by helping you move past your inertia and by quieting the chatter in your brain. And because caveats help you speak the truth, they also help you increase your credibility. In other words, using caveats to Name It and Claim It is a trust trifecta: you simultaneously increase credibility, increase intimacy, and reduce self-orientation—all in one or two sentences.

From the Front Lines: Telling a Difficult Truth

Lynn P., a career systems consultant serving largely government clients in the United States, tells a story about taking a risk under pressure:

"Eleven years into my career, I took over a major project. A key phase, testing, was way behind schedule, and the Testing Readiness Review was only two weeks away. Passing the review was a very big deal: It meant completing a milestone and getting a payment for my company.

"I was due to present to all the clients and the senior managers of my own company. It was intimidating—and I was intimidated.

"I was under significant pressure to keep the program moving by passing the review. I also knew that we were not ready to pass ....

"Knowing it could cost me my job, I went line by line through our assessment, citing the facts as I saw them. I said we did not pass the review and that we would need to delay to correct the critical items.

"There was complete silence in the room.

"My top executive asked, 'Are you sure?'

"I said yes.

"After the meeting, both my client and my senior managers approached me informally to commend me for 'sticking to my guns' and recommending what I believed to be right.

"Apparently, I had created trust—a lot of it. Over the next 18 months, I was given roles of increasing responsibility, and was eventually promoted to program manager.

"I now believe it was this event that drove the client to increase my role. The experience gave me greater confidence in my own judgment and skills. And finally, it was this program's success that ultimately propelled my career to the next level."

The willingness to take a risk by being principled can pay off hugely—as long as you're doing it for the principles, not the payoff.

—As told to Charles H. Green

"At the risk of" can be a useful way to caveat:

- "At the risk of embarrassing myself …"
- "At the risk of causing some momentary awkwardness …"
- "At the risk of overstepping my bounds …"

Other caveats might sound like this:

- "Since bad news doesn't get better with age …"
- "I pride myself in my subject matter expertise, and I may be on the verge of looking stupid here …"
- "This is awkward, and there's just no way around it …"
- "I just can't think of a better way to say this …"

Using caveats to name it and claim it is a trust trifecta: you simultaneously increase credibility, increase intimacy, and reduce self-orientation—all in one or two sentences.

You will notice that none of the examples use the word *but* as in, "This is awkward, but …." That's because the word *but* can have a negating effect on anything said before it. Steer clear of *but*, along with its close cousin *however*.

Worksheet: Risk-Taking as a Matter of Practice

Bring to mind a key stakeholder (e.g., client, prospect, colleague, staff member) with whom you have an exemplary trust-based relationship.

My stakeholder:

In what ways is risk present in the relationship? How do you take risks? How does your stakeholder take risks?

_____

_____

_____

Now, bring to mind a key stakeholder with whom you'd like to have an improved—or even transformed—relationship.

My stakeholder:

Consider each of the six ways to practice risk-taking as described in this chapter. Which ones do you regularly apply? What opportunities do you see to improve the relationship by taking more risk?

Ways to Practice Risk-Taking	Frequency	Opportunities
1. Be proactive about reducing ambiguity.	☐Y ☐N ☐Sometimes	
2. Acknowledge uncomfortable situations out loud.	☐Y ☐N ☐Sometimes	
3. Deliver hard news promptly and concisely.	☐Y ☐N ☐Sometimes	
4. Take responsibility for mistakes.	☐Y ☐N ☐Sometimes	
5. Be willing to express your own emotions.	☐Y ☐N ☐Sometimes	
6. Share something personal.	☐Y ☐N ☐Sometimes	

What actions will you take as a result of this reflection? Be specific.

What	By When	With Whom	Support I Will Ask For

What do you notice as a result of examining this relationship that might apply to other relationships?

_____

_____

_____

Worksheet: Name It and Claim It

Think about a challenging business relationship where topics are being avoided or negative patterns aren't being called out. What isn't being said that needs to be said? Describe it briefly:

_____

_____

_____

Use the four steps to Name It and Claim It in this chapter to imagine a way that you might put this hard truth on the table with your partner.

	Example	Your Situation
Step 1: Define the issue, clearly and simply	*We don't have the executive sponsorship we need.*	
Step 2: List all your concerns about speaking the issue	• *I might be wrong.* • *I'll step on someone's toes.*	
Step 3: Turn your concerns into a caveat	*I may be completely missing the mark here, and I sure don't want to step on any toes.*	
Step 4: Put it all together	*"I may be completely missing the mark here, and I sure don't want to step on any toes. I'm concerned we don't have the executive sponsorship we need."*	

What next steps will you take from here?

Know Yourself

Introspection, the act of looking within, helps you lead with trust. Knowing yourself makes it possible to adjust to people and situations, facilitates empathy by making it easier to relate to others and be related to, and paves the way for more rewarding working relationships. This chapter offers practical ways to increase your self-knowledge with guidance on how to look inward, turn blind spots into insights, and experiment regularly. We also suggest ways to use expanded self-awareness to increase your integrity and build trust.

The basis of Emotional Intelligence is self-awareness,[1] and trustworthiness operates in much the same way. To *know yourself* (Figure 10.1) is to be cognizant of your weaknesses, triggers, and hot buttons, as well as your strengths, interests, and sources of passion and purpose. Knowing yourself is not about being narcissistic, self-obsessed, or perfect. It is about achieving a level of self-awareness that, paradoxically, lowers your self-orientation and improves your ability to connect with others. The more self-aware you are, the better you are able to manage yourself, and the less likely you are to act automatically from your blind spots.

How Blind Spots Impede Trust-Building

Blind spots, or aspects of yourself that others are aware of but you are not, keep you from applying the three trust models to your everyday life. Some examples:

> Without self-knowledge you run the risk of damaging trust without even realizing it.

- *You don't realize the full extent of your need to be liked,* and therefore you don't see how it keeps you from saying something unpopular. This, in turn, lowers your credibility and your overall trustworthiness score on the trust equation.
- *You are not aware of the intensity of your internal drive to achieve.* As a result, you don't realize you habitually move too quickly from listen to commit in the trust creation process.
- *You don't fully grasp your discomfort with feeling unprepared.* Your uneasiness prevents you from engaging in the messiness that collaboration—one of the four trust principles—often requires.

Figure 10.1

Five Trust Skills: Know Yourself

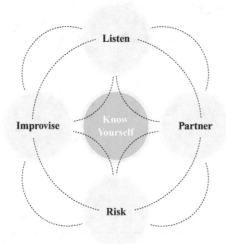

Without self-knowledge you run the risk of damaging trust without even realizing it. With it you can make choices that accentuate your positive traits and devise strategies for dealing with your weaknesses.

If you can take self-knowledge one step further and *accept* yourself, all the better. Consider the business value of integrity—being who you claim to be at all times to all people. It is a lot easier to be yourself when you know who you are, and when you have the capacity to accept yourself as is.

Three Approaches to Expand Your Self-Knowledge

Ways to expand your self-knowledge (see Figure 10.1):

1. *Look inward.* There are myriad tools to help you profile yourself. Use them. Discover your values, preferences, strengths, and weaknesses. Get familiar with your deepest inner voice—a critical guidepost for decision making. The part of your brain that hijacks you in a moment of crisis, the amygdala, is the same part of the brain that helps you develop hunches or "gut feelings."[3] Being able to tap into this part of you takes consciousness and practice.
2. *Turn blind spots into insights.* See yourself as others do by seeking and integrating feedback. Doing this takes confidence and humility. By bringing to light aspects of yourself that are hidden from you but apparent to others, you sharpen your trusted advisor skills while becoming a more well-rounded person.

CASE STUDY

From the Front Lines: Self-Knowledge Is Essential[2]

L.J. Rittenhouse has read and analyzed thousands of shareholder letters for The Rittenhouse Rankings Candor™ Survey, which correlates measures of CEO candor with stock price performance. She talks about the revelations that self-knowledge can bring:

"CEOs have been amazed when I show them how their shareholder letters compare to letters from other CEOs. They begin to see themselves as others see them. This isn't always pleasant: Sometimes the differences can be stark. But gaining self-knowledge is essential to maintaining dynamic and effective leadership.

"As Warren Buffett reminds us, the CEO who misleads others in public may eventually mislead himself in private. By observing what topics have been left out of their communications or were not fully developed, my CEO clients have stretched their perceptual boundaries so they could more effectively engage with their stakeholders and build trust. I am consistently impressed with the CEOs I work with and proud of them for their courage, their capacity to learn and change, and their willingness to know themselves."

—*L.J. Rittenhouse (author of Buffett's Bites and Do Business with People You Can Tru$t: Balancing Profits and Principles, and founder, Rittenhouse Rankings Inc., New York)*

---

3. *Experiment regularly.* Over time, you have developed habitual ways of thinking, doing, and being. Some of those may be productive, like the habit of listening first before problem-solving. Others may be limiting, like a habit of investing all your relationship-building time in people you already know. Move away from the familiar and comfortable. Test out new skills, experiences, and relationships on an ongoing basis.

> Expand what you know yourself to be capable of. Test out new skills, experiences, and relationships on an ongoing basis.

Figure 10.2 provides 11 specific practices to make these steps more concrete.

Approach	Practices
Look inward	1. *Articulate your personal values.* What matters most to you? A good way to find out is to write your own eulogy at your funeral. What would you want others to say about you and about what you stood for in your lifetime? Another practice is to develop a personal mission statement.[a] 2. *Learn your Trust Quotient and Trust Temperament.* Know which variables of trustworthiness you tend to lead with and which ones you are more likely to de-emphasize or ignore. Pay special attention to doing what it takes to have consistent scores across all four variables.[b] 3. *Delve into your working style and personality preferences.* There are dozens of frameworks available to help discover yours, including Tracom's Social Style(sm) Model, the Thomas-Kilmann Conflict Mode Instrument, the DiSC Profile, and the Meyers-Briggs Type Indicator, all of which can be useful. Choose one or two that align with your organization's programs and/or your personal interests. 4. *Use a journal to record your feelings.* Write about your experiences and your feelings about your experiences for several days or weeks. Let your thoughts and emotions flow freely. Create a private space for you and only you.[c] 5. *Set regular time aside for reflection or meditation.* Take time away from the fray to reconnect with your deepest thoughts, feelings, and motivations. Try meditation. Or if sitting on a meditation cushion is not your thing, take long walks or drives, or pursue a hobby.
Turn blind spots into insights	6. *Seek 360-degree feedback.* Use instruments such as the Trust 360 and Emotional Competence Inventory[d] to collect feedback from internal and external raters. Compare their assessments to your own. What do you see? 7. *Conduct stakeholder interviews.* Whether you do this as part of a formal 360-degree assessment or as a stand-alone practice, talk to people you work with. Find out what they see as your strengths and your opportunities for improvement. Get specific. Check what you learn against your own self-perception. 8. *Record yourself.* Use video or audio technology to see or hear yourself in action. Watch yourself presenting or in conversation. What do you see that others see? What you are surprised by? Let those things motivate you to change. This highly effective means helps you quickly develop new and improved habits.

Figure 10.2

Specific Practices for Expanding Your Self-Knowledge

Approach	Practices
Experiment regularly	9. *Try something new that stretches you outside your comfort zone.* This could be anything from taking a new route to work to signing up for an improv comedy class to going skydiving. What you choose doesn't have to be extreme—it does have to be a step beyond what is typically comfortable for you. Choose something, do it, then reflect on it. What did the experience confirm about you? What did you discover or rediscover?
	10. *Develop a new relationship.* Get to know someone you wouldn't ordinarily gravitate towards. This could be a personal or professional relationship. What does interacting with this person teach you about yourself?
	11. *Develop mastery as a trusted advisor.* Regularly choose practices in the other skill chapters in this book—listen, improvise, partner, and risk— to hone your skills. Which is most comfortable? Least comfortable? How can you stretch beyond your current skill limits?

a. Stephen R. Covey, *The 7 Habits of Highly Effective People* (Free Press, 2004).

b. Consistency across all four trust equation variables is associated with higher trust quotient scores, presumably because consistency is another reflection of integrity.

c. In a study conducted at Southern Methodist University, half of 63 laid-off managers were asked to keep a journal for five days, spending 20 minutes every day writing about their emotional responses to their circumstances. Those who kept journals found new jobs faster than those who didn't (Daniel Goleman, *Working with Emotional Intelligence* [Bantam, 2000]).

d. Fabio Sala and Steven B. Wolff, Emotional Competency Inventory (ECI) Technical Manual (Hay Group, 2005), www.eiconsortium.org/pdf/ECI_2_0_Technical_Manual_v2.pdf/.

How to Use Self-Knowledge to Increase Trust

The heightened self-awareness that comes from knowing yourself inside and out makes it possible to make better and more conscious choices to promote trust in your relationships. Returning to the examples earlier in this chapter:

- *When you realize the full extent of your need to be liked,* you see the importance of developing comfort and skill with saying unpopular things. You can then expand your risk-taking portfolio and practice using caveats to deliver tough messages.
- *When you are aware of the intensity of your internal drive to achieve,* you see the negative impact this has on your ability to be a masterful listener. You can regularly practice three-level listening and devise tactics like crossing your fingers as a reminder that you have something to say—later.
- *When you fully grasp your discomfort with feeling unprepared,* you see how this degrades your ability to improvise and partner. You can practice your reactions during a moment of truth through role-playing, and become adept at thinking out loud.

Worksheet: Self-Knowledge Is Power

This chapter identifies three approaches to expanding your self-knowledge: look inward, turn blind spots into insights, and experiment regularly. For each, choose one practice based on the ideas provided. What specifically will you do to achieve a level of self-awareness that, paradoxically, will lower your self-orientation and improve your ability to connect with others?

Approach	Description	Your Actions
Look inward.	There are myriad tools to help you profile yourself. Use them. Discover your values, preferences, strengths, and weaknesses. Get familiar with your inner voice—a critical guidepost for decision-making.	
Turn blind spots into insights.	See yourself as others do by seeking and integrating feedback. Bring to light aspects of yourself that are hidden from you but apparent to others.	
Experiment regularly.	Move away from the familiar and comfortable. Test out new skills, experiences, and relationships on an ongoing basis.	

Developing Business with Trust

Part **III**

Traditional approaches to marketing, business development, and sales too often create an adversarial relationship between buyer and seller: one *does to* and the other is *done to*. The trust-based view of these critical business functions centers on creating relationships and being of help.

Section III explores specific ways to use trust to radically alter the traditional dynamic and exponentially improve results. This section uses real-life examples to explore a full range of challenges, from trust-based networking to talking price to selling to the C-suite.

Trust-Based Marketing and Business Development

11

Chapter

Demonstrating that you are trustworthy starts long before you land the job; in fact, it contributes to whether you land it in the first place. Trust-based marketing and business development helps to build your brand, gain sales, and create enduring client relationships. After all, people genuinely prefer to do business with those they trust. This chapter shows you how to apply trust principles in the early stages of new business relationships.

Professionals in every marketing and business development department face the same concerns: How can I find new clients? How can I differentiate myself and my organization from the competition? How can I get referrals? How can I better cross-sell?

In the following sections, we explore specific ways to apply four trust principles to sales and business development:

1. A *focus on the other* for the other's sake, not just as a means to your own ends.
2. A *collaborative approach* to relationships.
3. A *medium-to-long-term perspective*, not a short-term transactional focus.
4. A *habit of being transparent* in all your dealings.

Focus on Your Customer

The terms *client-focus* and *customer-centric* are too often framed in terms of economic benefit to the person trying to be trusted. In contrast, focusing on the other for the other's sake is not just a means to your own ends. It focuses on what is best for your customer—even when that may not appear to be what is best for you and your organization.

Here are four specific ways to implement this principle:

1. *Share ideas.* Whether you are a solo practitioner, an account manager, a value-added reseller, or a small business owner, you probably have a lot of great experience and ideas about how your approach can really help your customers. Don't sit on those ideas; share them in ways that may help your potential customers.

2. *Give away free samples.* There is no better way to communicate your value proposition than to give away a sample. The impact of samples is even greater for the complex and intangible services that make up so much of today's business.

> Instead of thinking about cross-selling as "who else can we sell this to," think of what your client needs.

3. *Tell your prospects why they don't need you.* Be willing to walk away from business if it is not right for the customer. If there are reasons why your prospect may not need you, let her know. You have not wasted each other's time, you have established initial trust, and you are one step closer to a future productive relationship.

CASE STUDY

From the Front Lines: Building a Trust-Based Brand[1]

Sir Richard Branson's philosophy of differentiation and marketing for the Virgin brand consistently links to two of the four trust principles: customer focus and transparency.

Customer Focus: "[One] secret to lasting success: securing your customers' trust, which should be part and parcel of your differentiation and marketing. At Virgin, we first did this somewhat accidentally, by relying on openness and simplicity when we communicated."

Differentiation: "Since we'd created companies everyone on staff was proud of, we were all deeply concerned about quality and customer service, and our marketing focused on why the businesses were different and special."

Transparency: "Many of our ad campaigns play off this open, frank communication. Our mobile phone companies offer straightforward bills with no hidden charges; our credit card agreements are easy to understand; our health club members are not locked into lengthy contracts."

Trust-Based Marketing: "This strategy of differentiating and marketing your product with a view to winning customers' trust is the only way to build a sustainable, lasting business."

Build your marketing approach on the trust principles and you will be well on your way to a strong brand, a full sales pipeline, and client relationships that stand the test of time.

Insight: Client Focus in Action[2]

- You're an accounting firm. It's tax season. Everyone thinks you're busy. Surprise them with a two- to three-hour clinic for your clients' kids who are now college graduates on how to do their own taxes.
- You're a restaurant owner. You know who your good customers are. Surprise them next visit by picking up the tab. Quietly.
- You're a doctor. When you have good test results for a nervous patient, don't wait for the next visit. Call and celebrate together.
- You're a development director for a charitable organization. Your donors are your customers. Instead of asking them for money, turn the tables—ask how a particular donor is affected by the economy. How can you add value to his life? Who can you put him in touch with?
- Go drop coins in someone's parking meter or pay the toll for the guy behind you. It's cheap behavioral training for client focus. And it makes two people feel good.

4. *Make cross-selling about your client.* Instead of thinking about cross-selling as "who else can we sell this to," start with client needs. If you broadly consider, "How can I help this client?"—not just in terms of your products and services—you will have conversations that deepen your relationship. As a result, you will come up with great ideas for your client that may occasionally align with something you offer. Share *all* your ideas freely to build a long-term relationship founded on trust.

Collaborate to Drive New Business

The principle of collaboration refers to your willingness to work together, to create joint goals, and construct joint approaches to getting there. Here are three ways you can adopt a collaborative approach to business development.

1. *Collaborate internally first.* Your intention to collaborate with customers can be undermined if your people don't collaborate with each other, and if you don't collaborate with other stakeholders in your marketplace. The law firm partner who jealously guards her client relationships, the financial planner who always seeks to increase share of wallet, the client relationship manager who doesn't want his colleague to cross-sell—these situations telegraph an unwillingness to collaborate. Take a hard look at your organization: Are you falling into the same traps? How well do you collaborate, both within your organization and with all your partners?

2. *Approach networking collaboratively.* Rather than think of networking as prospecting, redefine it as actively practicing collaboration. The next time you attend a networking event, instead of focusing on how you can develop new business,

> Rather than think of networking as prospecting, redefine it as actively practicing collaboration.

Insight: Collaboration in Action[3]

- You're a speaker or trainer. Put together a speaking tour or a combined webinar of like-minded people—including those you used to think of as competitors.
- You're a business-to-business (B2B) manufacturing salesperson. Call a key customer. Suggest the two firms sit down together offsite for a day and discuss what you could do better together to make things cheaper, faster, or more profitable for *both* of you. Be prepared to share your manufacturing process, costs, and profit margins, so you can figure it out together.
- You're in an internal staff group of a large company (HR, Legal, Finance, IT, and so on). Identify three or four of the same departments in other large companies in your geographic area. Create a collaborative work group across the companies that meets (within bounds of legal agendas) to share best practices and work opportunities.
- You're a professional services firm with underemployed staff. Offer to swap similarly underemployed staff with a client. Both will gain valuable perspective and experience without being taken off critical work. The employees involved will feel grateful and challenged. And the linkages between the firms will be strengthened. None of which would easily happen in good economic times.
- You're in a business where sales are large and take time. At the next sales presentation meeting, have a client co-present with you. And make a point of it, saying, "Working collaboratively with you is what we believe in."

ask yourself: "How can I help the people in this room? For whom could I broker an introduction? How can we work together?" Thinking of new contacts as collaborators makes them appear less threatening than they might be as prospective clients, and gives you an opportunity to practice your partnering skills.

3. *Collaborate your way into referrals.* Who would you more likely refer to one of your clients: someone who has worked collaboratively with you or someone who is technically proficient but comes off as aloof, distant, and critical? Be mindful that the way you conduct yourself with others doesn't just affect your relationships with them—it affects how they characterize you to colleagues, and whether they are willing to refer you. Taking a collaborative approach with both your existing clients and prospective clients improves not just your immediate working relationship, but also generates more referrals.

> The way you conduct yourself with others doesn't just affect your relationships with them—it affects how they characterize you to colleagues, and whether they are willing to refer you.

Focus on Relationships, Not Transactions

The most beneficial relationships for both you and your clients are those where multiple transactions take place over time inside a framework of mutual trust. Here are two ways to embed this principle in your business development practices.

1. *Build relationships with those you've screened out.* Countless sales programs and literature focus on sales efficiency—they tell you to screen leads so that you don't waste your time on those who will never buy. The problem is this: while screening out unlikely buyers, you are bypassing opportunities for discovery and dialogue—and probably irritating some of them at the same time. Girard's Law of 250[4] states that if a prospect has a bad experience with you, on average he will tell 250 people; and with online social media, that number can mushroom rapidly. Suddenly an isolated act of sales efficiency threatens to destroy your reputation among a vast number of potential customers. You may not have thought

> Force yourself to think long-term—see every business act in a relationship context.

Insight: Long-Term Focus in Action[5]

1. Pick your top three clients and strategize internally on how you can strengthen your relationship in the long run. Then discuss those plans with those three clients, telling them exactly what you've done, and why.
2. Help everyone you know who has been laid off. Provide advice, contacts, and just listen. These are people who are potentially great customers down the road, but don't do it for that reason, do it because you care.
3. If you're a consulting organization, establish your alumni network. If you already have one, kick up the level of involvement. Facilitate their networking by updating your directory, hosting events, and creating online collaboration and conversation spaces.
4. If a key customer is in the middle of an important job with you and they can't afford for you to finish it, talk it over with them and offer to defer payment until such time as the customer can pay. It doesn't cost much to be generous; it lowers credit risk by creating trust and reciprocity. And showing a little faith and courage does wonders for the relationship.

From the Front Lines: A Personal Touch[6]

Our colleague Hazel Thompson in Australia tells a story about the difference a personal touch can make.

"A number of years ago I asked a friend what criteria he had used to decide on a service provider for a facility management contract. He said it was a difficult decision: The three tender documents he received were similar, and the people he met from each firm were all credible and seemed to be people he could work with. The clincher for him was that only one of the tenderers sent him a best wishes card for the holiday. That's the firm he chose."

—Hazel Thompson (Trusted Advisor Associates, Australia)

that your sales drove your marketing, but in the case of reputation, it does. Force yourself to think long-term—see every business act in a relationship context.

2. *Promote relationships.* Make it clear to everyone that you value relationships. Share stories about your relationship successes; talk about them inside your organization and in your literature. Mentor others in valuing relationships over immediate return.

Be Transparent with Prospects and Clients

Transparency preempts any concerns your buyer may have about being manipulated. If you are transparent about your activities, you show you have nothing to hide. If you have nothing to hide, people trust what you do and say. Be honest, open, and candid, except when illegal or injurious to others. Here are two ways to do it.

1. *Share your business model.* Sharing your business model means being open about how you do business. How do you make money? How do you give value to your clients? Make your financial statements transparent and your commentary candid. Unless your industry demands confidentiality, don't obsess over secrecy. Do you work with billing rates? Be open about them. When it comes to intellectual property, protect yourself, and respect others—but at the same time, do not overestimate the importance of your intellectual property. Owning a trademark doesn't guarantee you business; it is the art of management and marketing that will make your business work.

> If you are transparent about your activities, you show you have nothing to hide. If you have nothing to hide, people trust what you do and say.

2. *Share information.* It can be tempting to hold information for ransom. This is particularly true on websites—it may seem appealing to hold back certain information from potential customers so that you can deal with it in real time. Instead, be free with information that the customer is going to receive eventually. If you have a cancellation policy, then provide information about the terms. If you think the customer cannot handle price without understanding value, then work on more clearly articulating value instead of hiding your price. If you think the customer cannot comprehend a key idea in print format, maybe better copywriting is called for.

Being transparent with information distinguishes you from everyone else. Think of competitive differentiation as a bonus prize in addition to all the other benefits of transparency.

CASE STUDY

From the Front Lines: When Truth Matters More than Experience[7]

Our colleague Stewart Hirsch tells a story of transparency as a critical business development skill.

"I was referred to an international women's organization as a potential speaker to its chapter heads on leadership. Since I hadn't designed or delivered a leadership program before, I had two different reactions to the request: (1) fear and (2) interest in the possibility. I told the event chair the truth about my experience level, and asked about what the group wanted to accomplish at the event. Then, in order to help them find a good presenter, I offered a couple of other people who I thought would be great speakers for them.

"A week later, the event chair came back to me and asked what I would do if I was given the opportunity to speak. I designed a very interactive program on the spot and got the job. I loved doing the work, and some participants said it was one of the best workshops they'd attended.

"It was a real paradox: Being transparent about my lack of leadership training experience did not cause me to lose the opportunity. In fact, it had the opposite effect. While my natural tendency is to be open, I keep the lesson I learned from this experience in mind whenever I feel that I should have been more aggressive or less transparent. Being open and honest feels good. And the result was right for both the client and me."

—*Stewart Hirsch (Trusted Advisor Associates)*

Insight: Transparency in Action[8]

1. Share your cost structure with your customers. This will eliminate any suspicions they have about your pricing. They will also appreciate your candor and come to trust you more.
2. In sales conversations, compare your product or service to others. Include all relevant information—the good, the bad, and the ugly—to help your customers make informed choices. Some buyers will go with your competitors as a result of what you've shared. Even so, you will still end up with more and better business in the end.
3. Tell the truth about your own emotional reality. You are far more likely to get the straight scoop from your client about her reality, which puts you in a much better position to be of service.
4. Share information about your backlog, prospective orders, or plans as they affect vendors and suppliers. Having advance, nonbinding discussions about the future is invaluable to those who sell to you. Help them, and they will help you.
5. Share your product development plans with your customers before the products are ready for prime time. The software industry figured out long ago that users are more likely to buy what they've had a hand in developing, if you give them the chance. If you're in professional services, sharing the early version of a new service with potential clients will give you invaluable insight, help educate your buyers, and increases trust.

Worksheet: Putting the Trust Principles to Work

Consider the myriad ways to apply the trust principles in the early stages of new business relationships to help to build your brand, gain sales, and create enduring client relationships. Use the examples provided in this chapter to identify areas of strength as well as areas of opportunity. What works for your business? In what ways could you take your business development and marketing to the next level?

Trust Principle	Areas of Strength	Areas of Opportunity
Focus on your customer.		
Collaborate to drive new business.		
Focus on relationships, not transactions.		
Be transparent with prospects and clients.		

What actions will you take as a result of this reflection? Be specific.

What	By When	With Whom	Support I Will Ask For

Trust-Based Networking

12

Chapter

Networks and community have always been important in business. Technology has changed some mechanics of networking, but not its fundamental nature. Trust-based networking is still about focus on the other: listening, respect, low self-orientation, and transparency. This chapter explores trust-based strategies to help you network in any context, and shows you how the Internet has and hasn't changed how you network.

The goal of most business networking is to make new connections to get more business. The goal of trust-based networking is to help *other* people develop *their* businesses. As a collateral side effect, when you behave this way your own business benefits as well.

> The goal of most business networking is to make new connections to get more business. The goal of trust-based networking is to help other people develop their businesses.

Trust-based networking presents precisely the same dynamic we have pointed out elsewhere in this book: in delivery, in business development, in interactions. In a series of many short interactions, you practice the same principles that apply to longer, deeper interactions. Those principles are familiar by now: focus on the other person, be willing to share and collaborate, assume that relationships will continue in the future, and believe that by serving others, you will be well-served yourself.

Properly used, technology can greatly support and amplify trust-based networking. Improperly used, technology can undermine credibility and destroy trust. Either way, technology is an enabler, a tool—it does not redefine the nature of relationships, which remain at the heart of networking.

Networking falls apart, like most relationships do, when you are overly focused on your own needs and put them ahead of the good of the relationship. Picture someone whose only goal at a networking event is to collect as many business cards as possible, engaging in shallow conversation aimed at spending the minimum time possible before flitting to another business card opportunity. By contrast, trust-based networking puts the focus back on building relationships.

The math of basic networking is compelling enough: The more people you know, the more likely you are to get mentioned, talked about, and thought of for future business opportunities. Basic networking adds numbers to your contact list, and your level of fame adds something of a multiplier on top. It helps develop business in conventional free-market economic

From the Front Lines: Selling by Not Selling

A key salesperson for a service firm from India tells this brief and compelling story about making introductions:

"It was a new prospect, with a major organization. We decided to let go of any need to sell in the short term. Instead, we simply met with many of the senior- and middle-ranking executives to find out what they were preoccupied by.

"We offered help, but in the main, in those early days it was largely help in the form of introductions to others in the 'ecosystem' who were better placed than we were to help on particular points.

"Over time, this start has developed into a very strong, lucrative, and satisfying relationship for us both."

—As told to Julian Powe (Trusted Advisor Associates, UK)

terms: As your network grows, the market becomes more aware of your services, individual players become more knowledgeable about your capabilities, you gain scale economies of communication, and so forth. Networking lowers costs and increases market share.

Trust-based networking, on the other hand, aims to increase quality as well as quantity. It goes *beyond* free-market economics by including a pattern of ongoing, reciprocal favors and mutually-beneficial obligations that is naturally self-reinforcing. When you are networking with trust, you are also leading with trust.

Trust-based networking manifests in many ways including:

- Personal commitments to other networkers.
- Greater responsiveness to you in times of need.
- Richer and more positive responses when you request a reference (see Seek Referrals in Chapter 17 "Developing New Business with Existing Clients").
- Calls returned faster when you need a favor.
- A genuine sense of well-being that comes from helping others you care about without strings attached.

Ten Best Practices for Trust-Based Networking

Trust-based networking is a short form of longer trust-based relationship development. All these practices involve finding personal connection.

> What you take away from a networking interaction is directly related to what you give away during a networking interaction.

1. *Be present.* The key to great networking is paradoxical in the same way that trust-based selling is paradoxical: If you focus on the other person, the benefits to you happen as a secondary effect. Just *be there* with the person you are talking to. Be interested in what he has to say, be curious about what interests him, and be generous with your attention. What you *take away from* a networking interaction is directly related to what you *give away during* a networking interaction. Give the gift of your attention.

2. *Recognize others' contributions.* Nothing else in your networking strategy is more important than overtly recognizing others. Both internal and external communications can be used to recognize, mention, or elevate their work. Give credit, give thanks, and give public praise.

3. *Collaborate.* Establishing a joint project is the business equivalent of socializing: You develop a relationship while engaged in a supposedly nonrelationship activity. The subject matter on which you collaborate serves as the social lubricant. By working together you foster connection.

4. *Talk about yourself less and your partner more.* High self-orientation and shameless self-promotion alienate others and create a disconnect. Make a commitment in your networking activities to lower your self-orientation and focus on your partner by listening and engaging in her areas of interest. When you do talk about yourself, maintain your partner-focus: Frame your comments in terms of bringing value. Do not dominate the conversation—in that way you earn the right to be heard. Not sure if you are getting the balance right? Ask a friend for help.

5. *Add value.* There's a reason samples selling is so powerful: Nothing beats personal experience of a product or service. So be open to ways of adding value from your product or service while interacting in a networking situation. Rather than talk about how great your products or services are, offer practical information and advice to suit your partner's specific situation—*when asked*.

6. *Diversify your network.* You can easily get stuck in ruts, such as hanging out only with people just like you, or those above you who can do you a favor, or those who look up to you. For everyone's benefit, mix it up. You don't want to get stale, or typed as a sycophant, or hooked on praise.

   • Identify some people whom you admire and want to know more about. Find out whom they admire and follow those people.
   • Have a look at who has been contacting you lately—find some time to share with them.
   • Identify a few people with whom you can let your hair down and have honest conversations. Enjoy your time with them.

   If you do all this, you will be positioned to help others in ways only you can, and as a byproduct, you will grow personally as well.

7. *Research.* Do a little advance work. Information is widely available and it is a fundamental sign of respect to do your homework. On a regular basis and certainly before any explicit networking event, make the effort to learn about the people you want to meet.

8. *Make introductions.* Our colleague Stewart Hirsch talks about the importance of "working the room," meaning doing service by performing introductions, whether in a face-to-face meeting or online. The purpose of trust-based networking is to help others: One of the best ways you can help others is to help them build *their* networks. Review your connections from time to time: Who among your relationships might benefit from being directly connected with each other?

> One of the best ways you can help others is to help them build their networks.

   (Note: Working the room this way is also a great means for forgetting any anxieties you may have about being in a room of strangers.)

9. *Take better notes.* You may wish you had better recall of past networking interactions. The notes you scribbled on business cards are hard to read; the notes you meant to take after a phone call never got taken. Trust-based networking thrives on having a rich memory—the quality of your relationships improve, as well as your ability to provide detail and context in the introductions you make to others. Nurture your relationships by helping your memory. Get into the practice of taking more notes, immediately after your interactions, using better media.

10. *Keep making contact.* The purpose of networking is not to "capture" a name for your database, but to develop a relationship. To define your relationships solely in terms of numbers is to dehumanize them. The true tools of networking are lunch dates, drop-in visits, calls, e-mails, handwritten thank-you notes, congratulations, thinking-of-yous—in short, human contact—not business card scanning software or integrated databases.

People don't care what you know until they know that you care. Go show them.

> Nurture your relationships by helping your memory. Get into the practice of taking more notes, immediately after your interactions, using better media.

Technology and Trust-Based Networking

Networking has always been about extending and deepening business relationships—both quantity and quality. As great as technology may be, it doesn't alter the basics of human interaction, which is what networking is about. But technology undeniably removes some constraints, and adds others. Technology tends to amplify dynamics that already underlie networking. It's important to get them right.

Impact of Technology

Communication technology lets you overcome distance and time. You can now communicate instantly, to larger audiences, and with total strangers.

CASE STUDY

From the Front Lines: When People Know You Care[1]

Michelle Peluso, retired CEO of Travelocity, tells a story about how genuine interest in others generates powerful personal connections.

"A few months before I was born, my father founded an environmental-engineering firm. I literally grew up watching him build it. Even as a little kid, I was struck by Dad's obsessive interest in and care for the people who worked for him.

"Nights when our family's dinner-table conversation didn't include discussion of his employees were rare. 'Sally's gotten accepted into an MBA program,' he'd say excitedly, 'and we're going to figure out how she can do that part-time.' Or 'John's wife just had a baby girl! We're going over this weekend to see her.' His concern was authentic and unwavering, and it extended to all aspects of his employees' lives.

"Now, my father's attitude and behavior were just part of his personality, not some maneuver to produce results—but they produced results all the same. He grew that start-up into a thriving 300-person business and then sold it to a larger company but continued to run it successfully for two years. When he left to begin a new venture, more than half of his former employees sent him their résumés. So although my father never gave me management advice directly, his example provided a profound lesson."

—*Michelle Peluso (CEO [retired], Travelocity, Southlake, Texas)*

For networking, this raises one trade-off over and over: breadth vs. depth. For example:

- If you have 5,000 "friends," are they really friends?
- Can you have "relationships" if they are conducted without face-to-face interaction?
- As networks scale, can they still embody deep connectivity?

While those questions are under debate, you can be clear of one thing: Human beings want to do business in a social context. The Japanese may take longer than Americans to act out their social rituals, but every culture has its own definitions of appropriate behaviors that govern social interactions.

Traditionally the balance between the commercial and the social has been served by building networking around "events" or themes—athletic events, speeches, charity concerts. By focusing on the social aspect, all parties can increase networking quality and quantity without the social discomfort of appearing to be nakedly self-serving.

Technology has made it possible to strip out either the social or the business aspects of networking. Focusing only on the social feels like trivial gossip—think of the chit-chat on today's social media. On the other hand, focusing only on the business feels like crass self-promotion; think of robot programs that collect "followers" for those same social media (the equivalent of the aggressive business-card collector at a networking event).

Online dating networks have struggled with this problem in a much more complex arena and found a balance between the "business"—finding a match, in their case, and the "social"—doing so in a socially acceptable manner. If they can find solutions, surely businesses can and will as well.

Five Pitfalls of Online Networking

As these trade-offs sort themselves out, they suggest a few specific challenges in the online world. Here are five traps to watch out for:

1. *Getting down to business too soon.* Human interactions have rules of etiquette—jumping too quickly to business can be perceived as rude. It takes some time to get to know people, even online. Find out where the line is on a specific medium, in a specific community, in your specific industry or culture, and with your specific audience, and don't cross it. Once you have crossed it, you are spam.

2. *Promoting yourself too much or too aggressively.* People know you are in business, they all know you are networking—you don't have to push it in their faces every minute. Take some time to get to know who you are talking to. Talk about subject matter expertise, not about your selling it. There are plenty of people off-line who obsessively turn every conversation to themselves. It's even easier to do online, with fewer cues to counteract the inclination. Be aware of how much you talk about yourself while networking.

3. *Faking sincerity.* There is a level of sincerity that is unique to a one-on-one interaction. Once you change modes from one-to-one to one-to-many, something changes. Just as many trust issues are best dealt with individually, watch out for presuming an individual level of intimacy when dealing with groups. Just because tools are available that emulate personal connection doesn't mean you should misuse them.

4. *Indiscriminate connection.* Views on what it means to "connect" or to "friend" or "follow" online are changing. If you are inclined to connect with everyone, you may easily offend those who are more selective. At the very least, you may reduce the perceived value of connecting with you. Learn the cultural norms and expectations of the people you truly want to connect with and respect them.

> Learn the cultural norms and expectations of the people you truly want to connect with and respect them.

5. *Confusing party lines with private lines.* In the United States, before World War II, most households acquired telephone service through a party line, a single phone line shared with several neighbors. Radio and movie comedies had fun with the social implications of people listening in on conversations that were supposedly private.

There is a similar continuum across and often within various online communications media. At one extreme, there are private one-to-one communications such as SMS, or Short Message Service, the text message component of phone, web, and mobile communication systems. At the other extreme, there are publicly broadcasted one-to-many communications such as public messages on social media networks. Sending private messages via public mode can be embarrassing to the other party, and is often annoying to the public (think cellphone conversations on the train).

Pick the right place on the continuum to reflect your respect for your networking partners and for the other partners involved in the broader medium. And remember to take into consideration the nature of your message. Transparency is a virtue, as is intimacy—but sometimes you have to choose between the two.

Ten Best Practices for Trust-Based Networking Online

Best practices in emerging technologies will look a lot like those in the broader world, but it is worth highlighting a few for specifics.

1. *Engage.* Start a conversation by commenting on other people's websites and broadcasts, either directly or through other connective programs. If you have ever started a new blog or online venture, you know how good it feels when other people show up to support you by leaving comments or participating actively in other ways.
2. *Return comments.* This is an exact translation of the more general trust recommendation to "return calls unbelievably fast." Most web commenters don't expect instant response, but a good guideline is to reply to people within 24 hours. Reciprocity and interaction foster great connection and help transform isolated interactions into relationships.
3. *ABC: Always Be Crediting.* Use all your communications tools to acknowledge real contributions. Pin the credit on someone for good things well done. Don't just rebroadcast the interview someone did with you—thank them for doing so, publicly. Share information about the good things that other people are doing. Link to other people and send them traffic as a form of recognition and appreciation. Recognition at the media level mirrors the role that listening plays, as a sign of respect, in one-to-one conversations.

   > Use all your communications tools to acknowledge real contributions. Pin the credit on someone for good things well done.

4. *Collaborate.* Collaboration can work in three ways: contributing to other people's projects, inviting people to contribute to yours, and launching online projects together. Collaborating can look like:
   - Contributing to other people's websites and web projects.
   - Acting as the guest host for a blogger when she goes on vacation.
   - Submitting work to quality aggregator sites—those that collect and share content from diverse sources.
   - Inviting others to contribute to your projects.
   - Interviewing people for your newsletter or website.
   - Launching a new project like a podcast with a strategic partner.
5. *Increase your other:self ratio.* Generous gestures are harder to read at lower levels of interaction, and your comments are much more likely to show up out of context. Hence you need to increase the ratio of comments about others to comments about yourself.

> Give away free samples of your expertise—this might take the form of online diagnostic tools or advice. Provide real value.

6. *Set knowledge free.* Be generous with sharing your information. Make case studies, whitepapers, and articles available on your website. Give away free samples of your expertise—this might take the form of online diagnostic tools or advice. Provide real value.

7. *Diversify your online network.* When you link to or highlight other people in your web activities, don't act like an echo chamber and simply amplify the voices of the same handful of Internet celebrities. Expand your media diet: Introduce new and varied ideas and people to your audience. Draw attention to people you consider your Internet peers and to junior people who are starting out. Send the gift of traffic and attention where it can do the most good.

8. *Connect within networks.* Take advantage of new media tools to make introductions inside your network. You know Joe, you know Susie. You can see how both Joe and Susie could benefit from knowing each other, and now you can introduce them easily even if you cannot arrange for them to meet face to face. It is possible to be overeager in connecting other people—the downside is resentment at an unrequested social obligation. But with care and sensitivity, it is also possible to generate great value for those in your network by exploring the synergies with others in your online network. By actively increasing the value of your network to others, you are leading with trust.

9. *Automate your research.* Use online monitoring tools such as Google Alerts to keep track of online conversations about your contacts and their organizations. Don't sit on that information: Use it as a trigger to get in touch and send your congratulations about good news. Give the gift of attention. Don't forget to add relevant new details such as promotions and new titles to your contact management system.

10. *Keep making contact.* Don't be a one-hit wonder: Keep coming back so you can cultivate a real relationship over time.

Worksheet: Trust-Based Networking in Practice

Trust-based networking is about focus on the other: listening, respect, low self-orientation, and transparency. The goal of trust-based networking is to help other people develop their businesses.

Consider the 10 best practices for trust-based networking outlined in this chapter. To what extent do you already apply these practices? What opportunities do you see to take your networking to the next level?

Best Practices for Trust-Based Networking	Frequency	Opportunities
1. Be present.	□Y □N □Sometimes	
2. Recognize others' contributions.	□Y □N □Sometimes	
3. Collaborate.	□Y □N □Sometimes	
4. Talk about yourself less and your partner more.	□Y □N □Sometimes	
5. Add value.	□Y □N □Sometimes	
6. Diversify your network.	□Y □N □Sometimes	
7. Research.	□Y □N □Sometimes	
8. Make introductions.	□Y □N □Sometimes	
9. Take better notes.	□Y □N □Sometimes	
10. Keep making contact.	□Y □N □Sometimes	

Prioritize your top two opportunities for networking improvement, and note them here:

1. _____

_____

_____

2. _____

_____

_____

What actions will you take as a result of this reflection? Be specific.

What	By When	With Whom	Support I Will Ask For

Delivering the Pitch

13
Chapter

The way you conduct yourself in an initial meeting sets the tone for the relationship that follows. Some of the most powerful aspects of trust creation begin not after but during the sales process. In this chapter, we share nine rules for transforming the typical idea of the pitch into an activity that creates trust, transforms relationships, and differentiates your brand—to set you up for success from the outset.

The initial sales meeting where you make the case for your goods or services is generally known as the pitch. It also answers to a variety of nicknames: the dog and pony show, the beauty contest, the shoot-out. Whatever your industry, and whatever you call it, if you work in sales, you have to go through it.

Let's be clear: There is no single perfect way to pitch, since the pitch that ends up winning is situational to you and your client. This chapter explores guidelines for how to lead from trust when you deliver your pitch.

Here are nine rules for delivering your winning pitch.

Sometimes the Best Pitch Is No Pitch

Sometimes the best pitch is one that never happens because a provider is chosen without one—both parties find another way to make a good, collaborative decision. This outcome requires a relationship, not simply a face-off among strangers.

Think of a pitch without a relationship as a blind date. Each party is guarded. The quietly cautious buyer wants control and seeks it in an impersonal, formal event. The seller also wants control, and typically expresses it by being overly assertive. One fears being sold a bill of goods; the other fears losing. When both parties are fearful, decisions get made on price, features, and process rather than on value, long-term benefit, and relationship.

Unfortunately, both parties are better off starting from a strong relationship and although they both know this deep-down, they often don't admit it—the relationship resistance is subconscious. For example, sellers frequently seek inroads and try to gain advantage before pitch meetings; buyers typically tend to resist this because they fear being manipulated.

> ### Insight: Trust-Based Selling Is Like a Golf Swing[1]
>
> One of the reasons trust is so hard to get a grip on is that it's rife with paradox: The thing we're most afraid to say or do is precisely what will build the most trust. For example, the best way to generate sales is to have the courage to be brutally honest about your product's weaknesses and your competitor's strengths.
>
> The game of golf shares a similar paradox. From the perspective of someone who doesn't play golf, the logical way to get that tiny ball to travel hundreds of yards off the first tee towards that tiny cup is to hit it as hard as possible. If you're a golfer, you know what this strategy will yield: a nice left hook into a thick forest of trees.
>
> Trust-Based Selling is like a golf swing: Hype your product and you hook the ball; be honest and land it square on the green.
>
> Take a look at your approach to pitching. How might the lessons of golf improve your game?

The question then becomes, how do you get a relationship when you're presented with an opportunity to pitch? The key is to explore the viability of the pitch itself. Do this from a position of respect and honest concern for what is right for the client.

Here's what it might sound like:

> How do you get a relationship when you're presented with an opportunity to pitch? The key is to explore the viability of the pitch itself.

> John, thank you for considering us as your provider. We've always had a lot of respect for your organization. We've provided a lot of value for firms like yours facing similar challenges—given what I understand your challenges to be at this early stage. At the risk of coming off as uninformed, we don't know enough to be confident that we're the right choice for you—not yet, anyway. The last thing I want to do is waste your time and ours on a pitch that's misaligned. Could we talk some more about what you're in the market for and make an educated decision together about whether or not we should proceed?

Sometimes, the client will cancel the pitch meeting altogether, because they've found one provider that seems to uniquely understand them. That's generally a good outcome for both you and them—*even if you are not the provider chosen*. Remember, a trust-based approach to sales requires an unshakable commitment on your part to *help the buyer do what is right for her*.

This is vastly different from the traditional approach to sales where your primary purpose is to *convince the buyer to buy from you*. With service-orientation in your heart, along with words and actions that align, you won't go wrong.

Don't Skip the Pre-pitch Warm-Up

Any pitch will be improved by prior conversations with as many client people as possible. If you are literally meeting the client representatives for the first time at the pitch, your odds of being chosen are not great because when total strangers are just meeting each other, the do-nothing option frequently becomes the inevitable option.

Of course, not every client *wants* to meet you in advance. Often the intent of the pitch is to prevent such meetings in the first place, in pursuit of independent, fair competition. Pushing too hard for meetings can appear distasteful, disregarding the client's desire for fairness.

How do you know how far to push the suggestion for prior meetings? Simple—be collaborative and transparent, and simply ask the client. Point out advantages of offering *all* competitors a chance to talk with them in advance; then gracefully yield if the resistance is too strong. You get a few points for offering, if you do it respectfully. Remember, just because a client invites you to dance a certain dance doesn't mean you can't show them a new step or two.

Here's what your invitation might sound like:

> Emily, we're delighted to be asked and we wholeheartedly accept your invitation. I'd like to make a suggestion, if you'd be willing to hear me out. I don't want to suggest anything inappropriate in light of your standard buying procedures. I do think we'll make better use of your time and ours if we're able to deliver a pitch that's spot on for your needs. That's not only true for us, but for everyone in the running. Might you consider a couple of variations—for example, having a brief meeting before the pitch so we can get smarter about your business situation? Or perhaps you would allow us to design our pitch time to include a lot of dialog—maybe even some time actually working some of the issues? Would either of those options work for you?

Is it risky to talk to a client like this? It feels that way. But what is the worst that can happen? Probably that the client says no. That's really not the end of the world. And anyway, there is no trust without risk.

> Just because the client asks you to dance a certain dance doesn't mean you can't show them a new step or two.

If you can talk to people in advance of a pitch, you will improve the quality of the pitch itself—for both you and the client. Of course, you learn valuable information, and you get to call people by name. It also goes much further than that, because the next key to a great pitch is interaction.

Make It Interactive

Inevitably the client asks you to tell them about yourselves. And nearly all sellers assume that's what the client wants. Wrong!

In reality, listening to someone talk about themselves for 30 or more minutes is incredibly boring. Even more importantly, human beings are not persuaded by listening to others de novo. They are persuaded by listening to someone who has previously listened to them—someone who has already shown them the respect of understanding first who they are, before pitching.

Letting clients be heard is vital to successful pitches—even if you have successfully gotten meetings before the pitch. Here are some ways to do it:

- Tell the client ahead of time you would like to ask for reactions.
- Build "and-what-about-you?" questions into your pitch.
- Offer data about similar situations and ask for comment.
- Ask the client if they would consider a first-meeting approach: instead of a standard pitch, offer to treat the pitch like a first meeting as if you had already been hired. Request five minutes at the end to talk about how it went. This may sound like a crazy idea, but we have heard several success stories based on this approach.
- If you have had prior pitch conversations, refer to them during your time with the client. It shows you paid attention.

Remember: What you *say* in the pitch matters much less than whether you have *listened to them* first.

> ### Insight: What "Tell Us about Yourself" Really Means
>
> It seems perfectly natural. The prospect asks you to come in and give them a pitch and tell them about yourselves.
>
> It is expected you will bring along a PowerPoint presentation and some handouts. You ask the prospect if there is anything in particular he would like you to focus on, and his answer is something like, "No, just give us a general overview of who you are, what you do, how you work with clients. You decide what's most important for us to hear. Tell us about yourself."
>
> You arrive. There are handshakes and welcomes and coffee all around. They all seem sincere and interested. Everyone settles in, and you proceed to do the pitch.
>
> Later you decide it went pretty well, although not great. They seemed a little distant. It didn't help that two of them left to take calls. And their parting message of, "Thanks, we'll be in touch," didn't sound as sincere as you had hoped.
>
> Time goes on. You send an e-mail, but receive a perfunctory reply. Nothing ever really goes anywhere. Eventually, you cross this company off the prospects list and chalk up the failure to a window-shopping client.
>
> Don't blame the client. The mistake you made was to believe that they really wanted to hear about *you*. They were just being polite. What they really wanted to hear about was what you had to say about *them*.
>
> The lesson: "Tell us about yourself" means just the opposite. Don't mistake etiquette for a pitch design. If you want to succeed, make your pitch about the client.

Have a Point of View

Your excellent qualifications, credentials, and references are worth nothing if you cannot show relevance to the client. To walk in without a point of view on the client and the issues facing them is arrogant, disrespectful, and selfish. Those are strong words: Let us back them up.

If you want this job, you have hopefully thought about what you would do if you got it. So why wouldn't you share that thinking? The probable answers are because you are afraid you might have gotten it wrong, or you are afraid your ideas will get stolen.

That fear is all about you. Lower your self-orientation, check your ego at the door, and renew your commitment to being client-focused for the sake of the client. Now is the time when *not* to take a risk is risky. The client will be wowed if you are willing to do some homework on spec and if you are willing to engage in real-time thinking about it.

Sample selling is the way to differentiate. Showing up with nothing but a track record is like going on a blind date with lists and anecdotes from past dates. Even if you get it wrong, you will get far more credit than you think for your willingness to take the risk. If your ideas are subsequently stolen, get over it—there are very few new ideas in the world, and you can be glad that an idea-stealing client is now someone else's.

Take the Preoccupation Out of Price

Conventional wisdom says not to quote price until the client has heard benefits so they can properly calculate value. This makes theoretical sense, but it ignores human psychology—price is typically the elephant in the room during the pitch.

> The real point is not when you talk price—it is about who makes the decision to talk about it. Give up control over that issue and give it to your prospect.

While everyone listens or pretends to listen to your pitch, they are all mildly preoccupied with what your price is going to be. That preoccupation is death to their ability to listen to you. So air it.

Here's a suggestion for your next face-to-face pitch: When you walk in, place a five-page pile of paper on the table, face down, and say, "This is the price part of our proposal—the bottom line, and four pages of backup explaining it. We don't want to overly focus on it, nor do we want to keep it from you. At any point in the conversation today, you can ask us to turn the page over and we'll talk about it. Whenever *you* want."

The real point is not *when* you talk price—it is about who makes the decision to talk about it. Give up control over that issue and give it to your prospect.

With PowerPoint, Less Is More

There's a strong case to be made for skipping the slide deck altogether, or using it only as a leave-behind at the very most. The march of 1,000 slides has lost its luster.

There is an emerging consensus among presentation pros about how to make PowerPoint work for you:

- Most presentations are lengthy leave-behinds in disguise. Build your pitch on the presentation, not the leave-behind.
- Less is more: Limit yourself to six bullets per slide, six words per bullet.
- Do not read aloud what is written: Use stories and metaphors to make your points instead.
- Visuals are great, great, great—use photos, not clipart.
- Except for the title page, lose the logos and fancy backgrounds.

Stop Selling Your Qualifications

Most big sales these days proceed along a two-step process: first screening, then selection. Most screening is done on credentials. That means if you are in the pitch, your credentials got you there. The pitch is the sale you already got—stop selling it.

Insight: Buyer Psychology[2]

Ask a client what she wants, and she will tell you she wants someone with expertise and solid credentials: "Someone who will meet our needs."

Successful salespeople understand how buyer psychology really works. Clients only ask for credentials and expertise because they are not really sure what else to do. In truth, clients would rather find someone whose expertise falls within very broad acceptable parameters, and then choose whom to do business with based on their trust in the seller.

If you follow a sales script, you will have a canned dialogue with your client. You will take her request for credentials and expertise at face value, and not hear the undertone in the question. You will miss her boredom as she listens to your answer.

If you can engage your buyer in honest discussion, she will admit her uncertainties, and together you can discuss and discover what her needs really are.

If the client specifically requested a section on credentials, do not embarrass them by fighting the request. Instead, touch briefly on credentials and provide an ample leave-behind set of documents. Go through them if the client insists—if the client doesn't bring it up, don't you do so.

Do Not Denigrate the Competition

This is an easy one. Do not bad-mouth your competitors. Don't do it, don't go there, don't even think about it. If asked, demur by saying, "We respect our competitors. We encourage you to talk with them." Taking the high road never hurts and usually helps.

Sometimes you are actually better off referring the customer to a competitor. The most obvious one is when the customer is a very difficult buyer, one not inclined to work on the basis of trust relationships. In such cases, it is in your best interest—as well as the customer's—to put them in touch with a competitor who also is less focused on developing trust-based relationships.

> If a competitor offers a reasonably better service offering than you do and the client's success heavily depends on the quality of that service, then everyone is better off when you recommend the competitor.

The other case is less obvious, but far more powerful. If a competitor offers a reasonably better service offering than you do, and the client's success heavily depends on the quality of that service, then *everyone is* better off when you recommend the competitor. Of course, your client is better off—and of course your competitor will be delighted. But you, too, are better off—because nothing proves client focus and service like a willingness to forego short-term gains.

Such a selfless act speaks volumes about walking the walk as a trusted advisor. Even if your competitor performs a technically excellent job, you have gained the higher trust ground by being willing to risk your own benefits for the sake of client service. Make that kind of behavior your hallmark, and you will find your generosity returned—if not on this project or client, then on those to come in the future.

Be Willing to Ditch the Pitch

Imagine a pitch where an obstreperous client takes you off-script, away from your slide deck, or raises a point well in advance of when you had intended.

Disaster? Not at all. In fact, it is quite the opposite. This is client engagement—exactly what you want—cleverly disguised as an objection. Greet it with open arms. Ask the client for permission to go off-script and deal directly with the issue raised, for as long as the client wants.

> Remember: Despite what the client says, it is not your PowerPoint they want to see—they want to feel what it's like to interact with you.

Remember: Despite what the client says, it is not your PowerPoint they want to see—they want to *feel* what it's like to interact with you. If you respect their wishes, if you move your agenda to fit theirs, and if you respond directly with relevant content, you will address precisely that desire. Your chances of winning the pitch will increase greatly over someone who stayed on PowerPoint. The *real* win, anyway, is a relationship win, not a sale.

From the Front Lines: It's Too Hot to Pitch[3]

Craig Leach, CEO of Graham-Pelton Consulting, told me (Charlie) about making a sales presentation on a hot summer day, in a hot room, at the end of a long week. His team had the last slot on a four-pitch afternoon in front of the decision-making team of a dozen client executives.

"As we walked into the room, I saw a couple of execs wiping their foreheads, and everyone looked drained. In that moment I knew what I had to do. I quietly turned to my colleagues and whispered, 'Follow my lead.'

"I walked right up to the executives' long table and said, 'Folks—it's been a long, long day. How about we ditch the formal presentation and just talk? All in favor say Aye!'

"I got a shocked look from the table, and an instant later came thundering applause—just for making that offer."

Needless to say, he also won the job. Sometimes, the best pitch is no pitch.

—Craig J. Leach (CEO, Graham-Pelton Consulting, Inc.), as told to Charles H. Green

Worksheet: Transforming Your Pitch

Bring to mind a current sales situation where you see an opportunity to transform your pitch. Describe it briefly below, then answer the questions that follow. If you don't have a current situation, reflect on what you could have done differently in the past. The key is to bring a real and specific situation to mind.

Situation:

Of the Nine Rules for Transforming Your Pitch, which ones could you apply?

Rule 1: Sometimes the best pitch is no pitch.	☐Y ☐N
Rule 2: Don't skip the pre-pitch warm-up.	☐Y ☐N
Rule 3: Make it interactive.	☐Y ☐N
Rule 4: Have a point of view.	☐Y ☐N
Rule 5: Take the preoccupation out of talking price.	☐Y ☐N
Rule 6: With PowerPoint, less is more.	☐Y ☐N
Rule 7: Stop selling your qualifications.	☐Y ☐N
Rule 8: Do not denigrate the competition.	☐Y ☐N
Rule 9: Be willing to ditch the pitch.	☐Y ☐N

How would you apply the ones you selected? Be specific.

What actions will you take as a result? Be specific.

What	By When	With Whom	Support I Will Ask For

What do you see as a result of examining this situation that might apply to other sales situations?

Handling Objections

Working from trust means there are no objections in the traditional sales sense—there are simply issues of interest in an ongoing discussion. This chapter explores how to change your thinking from *handling objections* to *having conversations*. We identify the types of wrong thinking that underlie the negativity of objections and offer three alternatives: thinking of objections as invitations, as concerns, and as opportunities. You will be able to immediately implement three specific ways to improve the quality of your conversations. The result: greater trust and more satisfying long-term results for all.

As a child, did you ever ask adults to check for monsters under your bed before turning out the lights at bed time? Your caregivers probably tried all the rational arguments on you: monsters don't exist, and if they did you can see they're not here now, and if they show up mommy or daddy will protect you, and so forth. Logic works—sort of, a little bit, for a while.

> When you develop a richer view of professional relationships, you realize that what you used to think of as an objection is just another form of dialogue.

But the real cure for monsters is growing up. Only by maturing did you come to understand that monsters do not exist—and therefore nothing else needs to be said about them!

So it is with sales objections. The analogue to monsters and our maturity is that when you develop a richer view of professional relationships, you realize that what you used to think of as an objection is just another form of dialogue and the monsters disappear.

The Problem: How You Think about Objections

If you have taken sales training courses or read books on improving selling skills, chances are you have heard lots about "handling" objections. The objections are presented as obstacles to your ability to close a sale. This advice amounts to telling your childhood self to fight hand-to-hand with the monster under the bed. One of you is going to lose. *Handling objections* is the wrong means to the wrong goal for the wrong reasons.

You have probably been on at least one side of this kind of typical sales exchange at some point:

Salesperson: What is the reason you're not buying?
Customer: [states objection]
Salesperson: Is that the only reason?
Customer: Yes.
Salesperson: Then, if … [eliminates objection] … would you buy?
Customer: Yes.

And you have probably also been on the receiving end of these sorts of manipulative sales tactics:

The Boomerang. "Sure it costs a lot, but doesn't your wife deserve the best?"
The Feel-Felt-Found Model. "I sure understand how you feel about that. You're not alone; others have felt that same way. And what we have found is that…."
The Conditional Close. "So you like the metallic blue color. If I can find one from another store, will you take it today?"
The Deflection. "Yes, I see what you mean … hmm … well, let me show you the range of colors you can have…."

How does it feel to be handled? It probably does not feel genuine or respectful. And it reduces trust in the relationship—by a lot.

Besides being overtly manipulative, the problem with these techniques is it pits business against customer rather than putting them on the same side of the table. The customer is viewed as the enemy to be defeated or as a hill to be taken.

The first step in getting rid of the negativity of handling objections is getting rid of the two types of wrong thinking that underlie it.

Wrong-Thinking #1: The Win-Lose Mind-Set

Put yourself back on the side of the seller and think about how you feel when you are facing objections. What's running through your head? Most internal monologues about objections fall into the category of Closers or Cringers.

Closer. "All right, I'm getting close to closing the sale. I've got the customer to agree on the problem, I've got them hooked on some features, and I can see light at the end of the tunnel. All that's left is to karate chop a few objections, and we're home free. Bring it on, let's see what you've got—I can handle your objections!"
Cringer. "Omigosh, it's gone well so far, knock on wood. I hope they don't throw me some curve ball, this is the part I hate. I really want to close this one, if I can just get past the objections."

The first monologue sounds optimistic, if misguided, while the second sounds fearful, even defeatist. But what people do not usually notice is how much alike those two versions are: Both versions envision a battle between customer and seller—where one "wins" by subduing the other.

The win-lose mind-set dictates that only one person can come out on top—and the winner has to be you—which makes your customer the loser and ruins your prospects for a long-term business relationship.

Wrong-Thinking #2: Taking It Personally

Why is it that customer objections can feel so personal? Well, start with a win-lose mind-set. Add in some customer objections. Season liberally with your fear of losing the deal. Throw

> When you start from the win-lose mind-set, every objection threatens your ability to close the deal, declare victory over your customer, and announce yourself the winner. When you use this model, objections threaten your very identity.

your ego in there, too. Add some heat in the form of a lifelong fear of being a loser, and it begins to sound like a recipe for disaster.

No wonder you take objections personally: When you start from the win-lose mind-set, every objection threatens your ability to close the deal, declare victory over your customer, and announce yourself the winner. When you use this model, objections threaten your very identity.

The Antidote: Change Your Thinking

The way to make those monsters disappear is to change how you think about objections. When you lead with trust, the way to handle objections is this: Have conversations instead.

> The way to handle objections is this: Have conversations instead.

You no longer have to worry about being a loser when you let go of the false mind-set of winners and losers. You no longer have to be concerned about your ego when you take the focus off yourself and put it on the customer where it belongs. All those monsters under the bed disappear, leaving you finally free to get down to the important business of helping your customer.

There are three ways to think about objections that help, rather than hinder, your customer relationship:

1. Objections are invitations.
2. Objections are concerns.
3. Objections are opportunities.

Objections Are Invitations

Objections are an invitation for connection—something that human beings are hungry for. Objections mean that your customer cares enough about the sale to want to explore it—and he cares enough about you that he wants to explore the sale with you. It is an act of trust and a request for help.

Objections Are Concerns

Customers are concerned about changing—they want to know that they have covered all the bases and haven't left anything out. Your role is to help make sure your customers have indeed thought of everything and to uncover their concerns so they can be dealt with.

With trust-based selling, the purpose is not to convince your customer to buy from you—it is to help her make the decision that is right for her. Your objective is not to handle the objection, or to close the deal, or to get the sale. Instead, focus on helping to define and solve customer concerns. Let go of your own concern about the outcome—paradoxically, it is your willingness to let go of controlling that improves your chance of getting what you want.

> If you approach your customer with an open-minded, curiosity-driven, adventuresome attitude of mutual discovery, then objections are simply emotional statements about her readiness to buy.

If you approach your customer with an open-minded, curiosity-driven, adventuresome attitude of mutual discovery, then objections are simply emotional statements about her readiness to buy. Sometimes, those statements are about exactly what they claim to be—pricing, timing, politics. More often, those statements are about something else and what is expressed is covering up a more fundamental concern.

Objections Are Opportunities

When you hear an objection, recognize it as an opportunity. If you and your customer can resolve the objection, great! You will get a sale. And if you cannot resolve it, it almost certainly means the proposition is just not the right thing for your customer right now. Amazingly, you get even more credit if you back out gracefully when your offer is not right. Your customer will be surprised and appreciative. And you will increase the odds of getting the next sale and the one after that.

Insight: The Problem with Premature Solutions[1]

Neil Rackham has written three books on professional selling that were all *New York Times* bestsellers. Most famous as the author of *SPIN Selling*, Rackham's material is used in about half the Fortune 500 companies today.

When Charlie asked him what he sees as the most pervasive problem in the field of complex sales, Rackham replied:

"Perhaps the most pervasive one is also the hardest to correct. I'd call it 'premature solutions.' Most salespeople understand that their role in complex sales is to use products and services to solve customer problems. Many of them mistakenly believe that the sooner they can begin solving the problem, the more effective they will be.

"Our earliest research showed that top salespeople didn't focus on solutions until very late in the sale. Less successful salespeople couldn't wait to begin showing how their products and services could solve a customer problem.

"So most salespeople don't spend enough time listening and questioning. The moment they think they have the answer, they jump straight to talking about their solution. As a result they don't do a good enough job of understanding issues from the customer point of view. And if customers don't feel that they are listened to and understood, there's an inevitable loss of trust."

—Neil Rackham (founder and strategic advisor, Huthwaite, and author, Spin Selling, Major Account Sales Strategy, and Rethinking the Sales Force), as told to Charles H. Green

---

Three Ways to Improve the Quality of Your Conversations

Remember: Do not handle objections—have conversations instead.

Here are three ways to improve the quality of any conversation with any customer:

1. Change your language.
2. Actively pursue concerns.
3. Meet emotion with emotion.

Change Your Language

It is easy to get stuck in the old language of objection-handling and closing. New language serves not just to communicate new approaches, but also to signal to yourself and others that something fundamental has shifted.

Here are some *deadwood phrases to ditch*:

- Are there any objections left?
- If I could X, would you Y?
- Which address should I send that to?

And trust-building phrases to add:

- If I were in your shoes ...
- I sense you have some concerns ...
- Tell me how you feel about that ... (For more trust-building phrases, see Chapter 6, "Listen.")

Actively Pursue Concerns

Maintain an ongoing list of customer concerns. Keep a list of the issues that need to be addressed for your customer to make a decision. Share that list at all times with him and work on it jointly. Use an empathetic phrase to introduce issues, such as, "If I were in your shoes, I imagine I'd be concerned about..." Make sure to include some emotional and political issues on your list. For example, "I imagine you'd be concerned about how your internal customers will perceive the price you end up paying. Is that right?"

Review your list of concerns together. Discuss it on a regular basis.

Questions to Keep Current with Clients

- How are we coming along here?
- Is this process helping the decision?
- Are we meeting your time schedule?
- Since we last talked are there any concerns that have emerged to add to the list?

Meet Emotion with Emotion

Your customer's willingness to stay in the conversation in the face of his concerns depends directly on your willingness and ability to listen with openness and empathy.

It might sound something like this:

> Too expensive? Oh. Sounds like I misunderstood your situation, and I'm sorry about that. Would you mind backing up and going over again with me how you see your needs in this area?

Here's the point: Your true objective is not only to see what you missed the first time—it is to make sure that this time your customer *feels* really heard. He may or may not change his mind. Either way, you will have given him the experience of being genuinely cared for as a person—including his business issues. Prove you are committed to helping your customer rather than selling him and you are more likely to win a customer for life, whether or not you make a sale today.

> Prove you are committed to helping your customer rather than selling him and you are more likely to win a customer for life, whether or not you make a sale today.

Insight: Earning the Right to Be Right

If you try to persuade a client by telling her what she should do, she probably won't do it. Not because she is especially ornery—but because she is human. No one responds well to being told what to do unless she first feels heard.

Think about objections in light of this aspect of human psychology. When you are focused on being right, winning the argument, or showing others how smart you are, you are in effect objecting to *them*. And they, in turn, react by objecting to *you*.

When you listen first, you earn the right to be right.

Worksheet: Objection!

Write down the three statements that you interpret as objections—phrases you have heard in the past or anticipate hearing in the future. Pick those with the greatest emotional charge for you—the ones you least like to deal with or are most likely to take personally. Then translate these statements. How is each an invitation? What concerns or opportunities might be underlying what is being expressed?

Statement Interpreted as an Objection	How Is It an Invitation?	What Might be the Underlying Concerns?	In What Ways Is It an Opportunity?

How might you apply the best practices in this chapter—such as change your language, actively pursue concerns, and meet emotion with emotion—to interact differently with your buyers?

_____

_____

_____

What did you learn as a result of this exercise?

_____

_____

_____

Talking Price

Thinking and acting about price as a trusted advisor sets you apart from being just another sales rep. In this chapter we help you understand what is behind price concerns. We provide practical guidance on when to talk price, and offer a simple solution to price anxiety.

For many in business, talking about price is at best awkward; at worst a disaster. You know you have a great product or service, you believe in your company—but when it comes to talking price, you put it off as long as possible. You hesitate, you stammer. You shy away from bringing it up, especially early on when estimates are uncertain and customers may be ill-informed. You hope they will be so dazzled by your presentation that price doesn't even matter. But in the real world, price matters—to your customers and to you.

No business development topic, with the exception of closing, provides as much angst as pricing. How often do you hear (or voice) these kinds of pricing fears?

- "I don't want to mention price too early. Because if we lead with a high price to give ourselves bargaining room, they'll reject us before they understand the total picture. And they'll go with someone else."
- "We lost that deal on price. That's the third time this month. The salespeople are right—it's a very price-competitive market out there, and we are pricing ourselves right out of business."
- "I can't believe they objected to our price. We bent over backwards to make it a good price. They are just price-buyers. Either that or the competition is really out to get us."

> Price is very much about psychology—it's where money meets people.

Do these statements sound familiar? It's easy to take them personally. Talking price brings up a lot of confusion and anxiety. These statements *are* personal, just not in the ways you think. The fact is:

- You *can* talk about price right up front.
- Price talk is rarely about the price.
- There's a logical way to handle price concerns that keeps your emotions under control.

From the Front Lines: Talking Out Loud about Price

I (Charlie) once got into an argument with my boss over the price we were quoting the client—in front of the client.

We had agreed on one price, and my boss was reducing it on the spot, without having discussed it with me beforehand. This wasn't normal. Since I would be responsible for overruns, I chose to make an issue of it, despite the client's presence.

I would not typically recommend you contradict your boss in that way without prior permission, of course, but in this case, it had a good result. The client called us that night to tell us we had the job, and we had it at the higher price I had defended.

It was, he said, because "I could see you really had worked out the costs. And also—I want your butt on the line, no excuses."

If your pricing is honest, transparency is your friend.

—Charles H. Green

Price is very much about psychology—it's where money meets people. You don't want to get taken; they don't want to get taken. You don't want to lose the deal; they don't want to lose out. You don't want to give away too much; they don't want to get too little. You don't want to demand too much; they don't want to be controlled.

The Price Isn't the Problem

Put yourself in the position of the buyer.

You, the buyer, ask for bids on widgets from Seller A and Seller B.

Both sellers have a good product, but you feel better about Seller A. You get along with her, she seems sincerely interested in you, she's responsive to your questions, and she seems to get who you are and what your business is. Seller A is also priced 4 percent higher than Seller B.

The 4 percent price premium is worth it to you to sleep well at night because you are confident in Seller A. You might bargain her down, but you are willing to live with the 4 percent.

> If your customer says you lost on price, what it means is you lost on relationship.

Now what do you tell Seller B? You don't want to offend him—he's done nothing wrong. You want him around to bid again in the future. At the same time, you have no intention of getting into a fluffy discussion about organizational fit or chemistry with a losing bidder you don't know well. What do you do?

You probably tell him his price was too high. It is true enough. If his price had been 20 percent lower, you might have gone with him. It is emotionally safe to blame price.

Price represents many things: It is a cost to the customer, it is a competitive signal, and it is your profit. It is also a signal about your relationship.

> Price represents many things: It is a cost to the customer, it is a competitive signal, and it is your profit. It is also a signal about your relationship.

Price is the socially acceptable way of saying no. It's plausible deniability for the truth—they just didn't like you as much as the others. If your customer says you lost on price, what it means is you lost on relationship. Go work on your relationship, not on your price. If you have a good relationship, you will at least get an honest discussion on price, not an excuse.

Insight: The Truth about Losing on Price

We often do an exercise in our workshops that consists of asking people about their most recent competitive losses and wins.

Our participants report that about 30 to 40 percent of the time, according to the customer, the losses were based on price. But when we ask how often the most recent competitive win was based on price, they answer more like 5 to 10 percent of the time.

Let's explore that disconnect. In many businesses, the winning bidder is not the low bidder at all. The customer's suggestion that the seller lost on price is just a convenient fiction. If the buyer really wanted to do business with the seller, but price was an obstacle, he would find words to say so.

Price is quantitative (a plus in business), and only the buyer has all the cards. Most importantly, blaming a lost deal on price lets the seller save face and the buyer avoid a messy conversation. The truth is, the deal wasn't lost over price—it was a failure of relationship. Price is just the excuse.

When to Talk Price

If you work in a gas station, where laws require you to post your prices in very large type, you can skip this section. But for those of us in complex businesses, price often isn't written down for our customers to see. Knowing when to talk about price is important.

Conventional wisdom suggests that you do not mention price until the customer has understood the value. The thinking goes if you mention price too soon, before your prospect is sold on the value of your proposition, he will get sticker shock and you will lose the sale.

The Psychology of Sticker Shock

The conventional wisdom about sticker shock ignores two psychological issues:

1. The customer's desire to know the price now.
2. The customer's tension about whether his price expectations are reasonable.

The combination of these two tensions is potent.

Picture yourself walking into a high-end clothing store and seeing a very attractive coat with no price tag. A salesperson comes over and says, "You like that coat, eh? It's a great one, isn't it?" You feign calm while you ask the price, hoping it will be below $600. "That coat is $6,000," the clerk says, "and may I say, you have excellent taste." You nod your head, looking critically at the coat, and make sounds that suggest you'll think about it and that maybe you'll come back a little later. Then you walk away slowly, pretending lack of interest, but wanting to get away as fast as possible.

The same tension exists in the B2B (business-to-business) realm. The more you make others wait to find out the price, the more they hate you for doing it. And the bigger the gap between their price expectation and the answer, the more they hate themselves. This is not what you want them to be feeling toward themselves or you!

But these two tensions are in fact a great opportunity to create trust.

Don't Torture Your Customer

Conventional wisdom says a good salesperson should first talk about the value of the coat before revealing the price. We suggest that amounts to mental torture of customers. Who wants to be subjected to an excruciating monologue, while increasingly dreading the final answer, culminating in having to say no to a salesperson because you honestly cannot afford the price? No one we know!

Two dynamics are at play here:

1. The longer the wait between price question and answer, the more tension the customer feels.

2. The customer feels responsible and guilty for having been so far off in his initial estimate of the cost.

Together, these negative feelings fuel the enormous desire to shop online where people can avoid this kind of torment at the hands of salespeople.

> Price is the socially acceptable way of saying no. It's plausible deniability for the truth—they just didn't like you as much as the others.

The Simple Solution to Price Anxiety

There are two ways to reduce or eliminate price anxiety. First, talk about price early in the sales conversation. Second, make it safe for your customer to have inaccurate initial estimates about price.

Here are two sample statements to reduce the tensions and discuss price early:

1. "At the risk of raising price before we've talked about design or context or value, let me just make sure neither of us—mainly me!—is potentially embarrassed here. I'm guessing that this is going to be something like a low five-digit number. Is that different by a digit or two from what you're expecting? I just want to make sure we're all working in the same region on the likely cost here."

2. "You know, people have a hard time telling pricing apart on these services—they can cost a lot, or a little. They can range from $22,000 to $222,000, depending on a number of factors. We can hone in on what's right for you—I just wanted to let you know there's a big range."

> By getting price talk out into the open, and allaying your customer's concerns about pricing estimates, you have not only avoided the problem of sticker shock, you've also started to earn trust with your customer.

By getting price talk out into the open and allaying your customer's concerns about pricing estimates, you have not only avoided the problem of sticker shock, you've also started to earn trust with your customer.

How to Address Price Concerns

What if you get price talk out in the open early in the conversation, and your customer reacts negatively? The instinctive reaction of most salespeople to a price concern is to feel attacked, and then seek a rational response. (See Chapter 14, "Handling Objections.") This is precisely backwards. What you need to do is to rationally understand what is behind the concern, and then seek the right emotional response.

Let's first explore what lies beneath most price concerns, and then define how to respond.

The Three Primary Drivers of Price Concerns

Before you can respond effectively to price concerns, it is helpful to understand the three drivers of the vast majority of client demands.

1. *Fear of being taken advantage of.* If clients perceive that someone else is getting a better deal, they may react negatively. Clients who feel mistreated become very creative about attributing causes—blaming your rates, your profits, your margins, and so forth.
2. *Miscommunication about the project or process.* Problems can arise from project design issues, including the scope of issues addressed, the leverage of your team, the depth to which issues are explored, timing, and choices about staffing. If the client orders an apple and you price out an apple pie, the client may think you are charging absurd margins on fruit.
3. *Misunderstanding of quality needed.* You may be trying to sell the client on a Lexus/Mercedes solution when he thinks a Chevrolet/Volkswagen will do just fine.

When clients demand price concessions, they do not present the actual, underlying issue in these neat terms. They simply say, "Your price is too high, and you need to cut it."

Note: This does *not* mean your price is too high, nor does it mean you need to make price deductions. It does mean you would be wise to investigate what is really going on.

> The statement "your price is too high" is a smokescreen for your customer's real message. It's not about the price!

Five Meanings behind "Your Price Is Too High"

The statement "your price is too high" is a smokescreen for your customer's real message. It is not about the price!

Most price concerns are simply expressions of dismay or worry—emotional responses. The underlying concerns fall into five categories. Helping your customer identify these feelings and these categories is a positive step in and of itself.

Here are five buyer categories, along with how they object to price, and what they are really thinking. How many sound familiar? See Figure 15.1.

A Simple Solution

The good news is, while all these buyers are different, one simple question serves them all: "What do you mean when you say, 'the price is too high'?"

Here's how you might actually phrase it:

"Okay, so the price sounds high to you. Help me understand something, if you would. 'The price is too high' can mean several things. It could mean it's way more than you expected, it's beyond your budget, it sounds higher than someone else's bid, or it doesn't make sense. Now, I don't know if we can solve your concerns or not. I'd like to start by making sure I understand what you mean by 'the price is too high.'"

Your job here is simply to acknowledge that all reasons are valid, and make it comfortable for your customer to share which one is operative.

When they state their real concerns for what they are, the Uninformed and the Out-of-Budget Buyers feel relieved of their shame and embarrassment. And while their purchases won't happen today, you just vastly increased the odds of them buying from you in the future.

Figure 15.1

**What "Your
Price Is Too
High" Means**

		What They Say	What They Mean
1. The Uninformed Buyer		"Oh, that's way bigger than I thought."	"I feel ashamed. I didn't understand what was involved in making this purchase before talking to this person. I should have known. It's my fault."
2. The Out-of-Budget Buyer		"That's more than we can afford."	"I feel embarrassed. I invited this person in thinking we could do it in this year's budget. Now I see that won't work. How awkward."
3. The Engineer Buyer		"Wait a minute, competitors' prices aren't that high. I don't see why it should be that much. That doesn't make sense."	"I feel threatened. They must be quoting me a heavily loaded price. They can't get away with that!"
4. The Comparison Shopper		"Wait—how do I know I'm getting the best deal?"	"I will feel stupid if I don't get a good deal, so I need to know your real, true, best possible, final price—and I have to believe you."
5. The Bazaar Lover		"Oh we couldn't possibly go that high for this kind of service—it's just not worth it!"	"The game is afoot! I want to win. I don't care what you quote me; I'm going to get 20% off! I love this part of the buying process!"

Responding to the Engineer Buyer becomes a simple job of itemizing features and costs—as long as you are not attached to the margin on every little feature. (See "A Special Case: The Engineer Buyer" below for more details.)

The Comparison Shopper's issue is solved by your willingness to be transparent, within the bounds of what is legal. Another easy sale—as long as your price is fair.

Only the Bazaar Buyers will not give you a straight answer about what they mean—which is how you know you are dealing with the Bazaar Buyer! You may be tempted to pad your prices across the board to deal with this buyer—do not do it! Instead, build options into the design or quality or features. The customer can then remove, or otherwise alter them, thus allowing some room for him to positively affect the product-price package you have presented. That's what he really wants–to affect the offering. So let him. And enjoy yourself along with the buyer.

Insight: The Case against Discounts

The worst thing you can do when faced with a price concern is to give a discount. The predominant problem isn't lost profit: It is confirming your client's suspicion that you are untrustworthy. Discounting has the perverse effect of convincing all buyers (except dedicated hagglers) that—aha!—you really were hiding something.

Not only will discounting increase the odds this client will haggle with you in the future, but it will lower his trust in you.

A Special Case: The Engineer Buyer

One case merits further discussion: the (relatively) rational case of what we call the Engineer Buyer.

An Engineer Buyer who accuses you of high prices is likely to assume that rates, costs, and profit margins are the problem, and conclude she is being taken advantage of by a voracious provider. She may have particular experience with another bid or another seller, and use that as the basis for determining why your price is high. You as the seller are likely to feel you are being treated badly by a callous client playing you off against others. Both parties cast the issue in terms of greed and motives, and dig in for tough price negotiations.

The Heart of the Problem

Rates and margins are almost never the real problems. The real problems lie far more often in design issues and in misunderstandings. The worst response to an Engineer Buyer is to negotiate on a total price alone—it makes the client think you have been hiding something, and makes her wonder if she should ask for even more. Too often both parties try to negotiate price when they should be discussing design.

If the Engineer Buyer is citing another company with a lower bid, consider your economic model. Does it significantly vary from the competitor's? If not, that leaves two explanations: either the projects being discussed are just not comparable, or your competitor will lose money on this bid. (The latter is often true; many firms cut price to buy the business, perhaps even your firm.) The discussion you need to have with your client explores both options—in that order.

Above all, clients want to know they are being treated fairly. Fair starts with a fair price for work done, and the willingness to be open about how you arrive at that price. Very few clients will, in turn, be unfair to a provider who has treated *them* fairly.

How to Discuss a Competitor's Bid

1. *Commit to resolution.* Make sure you spend enough time understanding and empathizing with the client's concerns. Say you are committed to finding a mutually acceptable resolution—and mean it.
2. *Suggest a series of price drivers.* Commit to exploring each in turn.
    a. *Start with scope and design issues.* Ask the client to compare in detail your project design with what they had in mind. That means being specific about modules, scope of research, staffing levels—everything that might be different. Then compare. More than half the time, discussion will stop right here. Most fears are simply misunderstandings of design.
    b. *Move on to quality issues.* Determine whether quality in your proposal is higher than what they expected or want. If so, then ask whether the client is willing to pay for extra quality—or not. If the answer is "not," be ready to scale back or walk.
    c. *If the issue is not yet settled, put your business model on the table.* For example, if you are a services firm, tell the client your billing rate structure, base compensation structure, leverage model, and utilization rates. Explain why these numbers add up to a fair profit model for you and why they probably don't vary much by competitor.

As you become skilled at leading with trust, handling the price discussion can be your shining moment.

Worksheet: The Price Is Right

Being aware of your own uneasiness with discussing price is the first and critical step towards easing everyone's natural discomfort with the topic. What worries, fears, or concerns do you have about talking price—especially early in the sales process?

_____

_____

_____

_____

Bring to mind the last time you lost a sale and were told it was because of price. Looking back, what was the quality of your relationship with the buyer(s)? What evidence did you have of the presence or absence of a trust-based relationship?

_____

_____

_____

_____

If you had an opportunity to re-create that sales situation, what might you do differently?

_____

_____

_____

If you have had misunderstandings about scope, quality, or other factors related to price with past customers, what might you have done to prevent them?

_____

_____

_____

What do you see as a result of examining this situation that might apply to other relationships?

_____

_____

_____

Closing the Deal

The ABC mantra, Always Be Closing, typically destroys trust, along with the possibilities of future sales and repeat business. In this chapter we redirect you away from this counterproductive thinking and show you the value of leading with trust. You will understand the reasons not to Always Be Closing and you will benefit from specific ways to focus less on closing and more on helping.

It's often said that customers like to buy, they just don't like to be sold. We might add that buyers like to decide—but they don't like being closed. Yet many salespeople persist in believing that the buyer's to-buy-or-not-to-buy decision represents a pivotal moment at which sellers can and should influence the buyer. This moment has come to be called closing.

Closing has been cast as the dramatic end point to a transaction. That is a myth. The most influential moments in sales actually happen much earlier in the sales process.[1] In fact, most attempts at closing do more harm than good to the relationship.

The time when a buying decision is made is simply another milestone in the ongoing evolution of a trust-based relationship. Leading with trust means focusing on the relationship, not the sale, as your ultimate goal. Closing is therefore irrelevant; exploring, and moving forward is what matters.

> The time when a buying decision is made is just another milestone in the ongoing evolution of a trust-based relationship.

Six Reasons Not to Always Be Closing

The phrase Always Be Closing has positive connotations in some circles. It was taught for many years in the well-regarded Xerox sales system as a reminder to constantly explore customer needs. But more often than not, closing has both a negative connotation and negative impact, especially for buyers. Here are six reasons not to do it.

1. *Closing closes down the conversation.* Closing is typically used as a technique to get a buyer to take action. Consider the assumptive close, "Shall I start the credit check now?" and the either/or close, "Would you like that in red or green?" These questions are neither rooted in curiosity nor focused on discovery. They do not continue dialogue; they stop dialogue.

CASE STUDY

From the Front Lines: A Lesson about Closing

I (Charlie) got a call from a senior manager at a prestigious firm. He was very complimentary of my work, particularly of my suggestion that trust was the most effective driver of making sales, not techniques or processes.

We had an excellent discussion. It was clear he understood my services and that I could be useful for his organization. It was a very exciting opportunity for me.

As we moved from content to timing and pricing, the discussion began to bog down in indecision. Finally, I said, "Look, I think we both believe this would be good for your company. Tell me what it would take for you to agree with this."

There was silence on the other end of the line, then he said, "I think you just lost the deal. You tried to close me, the way I've been closed by some used car dealers. You just invalidated everything you've said to me about being client-focused and not closing."

I was crushed. He was right, and there was no point in my arguing. I never did hear back from him. But I've tried never to close again.

—Charles H. Green

2. *Closing is usually attempted prematurely.* When you try to close before the timing is right, you are doomed from the start. Readiness on the part of the buyer is actually a psychological state. The right time to make a decision is not when the seller sees the right solution—it is when the buyer feels heard and understood, and when *she* sees the right solution.

3. *Closing is seller-centric.* What all closes have in common is their attempt to persuade the buyer to do something—and that something is too often what the seller wants, or at best what the buyer wants *when the seller wants it.* Even with well-intended sellers, there is a whiff of coercion, trickery, and manipulation about the term *closing* and its connotations. The simple truth is that closing is not buyer-centric, it is seller-centric.

4. *Closing objectifies the buyer.* In the sentence, "I closed the customer," the subject is "I," the seller, and the object is "the customer." The subject does something to the object, meaning the seller does something to the buyer. This is antithetical to a collaborative relationship between equals, and adverse to trust. For most human beings, the only thing worse than being controlled is being controlled and being lied to about it at the same time.

5. *Closing is transactional.* Closing tends to be narrowly focused on getting a particular action today, rather than expansively focused on building a trust-based relationship over time. The celebration of closing—an institutional practice for many sales organizations—encourages sellers to declare victory for short-term results.

6. *Closing leads to fewer sales.* In Neil Rackham's perennial best-seller *SPIN Selling*,[2] he describes the results of research[3] on closing for high-priced goods.[4] His research reveals that training sellers in closing techniques resulted in shorter sales transaction times *and fewer sales.* The rate of sales was 42 percent before sellers were trained in closing; after training, the rate of sales dropped to 33 percent. For complex products or services, the better you get at closing, the less you sell. Closing, in effect, just gets you shot down faster.

Not only does closing making you less effective as a seller, it is in direct violation of at least three of the four trust principles: a focus on the other, a collaborative approach to relationships, and a medium- to long-term relationship perspective.

Five Practices to Stop Closing and Start Helping

There *is* a valid role to be played toward the end of a sales conversation: to help the buyer make decisions at a pace appropriate to him, while moving the relationship forward—not the sale per se. The goal of traditional selling is to convince the buyer to buy from you—the goal of trust-based selling is to help the buyer do what is right for him. The difference is a question of focus and motives. Helping, as distinct from closing, is other-focused, nonmanipulative, and trust-enhancing.

> The goal of traditional selling is to convince the buyer to buy from you—the goal of trust-based selling is to help the buyer do what is right for him.

We propose a new mantra: Don't Always Be Closing. Or, if you prefer a more positive acronym, Always Be Collaborating.

Here are five practices to help you stop closing and start helping.

1. *Let go of the sale itself.* Accept that you will not get every sale—including this one. Instead, focus on doing the right thing for the buyer, whatever that may be. Trust that doing so will gain you at least as many initial sales, more repeat sales, and far more referrals in the long run. Paradoxically, the best way to sell effectively is to stop trying to close. Just help your customer to do the next right thing. Period.
2. *Understand your buyer's motives.* Take the time to listen until you understand where she is coming from. Focus less on the answers, and more on empathy and understanding. When buyers buy, it is not because they have been persuaded by rational arguments—it is because they feel emotionally comfortable with the decision. Buyers who buy from you trust that:
   - You have their best interests at heart.
   - You understand their concerns.
   - You can be relied on.
   - You are committed to dealing rightly with the inevitable unforeseen circumstances.
3. *Envision a positive future.* When you and the buyer share a common perspective, the anxiety that naturally arises in the final stages of a sales conversation is reduced. Envisioning an alternate future reality—the result of implementing whatever solution you are exploring—creates a clear picture of what is possible and desirable.
4. *Keep your personal needs out of it.* Do not push for a commitment because of your own frustration or desires for closure. Instead, follow his lead. Work on her timetable.
5. *Replace closing language with action language.* When you sense it is time for committed action, ask questions like:
   - "What needs doing next?"
   - "Where should we go from here?"
   - "What makes sense now?"
   Then have a candid discussion about the answer.

Worksheet: Stop Closing, Start Helping

Bring to mind two situations: (1) a time when you or your colleagues successfully completed a sale with a buyer—that is, you were able to help the buyer make decisions at a pace appropriate to him, while moving the relationship forward—and (2) a time when you did not successfully "close" a sale.

Describe them briefly below, then answer the questions that follow.

Case 1: A Successfully Completed Sale
Description:

_____

_____

_____

Case 2: An Unsuccessful "Close"
Description:

_____

_____

_____

Using the five practices to stop closing and start helping in this chapter, how would you assess each situation?

Case 1: A Successful Close
To what extent did you:

Let go of the sale itself?	☐Y	☐N	☐Somewhat
Understand your buyer's motives?	☐Y	☐N	☐Somewhat
Envision a positive future?	☐Y	☐N	☐Somewhat
Keep your personal needs out of it?	☐Y	☐N	☐Somewhat
Replace closing language with action language?	☐Y	☐N	☐Somewhat

What other factors contributed to the positive result?

_____

_____

_____

How would you characterize the quality of the relationship with the buyer today?

_____

_____

_____

What practices do you want to carry forward into the next opportunity to successfully complete a sale?

_____

_____

_____

Case 2: An Unsuccessful "Close"

To what extent did you:

Let go of the sale itself?	☐Y	☐N	☐Somewhat
Understand your buyer's motives?	☐Y	☐N	☐Somewhat
Envision a positive future?	☐Y	☐N	☐Somewhat
Keep your personal needs out of it?	☐Y	☐N	☐Somewhat
Replace closing language with action language?	☐Y	☐N	☐Somewhat

What other factors contributed to the less-than-positive result?

_____

_____

_____

How would you characterize the quality of the relationship with the buyer today?

_____

_____

_____

What do you want to be sure to do differently the next time?

_____

_____

_____

Developing New Business with Existing Clients

17
Chapter

The best way to expand your business is to start with your existing relationships. In this chapter, we offer ways for you to nurture those relationships to make new business a natural progression of the relationship. We explore how you can sell upstream, effectively cross-sell, and request referrals.

From a purely business perspective, the most effective and efficient way to develop new business is to focus on existing relationships. This is not only commonsense, but one of the more widely proven facts in business.[1] Your current clients have a track record with you and can vouch for you. If you have been applying trust principles to your dealings with them, they have personally experienced you as a trustworthy professional.

There are three ways to develop new business by expanding existing relationships:

1. Move *upstream* in the organization.
2. Cross-sell *within* the organization.
3. Seek referrals *outside* the organization.

Each case presents opportunities to distinguish yourself by leading with trust.

First, Deepen the Relationship

Whether you wish to move up, across, or outside the organization, you will get there more easily if your existing clients are inclined to help you. And here's a principle we have found to be true: Existing clients are inclined to help you in direct proportion to how helpful you have been to them. If you have treated them with their interests at heart, worked with them collaboratively, focused on the relationship rather than the transaction, and been consistently open with them, then when you ask for a favor in return, you are likely to get a reciprocal response.

> Existing clients are inclined to help you in direct proportion to how helpful you have been to them.

If you have been just executing on the contract, working the transaction, and watching out for number one (yourself), then you are likely to get a negative reaction when you try to expand the relationship. As with trust-building itself, these steps will only bear fruit you if you actually *care*.

From the Front Lines: In It for the Long Haul

A savvy private wealth manager in Canada told me (Charlie) the long-term view he takes with his clients.

"I once offered to do some free investment planning for a client's 12- and 14-year-old children. My coworker was confused why I was wasting my time with children.

"That's easy! I regularly meet with clients' children and explain the concept of saving, investing and risk. Even at the ages mentioned I have had success in making the experience relevant for the children and ultimately appreciated by the parents.

"I believe in long-term focus and relationships. While working with clients' children has resulted in referrals (which is a happy outcome) that is never our primary intent. Our purpose is to build long-term relationships by continuously delivering a 'remarkable experience' for our clients and their families."

—As told to Charles H. Green

Move Upstream

At one time or another, you may have found yourself closed off from a business opportunity because you did not have a key relationship one or two levels higher in your client organization. Or perhaps you found out too late that you had not been invited to a meeting at which you could have influenced a crucial decision. Or maybe you have a product, the benefits of which are relevant only to a level above your existing customer.

From the Front Lines: Turning Down Business to Get New Business[2]

Sally Foley Lewis, an Australian management coach and trainer, remembers a story of turning down business:

"When I was working for a Middle Eastern company, I was often the 'expert' in the room to advise and guide a client on choices for services. My employer company already had a relationship with the client. As I got to know the client and what we delivered to them, it became clear that the client did not really need one of the services they were getting from us.

"In the contract renewal discussions, I told the client why they shouldn't bother with this one service; that the money, time, and effort would be better spent on other, more appropriate things. I suggested a few services we offered, but emphasized a range of possibilities, including some services we didn't offer.

"Not only were we successful in getting more work, they tripled their business with us."

—Sally Foley Lewis (management coach and trainer, Australia)

> Treat a potential upstream client the way you treat valued existing clients: with respect, authenticity, confidence, and caring.

If you want those higher-level business relationships,[3] you have to earn the right. Treat a potential upstream client the way you treat valued existing clients: with respect, authenticity, confidence, and caring. And then do a few other things unique to moving upstream.

When you are considering a move upstream, make sure you can answer the following seven questions to be certain you are making the most of your time and your clients' time.

1. *What is the need*? Can you explain in simple, nontechnical terms what's in it for them (not you)? Why should the client care about helping you?
2. *What is the want*? What is the emotional desire or wish behind the product or service? How will your offer make the upstream client delighted?
3. *What is the business case*? What's the payback? What needle gets moved, and how? How will you communicate that in a way that resonates for the new client you hope to gain?
4. *Who are the key stakeholders*? Whose buy-in is needed? What is the impact of your offering on all of them? What benefits will they receive? What risks are you asking them to take?
5. *If your existing client has not already raised the issue, why is that*? Is something preventing him? Is it against his interest? Is he afraid of something?
6. *What's in it for your existing client*? What does she get out of it? What is her incentive to help you? What is the risk to her, and what is your plan to mitigate those risks?
7. *How will you enlist the support of your existing client*? How will you address his concerns? What specific help do you need from him?

Once you have satisfactory answers to these seven questions, you can pursue and accept an opportunity to present your offer with confidence. In the special case of moving upstream, consider the extra value that often lies in presenting alongside your existing client, rather than without her.

Cross-Sell

To cross-sell is to suggest related products or services to an existing client or similar services to a new group within the broader client. Cross-selling implies working at the same level of the organization. It sounds simple and natural enough—you have a relationship and you invite a colleague in to help with another area—and yet it is rife with risk: risk to your client, risk to your colleague, and risk to you.

Say you ask your client Mary to meet your colleague Johann to talk about a new offering.

You are asking Mary to trust:

- That you are competent to assess the offering well enough to make the referral.
- That Johann is competent.
- That Mary and Johann will get along well.

You are asking Johann to trust:

- That you know the situation well enough to recommend he spend time on it.
- That he and Mary will get along.

And *you* are taking three risks:

1. Johann could fail—reflecting badly on you.
2. Mary could behave badly—reflecting badly on you.
3. Johann and Mary might get along famously, with Johann becoming the primary custodian of the relationship with Mary!

In light of this, it is tempting to simply hand off your colleague's business card—in other words, deliver the subject matter expert—and to say that what you have done is cross-selling. But this creates another risk: the lost opportunity to be your client's trusted advisor.

What clients really need from you as the existing relationship-holder is not a hand-off, but something else:

- Someone who can be relied on to do due diligence.
- Someone who understands her business.
- Someone who is on her side.
- Someone who knows when to call another expert on the team.

In cross-selling, the critical resource is not the new expertise being brought to bear—it is the existing relationship. The primary best practice for cross-selling, then, is the opposite of handing off the business card: You lead with your relationship, not with your colleague's expertise.

Take these three steps to be sure your cross-selling efforts are set up for success:

1. *Talk to your client about the new offering.* "Mary, I want to make sure I understand this area so I can best represent your perspectives to our internal experts, before I allow them to take up your valuable time."

> In cross-selling, the critical resource is not the new expertise being brought to bear—it is the existing relationship.

2. *Talk to your colleague about your existing client.* "Johann, tell me what you need to know from me. I want to make sure I have all the right questions answered for you before we both take the risk of you investing your time talking to them."

3. *Chair their first meeting.* "Mary and Johann, I've spent time with each of you to make sure this is a productive meeting today. If it doesn't work out, we can simply stop at any time, and it will have been my responsibility. I'll stay involved as long as it's helpful to each of you, because I am committed to you both."

> The primary best practice for cross-selling, then, is the opposite of handing off the business card: You lead with your relationship, not with your colleague's expertise.

Seek Referrals

The third source of new business from existing clients is referrals. Referrals are requests to an existing client or customer to introduce you to another possible customer outside of their organization. A request for a referral is a big deal. You are asking someone to take on all the risks of cross-selling with the added tension that the favor is now being asked about an *external* relationship.

It is a common misconception that deep trust must already be present in a relationship to ask a big favor. But paradoxically, asking a big favor actually builds trust. A bold request when a relationship is new or in some ways uncertain requires risk, and risk-taking increases trust. Do not get caught in the thinking trap that you have to wait to initiate a discussion.

Here are seven tips for requesting referrals in a way that builds trust at the same time:

1. *Be direct.* A trust-based request for a big favor doesn't beat around the bush. It might sound like this:

    "Mary, I know we have a strong business relationship. It's in that context that I want to ask you a big favor. Of course you can say no. I hope you'll be able to say yes. Would you

> It is a common misconception that deep trust must already be present in a relationship to ask a big favor. But paradoxically, asking a big favor actually builds trust.

introduce me to two potential clients? There are two in particular I'd like to discuss with you. I can offer some reasons why they might appreciate your calling them—after all, I want this referral to reflect strongly on you."

2. *Less is more.* A referral request is one you might make a couple of times over the life of a successful relationship. Referrals take time and effort on everyone's part to set up well, and follow through on. Think carefully whom you plan to ask, and when.

3. *Make it easy.* In your request, be explicit about what you expect. Research the organizations and the names, and prime your client with rock-solid things to say about you. The ideal result is a referral that eventually comes back to your client and says, "I have to thank you for referring [your name] to me, she was everything you said and more."

4. *Be whole-hearted about it.* It is all too easy to ask for a favor in a half-hearted way. You self-sabotage when you say things like, "I know you're incredibly busy," "Only if you have time," or "I don't want this to be inconvenient for you." If you ask in a tentative way, you tend to get tentativeness in return—your client notices your lack of confidence and the exchange goes the way of "Let's do lunch," where lunch never happens. This takes a toll on your relationship—it sets you up for low reliability and fake intimacy.

5. *Give your client a gracious way out.* It is possible to be clear and confident in your request, and still leave your client room to decline politely in a way that both increases trust and strengthens the relationship. Here is one version:

    "Mary, you may not be able to do me this favor, for any number of reasons. I believe that you will do it for me if you can, and that's good enough for me. If you can't, no explanations are required. I'm glad I feel comfortable enough with you to ask this. And I hope you'll feel free to ask the same of me some day."

6. *Build referral requests into your sales process.* When you engage with a new client, set the expectation that, if things work out and you end up doing work that they agree is great, you may come to them later and ask them for a referral. Be overt about it, and make it clear there won't be any pressure for your client to say yes. This might sound like:

    "Mary, as we're getting near the end of our buying experience together, I want to tell you about a practice we try to follow. We believe strongly in referrals as a way to do business. You may recall that Ralph X. referred us to you, and I believe it made an impact on you. If it turns out that we do business together, and if we end up doing very good work that you're pleased with, then I may come back to you and ask you to do us the honor of serving as a referral in turn. I would only ask this if I felt our work had been a great success, and of course you'd be under no obligation whatsoever to comply."

    By doing this, you model candor, show self-confidence, and demonstrate the importance you place on relationships, on long-term performance, and on commitment to your clients.

7. *Close the loop at the end of a project.* When you build referral requests into your sales process, it is important to revisit the conversation, regardless of how the project has unfolded and whether you choose to ask for the referral now or save it for later.

    - *If the project was a clear success*: "Tell me if I'm wrong, Mary, I think the work we did was valuable and very well received. I'm not going to ask you for a referral right now. I don't have a clear enough request for you just yet. If we continue to do the same caliber work together, I will come back to this topic, if that's all right with you."
    - *If the project was okay, not great*: "Mary, I don't think I've earned the right to ask you that big favor yet. The onus is on us to step up our game. I just want you to know I haven't forgotten our conversation."
    - *If the project went poorly*: "Mary, you may recall we had a conversation during the sales process about possibly asking you for referrals if you considered our work highly successful. As we've discussed, this was not one of those projects. I just wanted to acknowledge that with you, and restate our commitment to dramatically improving our performance."

Worksheet: Develop New Business Naturally

Examine an existing client relationship to identify opportunities to expand the relationship. For relationships that teams are assigned to, this is an excellent team exercise.

Organization/Client Name:

What opportunities are there to move *upstream* in the organization?

_____

_____

What opportunities are there to cross-sell *within* the organization?

_____

_____

What opportunities are there to seek referrals *outside* the organization?

_____

_____

By your assessment, to what extent is your existing client inclined to help you? In what ways?

_____

_____

What, if anything, is missing in the current relationship?

_____

_____

In what ways might you deepen the relationship before you attempt to expand the work you are doing?

_____

_____

What insight has this reflection provided about a conversation you might have with your client?

_____

_____

What actions will you take as a result? Be specific.

What	By When	With Whom	Support I Will Ask For

Selling to the C-Suite

18
Chapter

The challenges of selling to the executive level are unique, partly due to the distinct executive role and partly due to the ways you must adjust your thinking and approach. In this chapter, we explore what sets C-level executives apart and how you need to plan and respond accordingly. We focus on the mental preparation required to be effective at this level: managing your motives, your role, and your emotions. The chapter also includes a summary of best practices for making the most of your opportunity to enter the C-suite.

The term *C-suite* refers to the top levels of an organization—leaders who are generally referred to as CXO, where C stands for "Chief," X indicates the function (such as Finance or Marketing) and O stands for "Officer." The stakes are high when you are dealing with the highest level of an organization. Discomfort, anxiety, and the desire to compete and win are all reactions that are easily triggered, and all pose barriers to leading with trust.

There are many ways to build trust with a CXO, some of them unexpected. A CXO is approached by people trying to sell products, services, and ideas all the time. She is rarely approached by people willing to invest the time and effort it takes to understand her world. Consider that a lost sale in the C-suite is not a failure if trust is earned in the process.

> Consider that a lost sale in the C-suite is not a failure if trust is earned in the process.

What Sets the C-Suite Apart

CXOs really are different. If you start by understanding those differences, then you can align your actions based on trust. Five aspects in particular of the CXO's world distinguish them from other potential customers. Figure 18.1 shows what they are, and what they mean for you.

A Different Kind of Preparation

When building relationships in the C-suite, your mental preparation matters as much, if not more, as your slide presentation and leave-behind documents. Think about it: You probably

Aspects of the CXO's World	What You Can Do
1. **Sphere of influence.** The CXO has responsibility across the entire organization.	• Put more emphasis on the *why* of your proposal than the *how*. • Adopt the language of organizations: strategy, impact, change.
2. **Resource constraints.** A CXO works with inadequate resources under difficult deadlines. There isn't time, budget, or resources to say yes to many of the requests received.	• Be quick to demonstrate the value you bring. • Come prepared to directly describe a real problem and your solution. • Be concise and clear in your communications. • Serve as a sounding board.
3. **Data overload.** The CXO is besieged with data, though it is often incomplete, inconclusive, or contradictory.	• Help simplify, clarify, and focus. • Help identify the few critical factors in making a decision.
4. **Isolation.** It's lonely at the top. The information a CXO receives is often filtered by subordinates, suppliers, and others who have their own agenda, who don't want to deliver bad news, or who may be operating from fear.	• Tell the truth as directly and succinctly as you can. • Deliver bad news immediately. • Be willing to say, "I don't know." • Become someone the CXO can turn to for counsel. • Avoid "spin" at all costs.
5. **Complex decision making.** The CXO is faced with many complex decisions, and is ultimately responsible for them. The buck stops with her.	• Help the CXO make the decision that is right for the organization as a whole, not right for a portion of it, or right for you. • Sometimes the right thing for the CXO to choose is to do nothing. Respect this decision. • Focus on being a helpful part of the decision-making process, not on the decision itself.

Figure 18.1

Five Aspects of the CXO's World

know your offering inside and out; you have researched the CXO, and have had prebriefings with your team. You may also have spent looking at things from her perspective.

But how much time do you routinely spend on preparing your frame of mind for a C-level meeting? Probably very little. Yet your state of mind walking into a meeting can be critical. Why not spend at least as much time managing yourself as you do managing tasks? In particular:

1. *Manage your motives:* Think about when *not* to sell to the C-suite.
2. *Manage your role:* Are you presenting yourself as a salesperson—or a sounding board?
3. *Manage your emotions:* Keep your own personal reactions in check.

> How much time do you routinely spend on preparing your frame of mind for a C-level meeting? Probably very little.

Manage Your Motives

There are many good reasons to target your sales efforts at the C-suite, including the organization-wide benefit your product or service would have. On the other hand, there are

From the Front Lines: Asking a Simple Question

Paulo Novaes, a Senior Manager working in Mexico for a global consulting firm, tells a story about the power of asking questions.

"At the due diligence stage of selling to a global bank, I was gathering information on how they work: their existing skills and where the gaps might be. This was a company that traditionally did everything in-house, and we would be their first outsourcing partner.

"The executive in charge told me with great passion of all they had accomplished, the skills they had, and procedures they had put in place, and so on. It was impressive.

"I had to ask a simple, critical question: 'Why do you need us?'

"Once the client recovered from his surprise, he came back with a set of answers: 'You have the experience, the methodology, the capability to add to all we have built. Also, yes, we are good, we are proud, and have reached a limit in efficiency, with what we can do by ourselves. We need an external partner to complement what we've done, who is able to design a solution to fit our needs.'

"The client sold himself on our services in that moment.

"What I learned: Sometimes you have to ask basic questions. Simple and humble is often better. Rather than struggle to find what's beneath the surface or between the lines, the best way to advance is to be as direct as possible—even at the risk of going against cultural norms. If you speak directly—in a polite manner and with respect—the customer will thank you. You are saving their time and getting a better result."

—*Paulo Novaes (Mexico)*

several really bad reasons to explore before you walk through that executive door. Here are three.

1. *You have not succeeded at the lower levels of the organization.* If you are seduced by the persistent belief that *if only* you could reach some higher-up, she would appreciate the enormous value provided by your offering, think again. This optimism implies that your partner at the lower level is incompetent or ineffective—both of which are dangerous assumptions. If a lower-level partner has rejected what you are selling, invest your time and energy to find out how you or your offering are unattractive, rather than in blaming and trying to work around your buyer.

2. *You think the C-suite is the only place "real" work gets done.* An organization is a system: Everyone matters and everyone plays a part. No one knows this better than a CXO. Overvaluing the role and influence of the C-suite limits your view and diminishes your ability to be effective. Even if your relationship to the organization begins at the C-suite, you will inevitably need to build bonds at lower levels of the organization to be effective. It only takes the slightest bit of elitist attitude to impede trust.

> Overvaluing the role and influence of the C-suite limits your view and diminishes your ability to be effective.

3. *You want the badge of honor.* Let's be honest: It is seductive to interact at the senior-most levels of an organization. Do not let your ego run the show. Engaging with the C-suite gives you access to an organization's inner circle. This is a privileged place, from which you have the opportunity to serve the entire organization by influencing the agenda, introducing ideas, and bringing perspectives to bear. Treat it as an honor, not a trophy. Your motives matter. Be clear about your goals and your intentions.

Manage Your Role

A trusted advisor in the C-suite is a sounding board, first and foremost, not a salesperson. Leading with trust means you consistently value the relationship more than any one transaction or proposal. It means recognizing that the greatest value you bring to a CXO is to help his decision-making process. Being focused on a sales pitch limits your mind-set and narrows your role. Seeing your role as sounding board implies that you:

> A trusted advisor in the C-suite is a sounding board, first and foremost, not a salesperson.

- Facilitate a collaborative discussion.
- Explore strategic options from his point of view and yours.
- Listen with curiosity and interest.
- Come as close as you can to feeling what it must be like to be *this* CXO facing *these* issues or opportunities.
- Identify ways you can help him make a decision that is right for his organization.
- Speak the truth in a direct, respectful, and unvarnished way.
- Demonstrate a willingness to see things through.
- Recommend or support that no decision be made if choosing to do nothing is the best decision.

Manage Your Emotions

When working with a CXO, your own personal reactions may be different or heightened. You may be confident in your offering and still feel intimidated, nervous, or overwhelmed. Or your competitive nature may be overly fueled by the opportunity to engage at the highest level of the organization. As a result of this natural spike in self-orientation, you are more likely to act in ways that are neither in your best interests nor the CXO's:

- *You fall back into patterns or habits* that are comfortable, but not necessarily effective—like the march of a thousand slides, or being overly aggressive.
- *You fail to make an emotional connection* with the CXO because you are preoccupied with your own concerns and interests.
- *You allow the pressures of time to dominate,* attempting to get all of your credentials, your service's benefits, and the reasons for buying out on the table in the first 10 minutes of your meeting.
- *You overpromise out of anxiety,* and therefore sell something you cannot deliver.

While these reactions are natural, they pose a threat to your ability to be focused, centered, and effective. Bring self-awareness to your preparation by anticipating your tendencies and triggers, and devising strategies for managing them.

Nine Best Practices for Successful C-Suite Meetings

When you do have an opportunity to enter the C-suite, apply these nine best practices to help you make the most of it:

1. *Bring the right mind-set.* Be curious. Be helpful. Focus not on your sale but on helping the CXO do the right thing. Be a partner having a dialog among equals.
2. *Prepare, then adapt.* Prepare to your usual high-quality standards, and then be prepared to leave any or all of your preparation behind—on the table, in your bag, or on your laptop. Remember, the *relationship* is the customer. Focus there first and foremost.
3. *Make connecting a priority.* Even in a brief meeting, spend some time getting to know the CXO as a person. Be alert to all the cues that are available to you about who he is and what matters to him, personally as well as professionally. Without a more personal connection, you are just another salesperson. With a connection, you are someone who can be trusted to help define and shape the problems and opportunities.
4. *Bring five slides (if any), not 50.* Keep presentations brief and to the point. Do not revisit the technical sale you already made at lower levels. Make the conclusions the headlines. Offer leave-behinds or follow-ups to provide more information when needed.
5. *Listen with empathy.* Really listening to the CXO means understanding where she is coming from, and what it is like to be in her shoes. Listening builds bonds and fosters curiosity. Focusing on her perspective will earn you the privilege of being listened to in return. (For more on the power of listening, see Chapter 3, "The Dynamics of Influence.")
6. *Speak plainly and honestly.* CXOs often do not hear straight talk from their staff, and they appreciate it when they hear it from you. Have the courage to speak the hard truths. Say, "I don't know," when you don't have the answer or you are unsure.
7. *Master the 30-second answer.* When time is short—and it usually is for a CXO—there is no room for lengthy explanations or spin. Practice and master the 30-second answer: speak in headlines first, and dive into the details on her cue.
8. *Do your thinking out loud.* Demonstrate your partnering skills by sharing the very formation of your thoughts in a transparent way. If you get something wrong or make a mistake, you have proven that you are willing to be authentic, even at the risk of a little embarrassment.
9. *Watch the CXO's watch, not yours.* Be mindful of the time, and even more mindful of the CXO's attitude toward the time. If it is a 30-minute meeting, and the CXO is energized and engaged, you can say: "Do we have a bit more time to talk?" On the other hand, if he's looking at the clock after 15 minutes, ask: "Is this discussion on target for you? How can I best help?"

From the Front Lines: Taking a Chance on Connection

Gary Celli tells a story of the business value of building trust quickly with a C-level client.

"I was working in California for a multi-national high-tech company. I was a project manager at the time, and the project I was leading was rife with difficulties—nothing atypical, just the usual stuff. We were also trying to position additional work with the customer.

"One day, the CIO asked specifically to meet with me. Until that point I had been dealing with his directors, so he and I hadn't spent any time together beyond a brief interaction at the big project kickoff meeting. You can imagine I was a little on edge about the meeting.

"The first thing I noticed when I arrived at his office was what a mess it was. There were papers all over the place. One chair was so stacked with stuff it wasn't usable. I glanced around and noticed a copy of the *Scranton Journal* on the floor—the magazine for my alma mater, the University of Scranton, a small Jesuit university in Pennsylvania. I looked around for a diploma on the wall, but didn't see anything. So I asked about the magazine.

"It turns out that we were both graduates, now living nearly 3,000 miles away in California. Talking about that really helped break the ice and took the edge off. We spent 30 minutes reminiscing about the school, the campus, the local hang-out bar that all the kids went to. Then we spent about 15 minutes talking about project issues.

"It was a very successful meeting. The bond we had established made it possible for me to glean more information from him and he seemed very open to hearing my perspectives on the project. We got to the heart of the matter in no time. My company also got the follow-on work, and the CIO was a loyal client for years to come."

—Gary Celli

Worksheet: Get Ready for the C-Suite

Bring to mind a C-level executive to whom you would like to make a sale.

My C-level executive:

Spend some time reflecting on what it's like in her world. Write a vivid description below. Consider her sphere of influence, resource constraints, risk of data overload and isolation, and complex decision making.

_____

_____

_____

What did you learn as a result of this exercise?

_____

_____

_____

Think about how you might specifically apply the nine best practices for successful C-suite meetings from this chapter to help you make the most of a meeting with him.

Best Practices for Successful C-Suite Meetings	Specific Applications
1. Bring the right mind-set.	
2. Prepare, then adapt.	
3. Make connecting a priority.	
4. Bring five slides (if any), not fifty.	
5. Listen with empathy.	
6. Speak plainly and honestly.	
7. Master the 30-second answer.	
8. Do your thinking out loud.	
9. Watch the CXO's watch, not yours.	

What actions will you take as a result of this reflection? Be specific.

What	By When	With Whom	Support I Will Ask For

Reviving Stalled Relationships

When a buyer doesn't get back to you, you feel left in limbo. Your energy has nowhere to be directed—there may be no closed doors, but neither is there forward motion. The absence of a relationship is one thing, but a clear pattern of refusing to engage is something else. This chapter explores how to engage aloof partners. We discuss whether, and how to walk away from stalled relationships—and when to talk.

What happens when a relationship seems to stall—not ending with clean closure, but coming to an ambiguous halt? What do you do when nothing is happening, you don't know what is wrong, and you feel there is no good way to talk about it? For example:

- You want to get into an account and you are getting politely brushed off.
- You are at some point in the business development process, and the buyer stops returning your calls.
- You have requested an initial meeting. Despite your best attempts at engaging, you are not getting a reply back.
- You are nearing the end of an assignment and have requested a conversation about follow-on work. You are getting polite, late, or evasive messages, but no meetings.
- You know your buyer is working with a competitor. You have a feeling this has something to do with your buyer's nonresponsiveness, although you do not have proof.

A thousand factors could be at the root of the communication breakdown:

1. Your original message got lost in transmission.
2. Your buyer is in a new job and does not want to feel bound by past decisions.
3. A decision was reversed by his manager, resulting in embarrassment.
4. The budget got cut.
5. Your buyer just realized she does not have authority to make that decision.
6. Your buyer is overworked and simply has not been able to get back to you.

...
...
...
1000. You have horribly offended your buyer.

The factor you probably fear most is number 1000 (you have horribly offended your buyer), and your favorite excuse is probably number 1 (your original message got lost in transmission). The odds are great that numbers 2 through 999 are the real explanation—none of which have anything to do with you.

It is at times like this that the very human propensity to misinterpret outpaces your capacity to observe. Give most people one set of phenomena, and they are off to the races inventing storylines with themselves fixed at the center. Nothing fuels high self-orientation like a load of ambiguity.

The important thing to figure out in these situations is not the reason for the lack of communication, but how you will respond. After all, nearly all the reasons result in the same situation anyway—it is your response that matters.

How to Re-Engage

> The risk required to re-engage is far less than the risk of the relationship ending without closure.

Finding a different way to re-engage can help. This will naturally feel risky. Keep in mind that the risk required to re-engage is far less than the risk of the relationship ending without closure. Doing nothing about the impasse would preclude any opportunities for reconnecting and leaves baggage between the parties that could fester for months or years.

There are two basic strategies to revive stalled relationships:

1. Acknowledge the communication barrier.
2. Up the ante.

Acknowledge the Communication Barrier

Acknowledging the fact that communication has been hindered will likely feel risky. Paradoxically, it reduces risk by putting the lack of communication on the table as a subject to interact about.

The tool to apply is Name It and Claim It (see Chapter 9, "Risk"), using language that acknowledges the nonengagement in a direct and respectful way. A real-time conversation

---

Insight: Identify the Problem

When you want to reestablish communication, start by determining which problem you are really trying to solve. Are you trying to:

- Assuage your own guilt?
- Apologize to the client?
- Get an apology from the client?
- Justify your own actions?
- Engage in an argument against a concern you imagine the client has?
- Get a reaction from the client because you feel disrespected?

These goals all reflect high self-orientation. If you do re-establish communication and then proceed with these goals, expect the relationship to stall all over again.

If you want to move forward, focus on your client's needs and help fill them. That's the only problem you need to solve.

is the best option. Your second-best option is a recorded message, which, while not live and interactive, at least allows room for the nuances of verbal communication. Rehearse what you are going to say, and if the messaging system has a preview option, take advantage of it to get the tone and delivery right.

Your message might sound something like this, adjusted to your personality, your relationship, and the other specifics of your situation:

> Joe, this is Charlie. Hey, I realize we haven't been connecting over the last two weeks, and I just want to acknowledge there could be a thousand reasons for that. I can probably imagine ten of them myself, and I'm sure that's just the tip of the iceberg. In any case, I don't want to be pushy, or to be the cause of discomfort on the part of anyone, so let me do this: I will assume there are very good reasons that make it difficult or inappropriate for us to talk just now, and we'll just leave it at that. If anything changes, I would be happy to re-engage, at any time or manner of your choosing. You know how to reach me. I hope this finds you well.

This communication will likely spark one of the following reactions, all of which are a marked improvement from the status quo:

- *Suppose your earlier e-mail message really hadn't arrived* (the favorite though least-likely reason). Your message will provoke an immediate call back, asking to be reconnected.
- *Suppose you really had offended Joe* (your biggest fear). He is likely to be a little less angry at you as a result of your message, and therefore more likely to re-engage.
- *Suppose the problem was one of the other 998 possibilities.* Joe may now feel more comfortable reaching out, or he may feel relieved because you have given him permission not to do so. Either way, expressing your concern out loud eases the tension in the relationship.

Up the Ante

Upping the ante is about changing the problem statement so radically that everyone can disengage from the old issue with no trouble, and engage in a new issue with delight. Do this by raising the stakes, putting more work in, and coming up with a proposition for much greater value than what you had originally discussed.

For example, suppose you had been in early discussions to do a small piece of work, and it gets bogged down with no response. To up the ante, you would put more time and effort into a larger issue of potential interest and develop a powerful point of view on it. When you re-engage, say something like:

> Joe, this is Charlie. Listen, I realize we haven't been connecting over the last two weeks, and there are probably a thousand good reasons for that. But setting that aside, I wanted to raise a much bigger issue with you: We recently took some time to apply our White Paper findings on supply chain management to your specific situation, and I think we came out with some very interesting insights, and at least two powerful opportunities for you. Would it be useful for us to go through that information together?

When It's Time to Walk Away

Sometimes talking can help. Nearly always it can bring risk closer to neutral. But there are some times when you are better off doing nothing at all. There are three clear cases when it

> Patience and acceptance help you play the long game of trust-building, immune to temporary setbacks.

is best to walk away. All three offer you an opportunity to behave with dignity and grace:

1. *There's a competitor on the scene, and she is a trusted advisor to your buyer.* You know that when you have a trusted advisor relationship with a client you are in a position of security: He will never lightly consider someone else in your stead. The reverse also holds true. If your buyer feels the same level of commitment to your competitor, then she is no more likely to switch providers than your own clients would be. Go find a buyer where there is an opportunity for you to fill the trusted advisor role. Make your parting words ones of sincere congratulations for having found such a trusting relationship—and leave it at that.

2. *Your buyer is simply not interested.* It is tempting to blame lack of engagement on a client who is not sufficiently evolved, or wise, or intelligent. That would be a mistake. Blame-throwing is usually misplaced and never productive. There are better ways to invest your time and energy. Not every buyer buys from you; not everyone takes your advice. Look at it the way you might look at being assigned the middle seat on a full airplane, or being stuck behind a slow truck on a busy highway, as an opportunity to let go of the illusion of control. Patience and acceptance help you play the long game of trust-building and boost your immunity to temporary setbacks.

3. *You've made an unrecoverable error.* Sometimes you learn you have made a mistake that is, for practical purposes, unrecoverable—in other words, the benefits you can bring are just not big enough to redress the balance. In such a case, you may be tempted to have the last word, with some mixture of apology, justification, and forgiveness-seeking. Resist this temptation. Resolve to make a future client the beneficiary of the learning you gained at the expense of this one and move on.

Worksheet: Relationship Resuscitation

Bring to mind a relationship with a buyer that seems to have stalled—nothing is happening, you don't know what is wrong, and you aren't sure there is a good way to talk about it. Working independently or with your team members, reflect on the relationship using the questions below and arrive at a point of view about what actions to take, if any.

My buyer:

At what point did the relationship stall?

_____

_____

What specific evidence is there of a stall (for example, three unreturned phone calls)?

_____

_____

What assumptions have you made—mentally or verbally—to explain the stall?

_____

_____

Setting these assumptions aside, how might you *acknowledge the communication barrier* directly with your buyer? What words could you use?

_____

_____

How might you *up the ante* to inspire interest in a new, larger issue? What point of view do you have to share?

_____

_____

What actions do you need to take as a result of this reflection? Be specific.

What	By When	With Whom	Support I Will Ask For

Managing Relationships with Trust

When we ask our clients "What makes building trust so hard?" their answer is consistent and resounding: "Other people!" What they are really saying is that the complexity of human relationships is part of the challenge for everyone building trust. This extends beyond external customers, to include internal clients, colleagues, vendors, and more. And when you look honestly and objectively at the consistent factor in all of your relationships, what you find is yourself.

Section IV explores how to manage the full range of work relationships with trust, from how to kick off new relationships, to navigating client and workplace politics, to building trust at a distance for distributed teams. We provide real-life examples and specific strategies and best practices for addressing these relationship challenges.

Starting Off Right

20
Chapter

You've won the job. The celebrations are over; the contracts are being drawn up. Now it's time to actually begin the work. After the high tension and adrenaline of the sales process, you may be tempted to feel that you have accomplished the hard stuff and that you can now work on autopilot. And while it is true that you are probably more effective if you relax, it is not true that you can just kick back. In this chapter, we will point out the three most common pitfalls of the kickoff stage, and offer a practical approach to getting off on the right foot.

How you start a project can have an outsized impact on the result of the project. Let's do the math.

Ask yourself how your team's ability to work together will determine the success of this project—both in effectiveness and efficiency. What is the impact in terms of meeting deadlines? Quality? Friction versus ease of working together? Recommendations and likelihood of repeat business?

Say you have a project with a $1 million budget that's worth $2 million in value to the client organization. Conservatively, say the effectiveness of the team will impact both cost and value plus or minus 10 percent. Compare that to the cost of a well-run kickoff meeting. Suddenly the cost of kicking off *right*—including face-to-face with multiple stakeholders—pales in comparison to the relative upside/downside.

Whether you agree precisely with that order of magnitude, the point is that beginnings matter and should not be undertaken lightly because the way you begin sets the tone for all those variables. Here are specific ways to lead with trust to maximize your return-on-kickoff and avoid the common pitfalls to this early stage of any relationship.

Three Ways Kickoffs Go Wrong

There are three ways that project kickoffs typically go awry:

1. *Putting tasks before relationships.* After the commitment is made, it is tempting to jump right into tasks: After all, the sale feels like a license to get started. But that's a good way to foster resentments and dysfunctions.

We all make assumptions about other people. In the absence of any data, people tend to assume that others think as they do. Then when others turn out not to be the way you are, it is natural to get resentful—after all, you had assumptions, and your assumptions were challenged.

It is also true that people have to connect with others on some personal level if they wish to generate attachments or commitments. And when tasks require that you ask big things of people with whom you have little prior relationship, you risk generating opposition. "Who does he think he is, assuming we can drop everything to produce that in just three days?"

The bottom line is if you jump into task execution without getting to know each other at least a little, you are asking for trouble.

2. *Putting the present before the past.* Getting to know each other typically means learning about roles, jobs, interests, hobbies, routines, preferences, and history.

I (Charlie) learned some years ago from a wise industrial psychologist the value of understanding a partner's story. He suggested asking questions such as: Where did you grow up? How did you get to where you've gotten? What hurdles have you overcome? What did you learn along the way?

When you hear the answers to these questions, you have a dimensionally greater understanding of your partners' motivations. You have a context for knowing what they

---

CASE STUDY

From the Front Lines: Going around the Table

When I (Andrea) was 23 years old I got my first consulting job working for an information technology firm with about 9,000 employees worldwide. My first assignment was with the United States Navy. After just two weeks on the job, I was asked to join my team on-site for a kickoff meeting at a shipyard in Norfolk, Virginia. There I was, prim and proper and color-coordinated from head to toe, in the midst of the dirt and grime of this very industrial locale, surrounded by experienced and grizzled men.

The client lead facilitated introductions by going around the table, asking each of us how long we'd been "on the yard" and "what we brought to the party." I was panicked by the questions as the honest answers were "mere minutes" and "I'm not sure!" I decided to stall for time and positioned myself to answer last. By the time it was my turn to respond, I found out that every single member of the client team had been working in the shipyard longer than I'd been alive.

Of course it was obvious to everyone in the room that I was a complete newbie. I skipped the question about how long I'd been on the yard and, for the question about what I brought to the party, regaled them all with as much technical jargon as I could recall from my college curriculum in an attempt to sound qualified to be on the project.

They were gracious; and they weren't fooled. Imagine my relief and their appreciation if I'd just told the truth: "I've been a consultant for two weeks, been on the yard 20 minutes, and I hope to bring *something* to the project. Let's see what that will be."

What I know now that I wish I knew then: Honesty builds credibility as much as experience does.

—*Andrea P. Howe*

mean by various words and behaviors. And having told you their stories, your partners feel that you understand them more deeply (and you do).

> People have to connect with others on some personal level if they wish to generate attachments or commitments.

3. *Putting the plan before the culture.* Every organization has a set of rules governing behavior. Some of those rules are written, others are informally understood—in either case they are real. Because the rules are often not explicit, it is easy for outsiders to violate them and not even know they are in violation. He who violates the rules runs the risk of being presumed to be willfully disrespectful or ignorant—neither of which sets the stage for a trust-based beginning.

Insight: Getting to Know You

Here are two ways to get to know the team in a more personal way:

1. Allot a longer time for around-the-room introductions—four to five minutes each— and ask people to give a brief bio plus. Define this as, "In addition to your work role, tell us: where you grew up, where you went to school, your past work assignments, and how many years you've been at your present role. Tell us three things you're most proud of in your life."
2. Have participants pair off and interview each other. Tell them their job will be to introduce the other to the group, describing highlights from their bio plus. Allot about 10 to 15 minutes for the interviews, a few minutes for each introduction. Be sure to also include time for other members of the group to ask questions.

Going through this process of emphasizing unique personal information has two benefits. First, people get to know each other personally. Second, it serves to legitimize the discussion of relationships as valuable in itself. This legitimacy is an investment in the organization's commitment to fostering trusting and trustworthy behavior in its participants.

I (Andrea) have facilitated some variation of this activity hundreds of times. Without fail it is lively, interesting, and informative in ways that benefit the project for far longer than the investment of time required.

Four Key Ingredients for a Successful Kickoff

Project kickoff is a great opportunity to establish or deepen your credibility. By articulating a clear approach to a first meeting, you demonstrate mastery of something new to your partner. And if you do so in a sensitive and collaborative manner, then you also demonstrate your ability to take the lead comfortably in areas where your expertise is relevant.

Here are four key ingredients to a successful kickoff:

1. *Put the agenda on the agenda.* Make clear to your partner(s) that you don't just *do* work. Have a metadiscussion about *how* you will do the work. Then you can work together to define what the different types of meetings will look like, along with how they will be led and supported.
2. *Get to know the team.* Most initial meetings involve the standard ritual of name, rank, and serial number. Try adding a more personal dimension.

If the group is shallow—if it will not be in existence for long and/or doesn't require great depths of interaction—then you might simply augment the usual introductions. If the group is deep—if it will be in existence for a good while, and/or will involve considerable amounts of participants' work lives—then go one level deeper and find out something about participants' personal histories.

3. *Envision a successful result.* During the sales process, you very likely went through a process of envisioning the results of the project. Why should you do it again?

    First, things look different when you are across the table from a *potential* partner than when you are meeting with the one who has chosen you. Second, at this stage things have started to get more real for each party. You can use this to everyone's benefit in the initial meeting.

    Have someone lead a discussion of the to-be state of affairs after the project is complete. This does not mean talking about the benefits: It means describing, in some level of detail, how the process or organization involved will look, feel, or behave differently after the project is completed.

    > Little has more effect on getting things done than behaving in accordance with the unspoken rules of engagement.

    The reason for this discussion is to make the future results very real for all participants. Having a tangible sense of the target outcome makes it possible for organization members to begin to move in that direction.

4. *Articulate the Rules of Engagement.* Ask participants to describe the informal ways things get done at their organization. For example, "How are decisions usually made?" and "What happens when there are differences of opinion?" No judgment is called for here; this is purely informational. It is a chance to let participants articulate—for themselves as well as for others—the unwritten processes that govern how everyone will work together.

    The benefit of this discussion is partly to prevent unintentionally abrasive behaviors, and mainly to legitimize future discussions when real issues arise, as they inevitably will. Little has more effect on getting things done than behaving in accordance with the unspoken rules of engagement. Having the courage to ask about them up front will pave the way for candid conversations throughout the project.

A Word of Caution

Perhaps you do not believe in the value of overt discussion about interesting personal facts, history, values, and so forth. You may feel that your partner doesn't respect these kinds of issues—that they see them as too soft or a waste of time. You may be tempted to scale back on the level of effort you commit to it.

Be warned: you are compromising the success of your project right at the outset if you *don't* seriously pursue these themes. Trust is personal: pretending otherwise is never a good bet.

However good this sounds on paper, you may feel constrained by your own or others' limiting beliefs. Try these suggestions.

1. If *you* are skeptical, get the opinions of two other seasoned and highly successful project managers from your organization or others.
2. If *your team* is skeptical, then share this chapter with them and hold a meeting to discuss the issue.
3. If *your partner* is skeptical, hold a separate meeting with her to discuss the merits of the more personal dimensions of a successful kickoff.

Worksheet: Recognizing Project Start-Up Pitfalls

How you start a project can have an outsized impact on the result of the project. Bring to mind the last time you were involved in a project kickoff. Describe the project briefly below. Then, answer the questions that follow.

Project:

_____

_____

_____

_____

_____

In what ways did you fall prey to the common pitfalls of the project start-up stage?

_____

_____

_____

_____

_____

In what ways did the project start-up go well?

_____

_____

_____

_____

_____

What did you learn that you will apply to your next project?

_____

_____

_____

_____

_____

Accelerating Trust

It is often said that trust takes time, yet that is largely myth. In many ways, people form perceptions, trusting and nontrusting, with shocking speed. This chapter addresses how to help both you and your partner form quick, high-trust assessments of each other, which lay the foundation for more trust in the future.

At our Being a Trusted Advisor and Trust-Based Selling programs, participants are asked early on about the one big thing they want from their time with us. Invariably at least a quarter of people in the room will say something along the lines of "I need tools for building trust faster," and the rest usually nod their heads in vigorous agreement.

How many of these situations can you relate to?

- "We recently lost a key account manager, Ingrid, and I've been tasked with taking over her multimillion-dollar account. The primary client is Sara, a CFO with a reputation of being hard on her consultants. Sara had a lot of respect for Ingrid, and rumor has it she's not at all happy that Ingrid has moved elsewhere. How do I win Sara over quickly so we don't lose the momentum we've gained?"
- "I'm managing a technology implementation project with some really tight deadlines. The leader of the group of users, Amal, has some strong concerns about the project. We can't afford to miss a beat with him. How can we be sure to get off on the right foot—and stay on it?"

Insight: Does Trust Take Time?[1]

Researchers tell us that the propensity to trust can be increased by oxytocin,[2] or decreased by testosterone.[3] Both take effect quickly.

How about trustworthiness? Think about the reassuring symbols when you enter your physician's office: the white coat, the stethoscope, the degree on the wall. How long does that impression take? Not long.

Trusting quickly is profoundly common human behavior: we all make split-second decisions based on a variety of factors, few of which boil down to the kind of rigorous analysis we like to believe we follow.

Does it take time to establish trustworthiness? It depends on which elements we are talking about (see Figure 21.1).

Trust Elements	Time Required
Credibility	Not much
Reliability	Yes, by definition
Intimacy	Not necessarily, usually quick
Other-focus	Not necessarily, usually quick

Figure 21.1

Time Required to Establish Trust

- "I'm going on a sales call next week to pursue a major opportunity with Jorge, Director of Marketing. The meeting will be the first time I've interacted with him directly—until now he knows about me primarily through Aaron, his direct report, an old buddy of mine who made this meeting happen. Aaron says Jorge is a friendly, slap-'em-on-the-back kind of guy who likes to give business to people in his inner circle and doesn't have a lot of patience for people he doesn't know. How can I get a seat in the circle quickly?"

The key to creating trust rapidly in any situation lies in a simple three-step approach.

Three Steps for Creating Trust Quickly

Trust creation begins the instant you start interacting with someone. The key to accelerating trust is to hit the ground running with all your trust mind-sets and skillsets intact from the outset. Here are three steps to help you do just that:

1. *Mind your mind-set.* Being trustworthy is as much about attitude as it is about skill. What are the stories you carry in your head—about trust-building, about the people you meet, about yourself? Take stock. Be vigilant. Bust the myths. If you assume trust will take time, you will miss opportunities that are right in front of you. If you assume it will be difficult to bond with your prospective client, that assumption becomes a self-fulfilling prophesy.
2. *Set your intentions.* Be committed to a specific outcome—but not attached to it. Attachment equates to high self-orientation, and that is a sure way to lower or destroy trust quickly. Focus on serving your partner, not yourself.
3. *Demonstrate trustworthiness.* Now that you have completed the personal preparation in steps one and two, it is time to take action: prove that you deserve to be trusted by demonstrating your trustworthiness. The following strategies for creating trust rapidly are organized by the four variables of the trust equation: credibility, reliability, intimacy, and self-orientation. These are some of the highest-impact and fastest-payback actions you can take to build trust. Each of these takes minutes, if not seconds.

> When someone asks you a tough question and you do not know the answer, say so. And if you are embarrassed about that, say so, too.

What follows are some scripted suggestions that serve as concrete illustrations of these strategies in action. The words you choose should reflect your own style and personality. Authenticity is critical to creating trust.

CASE STUDY

From the Front Lines:
The Quickest Way to Create Credibility

Sriram, a consultant based in India who works for a global consulting firm, shares a story about an unexpected way to build credibility fast.

"I once had an opportunity to sell a significant piece of work to the Business Unit Director of a large pharmaceutical organization. At one point in our conversation, he asked me point blank, 'How many people do you have in India who have actually worked on improving revenue growth for companies in our niche area?' I knew the answer was zero, as most of our experts were abroad and very few existed in the firm in the first place. It wasn't an answer I wanted to give him. At the same time, I knew that putting any kind of spin on my answer would impact my credibility. So I simply answered truthfully: 'No one.'

"I fully expected our conversation would be over at that point. To my surprise, he replied, 'Congratulations. You're the first person I've met who has actually answered that question honestly.'

"We won the work, which was a significant piece in itself and more importantly the start of a great trust-based relationship over a long period of time. Our client was pleased with our candor to acknowledge a deficiency and was happy that we were already thinking about how we would work with them to fill the gaps while adding tremendous value in other areas. And I learned an important lesson that day about how telling the truth—clearly, succinctly, with no spin control—is a real differentiator in this business."

—As told to Andrea P. Howe

21 Ways to Build Trust ... Fast

Create Credibility

Six Fast Payback Actions to Create Credibility

1. *Show you've done your homework.* Note: That's show, not tell. Demonstrate your expertise by putting it to work to help your partner. Engage with something of value to him. Let him know that you may be able to help find a solution to a specific problem.

   "Jorge, I understand you have some concerns about your department's ability to scale in the coming year. Do I have that right?"

2. *Have and state a point of view.* The "advisor" part of "trusted advisor" requires that you put a stake in the ground by sharing your ideas, opinions, and perspectives. Even if what you say ends up being rejected or wrong, it will stimulate a reaction and crystallize issues, which is valuable in itself. Your point of view is a catalyst: a way of helping your client think and engage with you.

   "Amal, I believe the Help Desk is going to make or break this project, and that's where we should focus our attention first. How do you see it?"

3. *Speak the truth, always.* Remember, credibility is as much about honesty as it is about know-how. The courage to say something uncomfortable, difficult, or unpopular from

a perspective of genuine concern for your client is an instant trust-builder. It is natural to think you can't take this kind of risk until trust has been established—paradoxically, taking exactly this kind of risk builds trust quickly.

When someone asks you a tough question and you do not know the answer, say so. And if you are embarrassed about that, say so, too.

"Jorge, that's a great question and I'm embarrassed to say I don't know the answer." Then, don't be in a rush to say, "But I'll go back and get it for you"; this interchange is not about reliability; it is about credibility.

4. *Answer direct questions with direct answers.* People sit up and take notice when others speak frankly and honestly. Differentiate yourself as someone others can count on to speak directly, without spin.

5. *Express your passion.* Credibility is also affected by how you say what you say. If you like or love your work, by all means leave the reserved approach behind and let people know. From your partner's perspective, passion equates to commitment, enthusiasm, perseverance, and even the possibility of fun.

"I'm excited, Amal, about the opportunity to work with you on this. I've been leading successful implementations for over 15 years, but this opportunity is unprecedented in the scale of opportunity it represents.

6. *Convey confidence.* Offer handshakes, eye contact, and other interpersonal gestures as appropriate given cultural norms. Be confident, not arrogant. Let your presence underscore your professionalism.

Ratchet Up Reliability

Four Fast Payback Actions to Ratchet Up Reliability

> Reliability is rooted in a feeling of familiarity, and using your partner's jargon, not yours, is a great way to create that feeling in your very first encounter.

1. *Make lots of small promises.* There's no need to wait until the end of a six-month project to prove you can be counted on: start on Day One by making lots of small promises, then follow through on each one.

    "I'll be sure our white paper on organizational expansion is in your inbox, Jorge, by close of business today."

2. *Be on time.* Let your actions convey that punctuality is just one way you keep your word. Then go the extra mile by arriving in plenty of time to review your notes, get your mind-set and intentions in order, and take a couple of deep breaths, so you are fully present.

3. *Use others' terminology.* Reliability is rooted in a feeling of familiarity, and using *your partner's* jargon, not yours, is a great way to create that feeling in your very first encounter.

    If you say "po-TAY-toe" and Aaron says "po-TAH-toe," go with "po-TAH-toe."

4. *Dress appropriately.* Wardrobe choice creates another opportunity to make others feel comfortable around you. Dressing appropriately is not just about the style of your shoes or the color of your shirt. It also means not dressing way over or under your audience.

Increase Intimacy

Four Fast Payback Actions to Increase Intimacy

1. *Name the proverbial elephant in the room.* People want to know they can count on you to speak the truth, candidly and respectfully. If everyone is avoiding acknowledging an awkward or uncomfortable issue, be the one to tackle it directly—Name It and Claim It.

    "Jorge, at the risk of stating the obvious, you're a man who prefers, understandably, to do work with those in your inner circle. I'm not one of those people."

2. *Listen with empathy.* Empathy certainly takes effort and practice, but it doesn't take time. You can demonstrate empathy in your very first interaction with someone. Demonstrating empathy simply requires a willingness to tune in—and let on that you are tuned in. You do not have to agree with a single word the other person says—you simply have to understand it.

"Amal, I'm sensing your concerns about the project, along with some hesitation to focus on the Help Desk first. I'd like to hear more about your viewpoint."

3. *Tell your partner something you appreciate about him.* You may often think nice things yet fail to take the time to express them. It only takes a moment to pause and think out loud. As with any feedback, it helps to be as specific as possible; general statements make far less impact.

> You are who you are, and you aren't who you aren't. Pretending to be otherwise for the sake of building a relationship usually backfires.

"Sara, I really appreciate the leadership you demonstrated in yesterday's meeting. It was a tough crowd, and you stayed firm while being interested in every dissenting viewpoint that was expressed."

4. *Be yourself.* You are who you are, and you aren't who you aren't. Pretending to be otherwise for the sake of building a relationship usually backfires. If you walk into Sara's office and notice a photo of her three children but you know nothing about kids, don't pretend you do. Look for another way to connect on a personal level. If Amal mentions something in passing about his penchant for indie rock bands, and you share the same fondness, go ahead and admit it. You will be taking a risk *and* creating connection.

Shrink Self-Orientation

Seven Fast Payback Actions to Shrink Self-Orientation

1. *Give ideas away.* Recall these wise words from *The Trusted Advisor*: "Expertise is like love: not only is it unlimited, you destroy it by not giving it away." Bring three to five ideas to any interaction and be willing to share them unreservedly, and then generate more. If you give yourself permission to be both creative and generous, you will have more than enough ideas to go around.

> Bring three to five ideas to any interaction and be willing to share them unreservedly, and then generate more.

2. *Build a shared agenda.* Creating an agenda together is a simple strategy with big payback. When you share your ideas about how best to spend your time, your preparation shows respect. Next, find out what others have in mind and create a plan together. Be willing to let go of your own ideas about the right way. You will foster a sense of ownership in your partner while demonstrating an attitude of collaboration.

3. *Don't solve problems prematurely.* The second-biggest cause of broken trust, right behind not listening, is accelerating too quickly to a solution. The most pervasive problem in sales is "premature solutions": the mistaken belief that the sooner you can begin solving the problem, the more effective you will be. Do whatever it takes to slow yourself down:

   • Count to five so you don't interject too soon.
   • Cross your fingers as a reminder that when the other person has finished you have a comment or a question.
   • Take notes rather than interrupt.
   • Set clear expectations that the first half of the meeting will be dedicated to exploring the problem, not solving it.

4. *Ask open-ended questions.* Open-ended questions make it possible for your partner to respond on her own terms, without the constraint of being guided down a particular path.

Open-ended questions allow your partner to set her own frames of reference based on her own worldview, her sense of what is and isn't important, and what is cause and what is effect.

5. *Ask questions that may seem out of scope.* Most advisors focus on being of service by focusing on the issues and opportunities that are immediately relevant to the task at hand. Be willing to notice things outside of your particular realm of expertise and to naturally express that interest. It sends an important message. It shows that you care about more than your narrow assignment: you care about the big picture and about the person you are serving.

> The more distracted you are, the more your focus is on you rather than on others.

6. *Relax your mind.* The more distracted you are, the more your focus is on *you* rather than on others. That little internal voice clogs your brain with incessant chatter. While that little voice will never go away (it comes with being human), there are ways to minimize it. Train your brain to notice random chatter, and substitute some wisdom of your own choosing, such as:

   "I am not the center of the universe."

   "It's a 'we' game, not a 'me' game."

   "A point of view doesn't commit me for life."

   Take a deep breath and refocus on the person at hand.

7. *Practice thinking out loud.* Vocalizing your thoughts as they occur to you frees you up to be other-focused. Remove your own expectation that everything you say will be perfectly polished and articulate. That way you no longer have to spend your listening time formulating what you are going to say next. You can actually spend your listening time *listening*. Thinking out loud is also a way to collaborate with your partner by sharing the very formation of your thoughts in a transparent manner. It is also a great way to relax your mind by getting the chatter out of your head and into the conversation (see item 6).

   "Jorge, it seems to me that staff readiness is a critical success factor for your department's expansion, which requires not only a cohesive team, but a well-trained one. It's also very clear from this conversation that your confidence in your staff is at an all-time low. Putting two and two together, I'm thinking a key area of focus for you is going to have to be recruiting, along with professional development. There may be other focus areas as well, and as we keep talking I'll keep learning. Does this sound right to you as an area that's noteworthy for now?"

Worksheet: The Speed Pass to Trust

Trust creation begins the instant you start interacting with someone. The key to accelerating trust is to hit the ground running with all your trust mind-sets and skillsets intact from the outset.

What mind-sets do you hold that may be slowing you down when it comes to building trust rapidly—about trust-building, about your customers, about your colleagues, about yourself? What new mind-sets could replace your current thinking?

Current Mind-Set	New Mind-Set
Example: Trust takes time.	High degrees of trust can be established in an instant.
Example: I don't make friends easily.	I'm easy to approach; people like to spend time with me.

Bring to mind a key stakeholder (e.g., client, prospect, colleague, staff member) with whom you would like to accelerate trust.

My stakeholder:

Why is this relationship important to you?

_____

What outcomes are you committed to in this relationship?

_____

Using the resources in this chapter, what best practices could you apply to rapidly increase the level of trust in the relationship across all four variables?

_____

What specific actions will you take as a result?

What	By When	With Whom	Support I Will Ask For

What do you notice from examining this relationship that might apply to other relationships?

_____

Navigating Politics

22
Chapter

In your role as a trusted advisor, you do not need to be a skilled politician, but you must be aware of the role of politics and be respectful of, and not cowed by, its power. This chapter addresses why and how political situations present opportunities to serve others and create an environment richer in trust. We explore in depth the specific case of political situations when you are in a consultative role, and introduce a five-step model for navigating client politics. We also offer practical advice on what you can do when you are put on the spot, and best practices for dealing with organizational politics in any context.

The word *politics* has a negative connotation in organizations, and it really shouldn't. Politics is not a sign of dysfunction—it is an inevitable dimension of organizational life.

In this chapter, the word politics is used in these senses:

1. Competition between individuals or groups for power and leadership.
2. The total complex of relations between people in an organization.

There has probably never been an organization that didn't naturally deal with issues of power, leadership, competition, and the myriad other concerns that arise when groups of people come together to pursue a common purpose.

> Politics is not a sign of dysfunction—it represents an inevitable dimension of organizational life.

Typical political challenges include:

- Dealing with multiple agendas, opinions, priorities, goals.
- People who seek public acknowledgment.
- Corporate cultures that avoid blame or bad press.
- Leaders who avoid risk-taking or directive decision-making.
- Lack of transparency among others.
- More than one person who sees herself as your primary client.
- Getting stuck in the middle of an issue.

Politics is neutral in itself. It is how you pursue politics that can be negative or positive. Don't think staying out of politics means you are clean—it means you are sterile. The question is not if you get involved, but how.

> Don't think staying out of politics means you are clean—it means you are sterile. The question is not if you get involved, but how.

As with so many aspects of business relationships that seem undesirable on the surface, political situations are actually opportunities to create trust and better serve others. If you handle political situations well, you can engage with diplomacy, sensitivity, insight, and courage—and end up creating an environment richer in trust. This is true whether you are in an official advisory capacity with a client organization, in a leadership role within your own organization, or an everyday member of an organization. If you consistently lead with trust, then you can respect, interact with, manage, and influence organizational dynamics in ways that create positive outcomes.

Seven Best Practices for Dealing with Organizational Politics

These seven best practices for dealing with organizational politics apply regardless of your role or your relationship to an organization.

1. *See the organization as your client.* Whatever your relationship to the organization, your client is not the person paying the bills, the person who hired you, the one you will report to, the one to whom you will present results, or the one who has to implement whatever you end up influencing the organization to do. From the perspective of a trusted advisor, your client is the present and future organization as a whole. Or, in shorthand: Your client is the organization.

> If you handle political situations right, you can engage with diplomacy, sensitivity, insight, and courage—and end up creating an environment richer in trust.

2. *Put politics on the table.* Talk about politics freely: Politics loses its grip when it is handled openly.

3. *Stay neutral.* If someone invites you to take sides or to be the spokesperson for another person or group, be candid about the awkwardness and suggest ways that he might speak for himself. Do not risk the appearance of collusion. Sometimes the most trustworthy response is to respectfully decline to participate.

4. *Frame the issue.* Political issues are almost always about deeper issues of growth and security, opportunity and risk. You can do all parties a favor by helping to frame the root issue underlying the politics of a given situation. By helping people articulate the true issues, you defuse the negative connotations that so often accompany political interactions.

5. *Be a guide, not a decision-maker.* To build trust while navigating politics, help others recognize multiple points of view and build consensus. You can take this on as your job, regardless of your position in the organization, and regardless of whether you are acting in an advisory capacity. Explore advantages, disadvantages, risks, and costs together. Be a role model as well as a coach for good listening. Be willing to interrupt and redirect a conversation. Broker conversations between others. Unless you are the leader in the scenario with decision-making responsibility, it is up to them to choose.

6. *Envision a positive future.* Envisioning, always a useful technique, plays a particularly powerful role when applied to political issues. Because political discussions are so often symptomatic of deeper issues, the divisiveness they produce is hard to counteract. What's needed to turn negative political discussion into positive forward momentum is a commonly shared perspective. Envisioning a future alternate reality, based on the underlying issues identified in framing, does just that.

7. *Proceed with respect.* If your client/partner is the organization as a whole, then what is your obligation and role as a trusted advisor? At minimum it is similar to the guidelines posted in wilderness areas: "Leave it cleaner than you found it." At optimum, it is: "Make a positive difference." And the territory between the two is defined by: "Go mainly where invited."

> ## Insight: The Possibilities in Politics
>
> When you pay attention to the politics in client organizations, you can find powerful opportunities to deliver value to your client. For example:
>
> - Do you have a *family-owned company* as a client? Then you've almost certainly noticed parent-child or sibling dynamics that influence the business. Those dynamics are not pitfalls to be steered clear of: They are opportunities to improve the business. If you can make a small contribution to that improvement, you have done something very meaningful for the organization as a whole.
> - If you are selling into *three divisions of a company* and are painfully aware of the duplication and secrecy caused by those divisions competing with each other, you are in a powerful position to point out the values of collaboration.
> - If you are an *HR partner* in a company where the line organization treats HR badly and treats the IT function well, ask why that is. The whole organization suffers in such a case. Addressing the root issues offers an opportunity to improve the situation for everyone.
>
> We are not saying you should charge like a bull into a china shop at the first sign of conflict in your client organizations. We are asking you to see a chance to make things better. Look for ways to be a positive contributor for everyone's benefit.

The Special Challenges of Client Politics

Relationships between an advisor and client, whether that client is internal or external to your organization, carry their own particular set of relationship dynamics. Client politics, as opposed to political situations in any other kind of business relationship (such as with a manager, a colleague, or an external supplier) can feel perilous because you are not just involved as an organizational good citizen, you are acting as an ambassador for your own organization. In the case of internal service groups such as IT, HR, Finance, and Legal, you are acting as the official representative of your service group to your internal clients.

Key questions about navigating client politics that naturally arise include:

- What if you have a strong point of view about what's right?
- How can you protect your own interests while being of service at the same time?
- How do you remain professional and effective?

Fortunately, it is possible to think clearly about these issues by clarifying for yourself what it means to act as a trusted advisor. That in turn will guide your actions and make you a more useful and valued resource.

Avoiding the Extremes

When dealing with client politics, how often are you tempted to:

- Avoid conflicts at all costs, taking sides only if forced to take a position?
- Jump in when you know something about the issue, and/or when the situation has the potential to affect your own business interests?

Unfortunately, both options compromise your ability to be effective.

Here's the dilemma. On one hand, you cannot and should not avoid client politics. They are unavoidable to begin with, and if you try to avoid them, you put yourself in a passive role. You can run, but you cannot hide. On the other hand, if you are seen to take sides, you compromise your value as an objective party. Whoever's side you did not take will see you as just another player in the political game. Getting involved can mean stepping in quicksand.

A Five-Step Model for Navigating Client Politics

This five-step model provides additional guidance for how you can make a positive contribution in the particular dynamics of client politics.

Step 1: *Notice political flash-fires.* As a regular part of your internal meetings, schedule 10 minutes to reflect on active political issues with each client. Discuss them with your team or with a confidant if you are working solo. Do not try to address these issues—just identify them and become aware of them.

Step 2: *Reframe the issue.* On a regular basis, devote some time to developing a point of view about what is behind the politics.
- What are the business issues at stake?
- What are the economic drivers?
- What are the implications for other stakeholder groups, like employees or customers?

Step 3: *Determine key players.* At the same meetings as Step 2, spend a few minutes identifying who in the client organization will and/or should have the greatest influence on defining and resolving the underlying business issues for the client. It is your job to help those people.

Step 4: *Develop your own point of view on the best solutions.* Arrive at an informal agreement about your point of view of the best option for the client organization. At the same time, spend some time envisioning what a desirable future state might look like. Note that this point of view is not to be raised with the client except if the client asks you point-blank (see "Five Things to Do When Asked to Share Your Point of View" in this chapter). The

---

CASE STUDY

From the Front Lines: The Leadership Challenge

I (Charlie) once had a session with a group of high-potential future leaders of a company. They said, "Never mind the basics of trust, we pretty well understand that. Let's focus on some really difficult issues, advanced issues. For example, how can we identify senior leaders who are untrustworthy, and how can we protect ourselves in dealing with them when we have to?"

The ensuing discussion surfaced as a concrete example of a senior leader behaving in truly untrustworthy ways, with real and negative career consequences for one of this group's colleagues. If this group was a little paranoid, it wasn't without reason.

I asked them, "What if the CEO walked in right now and heard that question? Would he be pleased that future leaders of the company were trying to avoid confronting behavior that is hurting the firm? Would he be pleased that you believe the individual and the company are at odds—and that you'd choose to avoid the problem, rather than addressing it? Is that how he would want leaders to think and behave?"

—Charles H. Green

purpose of the point of view is simply to have a perspective to inform your group's work or to inform your own efforts if you are working solo.

Step 5: *Align your actions.* Given the common perspective above, be alert to opportunities to advance the discussion among the key players in Step 3 around the business issues you identified in Step 2. This doesn't have to be complex or Machiavellian. It can be as simple as saying, "Michael, your people are always talking about who is going to take over purchasing next year. You know that affects supplier relationships, so while you're in Pittsburgh next week, it might be a good idea to talk to ACME, our largest supplier. What do you think?"

Your goal here is not to get your clients to re-create your own brainstorming in Step 4 above, but rather to help them have the same experience of problem definition and envisioning.

Five Things to Do When Asked to Share Your Point of View

Here are five suggestions for how to respond when you are invited to express your point of view about a political issue:

1. *Frame your reply in terms of the root business issue* (as outlined in Step 2). For example, "Well, I think that's really about differing views on supplier economics, at root."
2. *When the invitation is genuine* (as defined as in Step 1 above), respond directly, and without a lengthy supporting argument. Wait to be invited before going into detail.
3. *When the intent is hostile,* decline politely. For example, "I'm really not sure it's useful for me to talk about any opinions I might have. I just can't see it doing a lot of good." If pressed, do not lie—state your point of view (as in Step 2 above). But keep it short, and don't get into arguments. Just repeat: "Again, I don't think it's useful to us for me to get into that."
4. *When you feel forced to respond* to an either/or question, refuse politely but firmly. When you are asked something such as, "Are you with us on this, or are you with Marketing?" say something like, "Look, I just don't accept that it's come to that. On any given issue I might take one view or another, but I don't buy that we're institutionally on opposite sides of all issues."
5. *If you are invited* to be a part of a conversation about the issue, jump at the chance to facilitate the discussion. If you strongly feel it is useful to share your point of view, or if you are strongly pressed, then make it clear you are momentarily stepping out of your facilitator role.

Worksheet: Possibility in Politics

Politics is an inevitable dimension of organizational life. It is neutral in itself—how you view and address politics can be negative or positive.

What mind-sets do you hold about politics that may be impeding your ability to be effective? Think about what words immediately come to mind when you think of organizational politics. What new mind-sets could replace your current mind-sets?

Current Mind-Set	New Mind-Set
Example: Politics is dirty business.	Politics is normal—it's a sign of life in an organization; nothing more, nothing less.

Bring to mind a specific situation that has a political dimension. Describe it:

Think about how you might specifically apply the seven best practices for dealing with organizational politics from this chapter to this situation.

Best Practices for Dealing with Organizational Politics	Specific Applications
1. See the organization as your client.	
2. Put politics on the table.	
3. Stay neutral.	
4. Frame the issue.	
5. Be a guide, not a decision-maker.	
6. Envision a positive future.	
7. Proceed with respect.	

What actions will you take as a result of this examination? Be specific.

What	By When	With Whom	Support I Will Ask For

Shifting from Tactics to Strategy

It's hard to lead with trust—and apply a long-term relationship focus—when you are working with people who pay greater attention to short-term tactics than to long-term strategy and pour their resources into immediate details. This chapter provides insight into how to engage with others at a level of shared strategy. It challenges you with four key preparation questions that help shift the conversation from a tactical orientation to a strategic one, and provides specific examples of how to engage in a compelling way.

One issue we hear from clients is that partners often get mired in the details and lose sight of the big picture. In other words, there is tension between strategy and short-term tactics. How often have you experienced the following kind of conflict?

> I'm working with a senior-level client on issues of strategic importance to his organization. He is very worried about a particular task on the contract. His sole focus is making sure we meet this one deadline, and I'm concerned it is preventing him from seeing and planning for the bigger picture. He isn't taking enough time to understand the lessons we're learning through this task so he can make an informed decision about downstream activities.

> I'm thinking this is an issue of my credibility. I need to do a better job of selling the bigger-picture issues I think we should consider in ways that he understands.

Whether you are consulting to an external client, working with a colleague who is a detail master, or trying to engage your boss in higher-order thinking, the same pattern of tactical paralysis will emerge.

The Strategy Blind Spot

Most professionals seem better at thinking strategically about other people's issues than at their own. It is easy to see behavior patterns, habits, and obsessions in others, and to see clearly where those patterns inevitably lead. Yet when it comes to addressing your own issues, it is common to get derailed by obsessions, fears, and old habits before you even get to strategy. There is an important place in business for tactics, as well as for strategy; but these are the kinds of tactical issues that are not important—they are truly distractions.

This shared blind spot about strategy provides a big tip-off: The key to shifting your conversations with others from tactics to strategy does not lie in engaging them about strategy directly—it lies in establishing a new, objective perspective. This new perspective requires letting go of self-orientation in the form of those obsessions, fears, and old paradigms. The gift that you *can* bring as a trusted advisor, then, is an attitude of calm, detached curiosity.

> The road to strategic thinking runs straight through curiosity.

If you can help other people see things objectively, as if from an outside perspective, they will generally discover new and different insights themselves. The road to strategic thinking runs straight through curiosity.

With that insight in mind, your job is to engage your partner in ways that encourage calm curiosity.

Four Key Questions to Shift the Conversation

Shifting a conversation from tactical to strategic starts with you. Begin by asking yourself four key questions:

1. How are you part of the problem?
2. What barriers are preventing your partner from thinking strategically?
3. What really matters to your partner?
4. How can you help clear the path for what matters to your partner?

If you are really curious about each of these four areas, you will find that whole worlds open up which were previously obscured.

Question 1: How Are You Part of the Problem?

The participant who submitted the example from the beginning of the chapter is right to be looking in the mirror. ("I'm thinking this is an issue of my credibility.") Looking within is an obvious place to start that is often overlooked.

It takes self-discipline to look at your role in the problem, particularly because by the time such a problem becomes evident, you are probably frustrated and impatient, which leads to high self-orientation and creates a breeding ground for blame. That's normal. Take a deep breath and start here anyway.

Here are some ways you may be part of the problem:

*   Your credibility is low—you have yet to establish yourself as a go-to person for strategic matters.
*   You are not being transparent about your concerns and frustrations and therefore are not proactively elevating the conversation.
*   You are not delivering your message in a way that is easy for your partner to hear it.
*   You are spending too much time trying to convince your partner to adopt your ideas, forgetting the power of reciprocity and the value of empathetic listening.
*   The majority of your time is spent being responsive to your partner's tactical requests, thereby reinforcing the tactical as what matters most.

- You are making assumptions about your partner's capabilities based on your observations, and sticking her in a box as a result.
- You are focused on your own agenda and therefore not really listening to what matters to your partner.

Question 2: What Barriers Are Preventing Your Partner from Thinking Strategically?

Try a little empathy. Sit in the proverbial seat of your partner and be him for a few minutes. Next, answer the following questions:

- How does the world look from here?
- What are the demands on my time?
- What distractions/challenges/pressures am I dealing with that make it difficult to focus on strategic issues?
- How does it feel to be in my seat?

Question 3: What Really Matters to Your Partner?

Stay in the seat you took above, as your partner, and consider these questions:

- What's important to me professionally? What's behind that?
- What's important to me personally? What's behind that?
- How does my tactical orientation serve me?
- Would a strategic orientation help me? If so, in what ways?

Imagining how a situation looks from your partner's perspective is a powerful tool to increase empathy and unlock insights. Better yet, validate your thinking through dialogue with your partner, being sure to ask your partner how she feels and what she needs.

There's a good reason Question 3 is phrased "what really matters to your partner," not "what do you really want." If what matters to your partner bears no clear connection to your strategic agenda, drop the topic entirely and engage with her on a topic of real interest, or find another audience for the conversation about strategy. If there are subtle linkages between what you want and what matters to your partner, clarify those connections. If there are obvious connections, speak up. The onus is on you to engage your partner by presenting your point of view in a way that aligns with her interests, not the other way around.

Question 4: How Can You Help Clear the Path for What Matters to Your Partner?

You've looked at the world from your partner's vantage point; you've asked what really matters to him. You have examined what's making it difficult for your partner to think strategically. And you have considered how you may be leading ineffectively in this situation. Ideally you have also raised these questions with your partner, too, and have confirmed what matters to him through direct conversation, not only through your own assumptions or conjectures. Here is your opportunity to put it all together and determine how you can pave the way for what your partner deems important.

Consider these questions:

- What are the connections between what matters to me and what matters to my partner?

> The onus is on you to engage your partner by presenting your point of view in a way that aligns with her interests, not the other way around.

CASE STUDY

From the Front Lines: Upping the Ante

Sarah Agan tells us about the conversation that changed everything with her client, John.

"I had just joined a new consulting firm and was asked to take over as the engagement manager for a project that I soon learned was in dire straits. My client John was happy—he was responsible for a high-priority government-wide initiative with the potential to catapult his career, he had a high-end strategy firm by his side (that was us), and he was getting everything he thought he wanted—a well-documented plan identifying key investments required to guard against terrorist attacks.

"The problem was this: My team was very unhappy. Imagine a group of super-bright, creative, energized young graduates, well-trained in strategy development and execution, assigned to a high-visibility project, sitting in a windowless conference room formatting Excel spreadsheets. It was a troubled project that everyone in my firm had heard about and no one wanted to work on.

"While it was tempting to step in and make a dramatic move, I bided my time. I focused first on developing my relationship with John, understanding his interests and priorities. In several of our initial meetings he made reference to our team as his 'administrative support.' At first, I just filed it away. He was happy with the arrangement. He had no idea what he could or should expect from us.

"I also made a point to find out more about how our company had ended up in this predicament. We had fallen into the trap of being seduced by a lucrative long-term contract, doing whatever it took to keep the funding coming.

"One day when John referred to us again as his 'administrative support,' I decided it was time to speak up.

"I don't recall being particularly nervous at the time. I just spoke from the heart: 'John, this is at least the third time I've heard you refer to us as your administrative support. If that's what you truly feel you need, let us help you find someone who does this as a core competency at a fraction of what you are paying us. If you're interested in doing things more strategically, I'd love to have that conversation.'

"From that moment, everything shifted. The nature of all our conversations changed. The team began to bring ideas to the table, like helping John host a national workshop—with representatives from across the government, academia, and private industry—so that John could engage all his stakeholders in a way that they would have some ownership for the nationwide plan. It was an extraordinary workshop that John's successor is still talking about years later.

"Now we were positioned to deliver the kind of value we were truly capable of. The project that no one wanted to be on became a project people wanted to be part of.

"The biggest lesson for me in all of this was the importance of being willing to interrupt the status quo and say what had been left unsaid for too long in order to focus on what really mattered to John. Looking back, it was a pretty risky move. It was also the *right* one. Nothing ventured, nothing gained."

—Sarah Agan

- What, if anything, about those connections are compelling from her vantage point?
- Where are the disconnects?
- Does it make sense to proceed? With whom?
- How could I open the conversation in a way that is both respectful and compelling?

How to Engage Strategically

Now you're ready. String together the hard work you did in steps 1–4 into a statement. Remember: Your job here is to re-establish curiosity and an objective perspective.

Here are three examples shown in Figure 23.1 of how to open the conversation in a respectful and compelling way, in light of the good thinking you have done to prepare.

Figure 23.1

Shifting Conversations from Tactical to Strategic

Scenario 1: Your partner is Amy, head of recruiting. You've been working with her to implement an executive directive to a smaller and more targeted set of colleges for the upcoming recruiting season.

Amy is expected to develop a strategic recruiting plan and she's getting lost in the details.

Your Part in the Problem	Barriers Preventing Your Partner from Thinking Strategically	What Matters to Your Partner
• You haven't taken the time to demonstrate empathy for the situation she's in; she doesn't see you as someone who really gets it. • You've been telling her what to do, not collaborating with her on the solution.	• She's a high achiever who derives satisfaction from excelling, so immediate details matter immensely to her. • She doesn't see how there's time to get it all done, so she falls prey to the Tyranny of the Urgent.	• Maintaining her well-earned reputation of excellence in all dimensions. • Solving problems in collaborative ways. • Integrating work life and family life. Managing the perceived time crunch.
How to Engage		

"Amy, I have a real appreciation for the pressure you're under to deliver the product by June 15. It's a high stakes project with an impossible deadline and you've worked hard to earn the reputation of someone who only delivers top quality results—all while striving to be a role model for work/life balance. I'm concerned that we're losing sight of the big picture in the meantime. I have some ideas for how we can achieve the best of both worlds and ease the pressure. I'd like to hear your ideas as well. I'm sure that, together, we can come up with a really good solution. Would you be willing to spend some time with me on this issue?"

Scenario 2: Your partner is John, who appears to be inconsistent and impulsive in his dealings with subordinates. Others have mentioned this to you. His management style is causing some tension in the organization. He's new to his role and doesn't appear to have a well-thought-out approach to managing his people.

(continued)

Your Part in the Problem	Barriers Preventing Your Partner from Thinking Strategically	What Matters to Your Partner
• You've been indirect. • You've been writing him off as incapable rather than seeing him as facing what all good managers inevitably face. • You haven't established yourself as a resource for management best practices.	• His organization doesn't offer much in the way of training and coaching for managers at his level. • He's feeling a bit lost but doesn't want to lose others' confidence.	• Being well-prepared. • Getting things done swiftly. Having a sense of accomplishment. • Being known as a good manager.

How to Engage
"John, how to maintain both a tactical focus and a strategic focus is a dilemma that every good manager faces. I know you don't have a lot of resources at your fingertips to help navigate the terrain. I can help you with that in some very specific ways that I think will take some of the immediate pressure off you and improve your ability to get the results you want, faster. Let's talk about it."

Scenario 3: Your partner is Pat, head of marketing for a medium-sized law firm. She's charged with increasing revenue, and the number of new clients, over a two-year period. She has a lot of flexibility and autonomy in terms of how to get there. For the past two months she's had you focused on drafting a brochure. You and your team have broader expertise.

Your Part in the Problem	Barriers Preventing Your Partner from Thinking Strategically	What Matters to Your Partner
• You've let your desire to please and be helpful get in the way of your commitment to providing maximum value. • you haven't been thinking and communicating in bottom line terms.	• There are so many things to focus on, it is hard for her to know where to start. • Pressure from her leadership team to fix the immediate problem.	• Getting what she pays for. • Demonstrating to her boss that she's a good custodian of the organization's resources. • Being a part of any solution, not just taking others' advice.

How to Engage
"Pat, the bottom line is you're overpaying me for the kinds of tasks I've been focusing on. I need to do a better job of keeping us focused on both the immediate problems and the longer-term picture. That way you will get maximum value for your investment and get help being responsive to what your higher-ups are demanding. I have some ideas. Can we talk?"

Remember, these are meant to be suggestions, not scripts. Bring your own words, voice, and style to this approach. And if you are realizing that to connect effectively requires you to stretch outside your comfort zone, it is best to acknowledge that ("Pat, I'm going to be uncharacteristically direct here," or "Amy, I realize I've been doing a bad job of putting myself in your shoes, and I'm committed to changing that."). That way your new approach doesn't come across as startling or, worse, disingenuous.

Worksheet: Shifting a Conversation from Tactical to Strategic

Shifting a conversation from tactical to strategic starts with you.

Bring to mind a current situation where you see an opportunity to shift the conversation from tactical to strategic. Describe it briefly, and then answer the questions below. If you do not have a current situation, reflect on what you could have done differently in the past. The key is to bring a real and specific situation to mind.

Situation:

_____

_____

Next, ask yourself four key questions. Get really curious about each of these four areas, and you'll find that whole worlds open up that were previously obscured.

How am I part of the problem? Use the questions in this chapter as your guide.

_____

_____

What barriers are preventing my partner from thinking strategically? Use the questions in this chapter as your guide.

_____

_____

What really matters to my partner? Use the questions in this chapter as your guide.

_____

_____

How can I help clear the path for what matters to my partner? Use the questions in this chapter as your guide.

_____

_____

What do you see as a result of examining this situation that might apply to other situations?

_____

_____

_____

My Client Is a Jerk: Transforming Relationships Gone Bad

24
Chapter

Difficult clients—and for that matter, bosses and colleagues—come in many different varieties. This chapter provides you with insight into what is really going on with the difficult people, as well as what is really going on with you. It offers specific strategies for turning difficult relationships into rewarding ones, along with a five-step technique for reframing problems that both invites and inspires collaboration.[1]

How many times have you experienced the following?

- A prospect who just *cannot make a decision*, regardless of how much data or analyses you provide at his request.
- A well-meaning boss who is *frozen by politics, fear, or ignorance* and as a result doesn't face facts about critical issues.
- A client who is *disrespectful to you and your team*.

The good news: All these cases have *something* in common that can almost always be transformed. That something is you, which is where the change must begin.

Consider this deliberately provocative statement: There is no such thing as a difficult partner—there is only a relationship that is not working well. Freedom from difficult partners lies in taking responsibility for fixing the relationship.

What Lies Behind Bad Behavior

If your client behaves in ways that seem unproductive, ineffective, uncooperative, or untrustworthy, it is easy to dismiss her as a "jerk." Lead with curiosity instead to look at what may be behind the behavioral issue—for her and for you.

What Is Really Going On with Your Client

Unfortunately, saying "My client is a jerk" (even just to yourself) is an ineffective problem statement, for three reasons:

1. It is highly subjective.
2. It is unverifiable.
3. The object of the statements—your client—is not likely to agree.

The very person whom you think of as a jerk has probably had some degree of success in life, and most likely has people in his life who love him. What we judge to be bad behavior usually comes from decent people who are stressed out, anxious, or fearful.

> If your client behaves in ways that seem unproductive, ineffective, uncooperative, or untrustworthy, it is easy to dismiss her as a "jerk."

What Is Really Going On with You

What is true for your client is often equally true for you. There is nothing like a close relationship to invite your own bad behaviors to surface. The assertion that "My client is a jerk" could be masking your fear of confronting a difficult topic, or anxiety about meeting a tight deadline, or stress about your ability to step up to a challenging task. And sometimes it is easier to blame someone else than to take responsibility for dealing with our own tough stuff.

"It was not my fault!"

"This sale was doomed because I got stuck with a difficult client!"

"The project is stalled because he can't make a decision to save his life!"

Blaming clients will never get you the sale; blaming your boss will never make him a better decision maker; and blaming your teammate will never help her face facts about critical issues—it will, however, definitely compromise trust in your relationships. Even if you think you are keeping your attitude to yourself, it usually finds a way to creep into your conversations with others. And even if you are only *thinking* blame, not speaking blame, a mind-set of blame hinders a mind-set of collaboration.

> There is nothing like a close relationship to invite your own bad behaviors to surface.

From Difficult to Rewarding: Three Steps

There are actually very few truly difficult clients, bosses, or teammates. Often what lies behind difficult people are relationships that are not working well. Since you are part of that relationship, you can be part of the solution.

In the case of relationships that are salvageable, use these three steps to transform difficult relationships into rewarding ones:

1. Reframe your thinking.
2. Reframe the problem.
3. Listen masterfully.

Reframe Your Thinking

First, notice your thoughts. Take a mental snapshot. Ask yourself, "What is the problem here?" If your answer starts with, "He won't ..." or "She doesn't ... ," or "I can't get him to ... ," then you are stuck in assigning blame. Step back and reframe your thinking.

CASE STUDY

From the Front Lines: Rogue Operatives

Jane Malin, a Principal with SRA International, tells a story of the power of reframing problems.

"I was working on a project for a challenging customer. The team that I was supervising included some very strong personalities, including four formerly high-ranking military officers. There was tension on the project. On one hand, these four team members were go-getters who wanted to seize initiative and make things happen, without interference from me or anyone else. On the other hand, the client sponsor needed time to process information and to work his own internal chain of command.

"While the foursome had good intentions, they caused some difficulties as a result of the tactics they used without my approval—sharing information and sending communications over the client's head up the chain of command with the hopes that this would facilitate action. I spent as much time solving problems of their making as I did working the real issues of the project. I worried, and witnessed, that all of this churn within our own team would cause problems with the sponsor and weaken his trust in us (SRA). They simply didn't think through the impact of their actions.

"I vividly remember the day I took a hard look at my own description of the problem: It was all about 'I don't know how to get these guys under control; they aren't doing what I need them to do.' I am a control freak; I know I am. It's what I do for a living—I'm an engineer by training, and I was the project manager on this assignment.

"And then it hit me: What if it wasn't about my finding ways to control them? What if I looked at the situation through their eyes? What if I cared about their challenges? What if I appreciated—and found a way to leverage—their best traits, rather than keeping them in a box? That was the key that unlocked the lock for me.

"I remember being conscious about changing my approach at the next team meeting—my tone, my words, my questions, my requests. In a short period of time, the foursome that had gone rogue got collaborative. They started asking me for my opinion: 'How do you think we should do this, Jane?' I went from being a thorn in their side to someone they wanted to involve. And suddenly there was no more damage to control. They also came to realize that I had their best interests, and the project's best interests, at heart. They slowly relied on me to help coordinate and orchestrate activities.

"Reframing the problem made all the difference. It made me more patient and more interested in what was going on with my team members. We became a real team, pulling together in the same direction. I trusted them more and, as a result, they became more trustworthy."

—Jane Malin (Principal, SRA International)

Being attached—to outcomes, to winning, or to being justified—may be holding your thinking hostage and making it difficult for you to reframe.

- *Are you attached to a particular outcome? Let go.* Yes, you should have points of view; that is part of your job. And you should stand behind what you believe is right. But you are not responsible for others' actions, only for informing their actions as best you can. Hold yourself accountable for being as effective as possible—do not hold yourself accountable for changing others.

- *Are you attached to winning? Check your ego at the door.* The best way to lose anything—the sale, the debate, the relationship—is to try very hard to win it. A desire to win is usually fueled by ego. Focus on what is best for all parties and collaborate to get there.
- *Are you attached to being justified? Be curious instead.* Make it a practice to wonder why your partner is acting this way. What is he afraid of? What is at stake for him? What is your role in the situation? In what ways are you contributing to his bad behavior? What are you afraid of? On what basic issues do you see things differently? What problem are you both trying to solve?

Reframe the Problem

Reframing is how two parties come to agree on an issue. When you frame a problem, you:

- State the true, root issue in terms acceptable to both parties, using problem statements, caveats, and hypotheses.
- Take personal risks to explore sensitive issues in depth.
- Articulate a point of view.

Framing an issue well can result only when you collaboratively and effectively address the matter at hand. How you think about and express the problem in the first place influences the solution. A problem statement defines the business issue that lies at the heart of all the symptoms you see.

> A problem statement defines the business issue that lies at the heart of all the symptoms you see.

A good problem statement has the following characteristics:

- It is a rigorous statement of fact, devoid of blame.
- It reflects a *we* approach, which means it has *you* in it.
- It reflects a longer-term, relationship-based perspective.
- It resonates emotionally as well as rationally.
- It imputes good motives.

"My client is a jerk" is a nonstarter as a problem statement. Unfortunately, it takes more than a little editing to gain traction. "She refuses to cooperate because she doesn't understand the importance of corporate governance," is simply a more polite version of "She's a jerk."

See "Reframing: Five Steps to a Better Problem Statement" in this chapter for a step-by-step approach to a more productive outcome.

Listen Masterfully

Sometimes, all that is required to transform a relationship gone bad is to jointly reframe an issue: Now your partner no longer seems so difficult. Other times, a good listening to is what is needed. One reason people act in unproductive ways is that they haven't really been heard and they need someone to really listen. Listen deeply. Listen without suggestions or action steps. Listen simply for the sake of understanding.

While framing is a pivotal step in the trust creation process, listening is the most powerful. Do not get so caught up in the analytical aspect of reframing that you forget to bring this critical skill to the relationship.

That said, you will set yourself up to have an easier time listening if you frame the problem well to begin with.

Reframing: Five Steps to a Better Problem Statement

Here's how to craft a better problem statement by reframing it, in five simple steps:

1. *Write down the problem statement as authentically as you can state it.* Define the issue, starting with the words, "The problem is...." If you are upset, do not mask it—work with it. What you are defining right now is only between you (or your team) and a piece of paper. Then, continue to Steps 2 through 5, crafting a new version of your problem statement with each pass.
2. *Take the (exclusive) focus off your partner.* Collaboration is reflected in language. Get rid of all instances of "he/she/they" and rewrite the statement to include "we" or "our." Try to get to the heart of the disagreement or disconnect. If you cannot make "we" or "our" work right away, at least change it to "I."
3. *Remove any version of the verb "to be."* In English, "to be" has several meanings, including a quality you attribute to someone or something. Removing "is," "are," "was," and "were" has the effect of eliminating the possibility of assertions, which forces you to state facts that are not in dispute. It's the difference between saying "That was a good movie" (which could be disputed) and "That movie had action in it" (which is indisputable).
4. *Revisit the subject of your problem statement and make sure your "we" includes both parties.* Often the result of Step 2 leads you to insert a "we" that refers to you and your team or organization and excludes the other party. Make sure you refer to the collective "we," as in:
   - "Our problem is we have differing views about the priority of A and B."
   - "We seem to have a problem in communicating when it comes to X and Y."
   - "It looks like we differ about the timeframe to be considered here."
5. *Imagine showing it (or speaking it) to your partner. Would he vigorously nod his head in agreement?* In other words, would it resonate factually as well as emotionally? This is a critical test. Without factual agreement, you run the risk of being diverted from the real issue. Without emotional resonance, you won't inspire interest in addressing the problem. If your problem statement doesn't pass this test, go back to Step 4 and try again.

Transform the Conversation: An Example

Let's walk through an example. Imagine you are frustrated because a key stakeholder—one who is senior to you—acts impatiently every time your team tries to present your recommendations. He interrupts you before you can get your points across. You feel disrespected, and you are beginning to lose respect for him because of his behavior.

Figure 24.1 shows how you can apply the five steps.

When you think you have found a problem statement that works, run through Steps 2 through 5 one final time to be sure it still meets all the criteria.

Words of Caution

Keep these tips in mind when crafting your new and improved problem statement:

1. *Reframing the problem statement to include both parties (Step 4) is often the hardest step.* It forces you to think about the problem from a joint perspective—it is not his perspective, or your perspective, but the collective perspective. This requires you to think about the problem fundamentally differently, which is when you usually get to the true, root issue. There is often a paradigm shift at this step that may take persistence. Don't give up! It helps to ask "So what?" or "What's behind that?" in your exploration of the issue. Keep digging until you get to the heart of what really matters to both parties.

2. *If you are dissatisfied with the final problem statement, you don't quite have it yet.* Go back to the drawing board. Maybe the problem statement seems indirect or sugar-coats the issue in some way. The purpose of this exercise is to get perspective, not to step so far back from the issue that it gets diluted. There should be as much emotional resonance for *you* as for your partner.

3. *There are times when a difficult issue needs to be put on the table and the best way to do that is to Name It and Claim It, not reframe the problem.* Chapter 9, "Risk," provides details on Name It and Claim It.

Remember, the ultimate goal is to define the problem in a way that both invites and inspires collaboration on the issue.

Steps	Problem Statement (Iterations)	Your Insights
1. Write down the problem statement as authentically as you can state it.	**"The problem is he doesn't get it and he's rude."**	
2. Take the (exclusive) focus off your partner.	"We can't get him to understand, and he is disrespectful."	Maybe we're not communicating in a way that works for him. Or maybe there's something going on with him that we don't know about, that has nothing to do with us.
3. Remove any version of the verb "to be."	"We can't get his attention or his respect."	There's a difference between him being disrespectful and our ability to earn his respect. Perhaps we aren't doing what we need to do to earn it. We haven't asked, so we don't know.
4. Make sure your "we" includes both parties.	"We have very different approaches to communication."	The fundamental issue is a communication issue. *That's* the real problem to be solved. And maybe he's as frustrated as we are.
5. Imagine showing it (or speaking it) to your partner. Would he vigorously nod his head in agreement?	**"We aren't communicating effectively, and that leads to frustration for us all."**	

Figure 24.1

Reframing Problems to Inspire Collaboration

Worksheet: Five Steps to a Better Problem Statement

Try your own hand at reframing a problem you are currently facing in one of your relationships. Use the example in this chapter as your guide.

Describe the situation:

_____

_____

_____

Apply the five steps to a better problem statement:

Steps	Iterations	Insights
1. Write down the problem statement as authentically as you can state it.	(ORIGINAL) The problem is:	
2. Take the (exclusive) focus off your partner.	(BETTER) The problem is:	
3. Remove any conjugation of the verb "to be."	(BETTER) The problem is	
4. Make sure your "we" includes both parties.	(BETTER) The problem is:	
5. Imagine showing it (or speaking it) to your partner. Would he vigorously nod his head in agreement?	(BEST) The problem is:	

What do you now see as a result of reframing the problem?

_____

_____

_____

What actions will you take as a result? Be specific.

What	By When	With Whom	Support I Will Ask For

Dealing with Untrustworthy People

25
Chapter

One of the most frequent reservations we hear about doing business with trust is: "I would love to conduct myself like that, but I don't trust my boss [or my colleagues] to act the same way." This sentiment generally underestimates what you can accomplish on your own. This chapter explores what you can do to lead with trust even when dealing with people in your workplace who seem untrustworthy. It explores strategies for dealing with trust conflicts, and offers criteria for deciding when it is time to walk away. This chapter will help you in cases where you feel personally conflicted, fearful, or compromised by the behavior of members of your own organization[1] and are not certain how to respond.

There is no organization with a perfect track record on trust. And there is no denying that there are real challenges facing you when you want to behave in trustworthy and trusting manners.

When you feel surrounded by untrustworthy people, your first instinct may be to minimize your risk. Here's the result if you follow that instinct—you will be sucked into the vortex of low trust yourself. The solution to low trust does not lie in prevention, risk-control, or avoidance—it lies in selectively taking risks in order to build trust.

Remember, there is no trust without risk. It is the act of taking risk that creates trust, and there is no more powerful application of this principle than your relationship to others in your own organization.

People sometimes behave badly. The question is: What will *you* do in response?

> The solution to low trust does not lie in prevention, risk-control, or avoidance—it lies in selectively taking risks in order to build trust.

Blame and an Inability to Confront

You may find yourself expressing reservations like these about your ability to lead with trust:

- "You don't understand my boss. That just wouldn't fly here."
- "Oh, that would be a career-limiting move."
- "I would love to work that way, but that's just not how people do things around here."
- "Until the CEO changes things, who am I to buck the system?"

> ## Insight: Disagreeing with the Boss[2]
>
> There is never a guarantee that you can persuade your boss to see your side of things, but you can dramatically improve your odds for a positive outcome.
>
> Start by getting really clear on these three ideas:
>
> 1. You are not the boss of your boss. Your boss is the boss of you. So if the issue ever comes down to who wields the most power, you might want to remember that.
> 2. You will rarely convince anyone that you are right, particularly your boss, as long as that equates to convincing her that she is wrong. If your objective involves being right, then you may have an ego problem.
> 3. You have to earn the right to be right. Your boss won't listen to you until you listen to and understand her.

These are all examples of what Phil McGee, CEO of The Wall Street Group in Jersey City, NJ, suggests are the two most corrosive qualities to be found in an organization:

1. A tendency to blame others.
2. An inability to constructively confront issues.

The usual subjects of people's blame are their boss, their coworkers, or perhaps their organizational culture. The things most people are bad at confronting are the things they fear most: disapproval, rejection, disagreement. The result of blaming others is pervasive, toxic distrust.

If you are serious about increasing the level of trust in an organization, *you* have to help lead the change. Here's why:

- *Trust requires truth-telling.* If you blame others, but fail to confront them with issues, you are adding to the distrust by failing to speak the truth.
- *Trust requires relationship.* If you talk about others behind their backs and fail to engage them, you are adding to the distrust by failing to create relationships.

That's the hard-to-hear news.

The good news is, if you are willing to lead with positive actions like truth-telling and constructive confrontation, trust is not only created—it becomes contagious.

> If you are willing to lead with positive actions like truth-telling and constructive confrontation, trust is not only created—it becomes contagious.

Imagine you are a project manager, reporting to a senior person in charge of the customer relationship—the Client Relationship Manager or CRM. The project is scheduled to run 18 months. At the 5-month mark, your projections show that you are going to be 2 months late and 13 percent over budget on costs.

You feel the right thing to do is to openly discuss the situation with the client. Your CRM, however, wants to work on correcting the trends internally over the next six weeks, saying, "We can fix this, and there's nothing to be gained by getting the client upset. Let's not mention the problem to them."

What do you do?

Constructive Confrontation

You are probably tempted to do nothing. Inaction would avoid an uncomfortable argument with your CRM, as well as other potential unpleasantness. But if you give in to that temptation, you will fail to confront something you believe to be destroying trust. So will your CRM. And you will probably end up blaming someone else (the CRM, most likely, behind his back). This is not a good outcome.

Notice that your fear of confronting your CRM is identical to your CRM's fear of confronting the client. The same three-step approach works in both cases:

1. Assess the risks.
2. Make a sincere attempt at understanding the other party.
3. Make a decision.

Assess the Risks

Do not try to keep evaluating this issue in your head. Instead, make the issue tangible, in a very simple way. Get out a pencil and paper. Yes, seriously.

1. Draw two columns. Start with the negative because it is uppermost on your mind—it will preoccupy you if you put it off. In one column, write "Talk to CRM: Minuses and Pluses." In the other column, write "Don't Talk to CRM: Minuses and Pluses."

> Forcing yourself to write out your assessment can bring you back to a more reasonable balance.

2. Write down the worst-case result of talking to your CRM. Write as much detail as you need to get the thought out. Now add the probability of that worst-case scenario actually happening.
3. Move on to the pluses of talking to your CRM. Assign probabilities.
4. Then move on to the pluses and minuses of *not* talking to your CRM. Assign probabilities.

People almost always overstate the consequences of near-term negative emotional interactions, and they understate the long-term positive business consequences of those same interactions. Forcing yourself to write out your assessment can bring you back to a more reasonable balance. If your page still suggests you avoid the conversation, review it with a trusted friend or two. Assuming you arrive at the conclusion to talk to your CRM, go on to the next step.

Understand the Other Party

Start by accepting that you may not convince your CRM. You have very little power to force change on other people. Our CRM is as prone to pressure and stress as you are: if you go in with arguments for your position, he is likely to dig in to his position. But if you go in sincerely listening, you will end up being listened to as well.

Now you are ready. Approach your CRM with a request for help and an honest willingness to listen. You might say something like this:

> Bill, I need your help on something: I can't solve this problem on my own, and I very much want to solve it. The issue is the budget overrun projection. My instinct is to talk to the client. I'm pretty sure yours is not to do so.

> Where I need help is in truly understanding your thinking on this—I realize that I only really know my own point of view. I ultimately want to be of one view, and that has to start with me better understanding yours. Will you help me?

> If I may suggest, could you approach it in simple pro/con terms for me—the pluses and the minuses of bringing it to the client now vs. later? Again, I'd appreciate your helping me to understand your viewpoint here. I want us on the same page.

As you are saying this, sketch out two columns on a piece of paper—exactly as you did for yourself in making the decision to constructively confront the CRM. Those two columns—pro/con for go/no-go decisions—are the same in all low-trust discussions. It is a discussion that is all about risk and reward, now and later.

Make a Decision

Be very careful not to be judgmental as you hear your CRM's response. If your CRM changes his mind in the meeting to your point of view, do not gloat. If you have questions of clarification, ask them calmly. If your CRM has suggestions that seem unreasonable to you, ask for clarification with words like, "Help me understand how you would deal with the issue of...." Do not get into an argument in this meeting. If your CRM asks what you think, be brief and factual, and then listen to what he says in response. This is not the time for you to make your case.

If you are very calm and happy with the result, say so. If you are still on the fence and feeling unresolved, you can say, "This has been very helpful. I want to sit on it for 24 hours, if I may, and get back to you."

If you end up disagreeing, remember who is the boss here (not you), and think of all you have learned for the next time. Then salute and carry on.

When You Can't Confront

Sometimes you cannot engineer a constructive confrontation—you have tried everything and the other person continues to be untrustworthy in your view, yet you must still work with her. You still have several options:

1. *Assume responsibility.* If the other party is concerned about the effect of an action you propose, offer to take on sole responsibility. You might say, "Give me six months to try out this approach to sales. I'll take responsibility for the results myself."
2. *Clarify boundaries.* This strategy effectively counters vaguely threatening suggestions. For example, if you are being pressured to mislead a potential customer, you might say, "I just want to be clear here: I'm sure you're not asking me to lie, are you?"
3. *Articulate your intentions.* This strategy helps clarify responsibility of others, as well as yourself, by stating out loud and for the record what you will do in a given situation. For example, "Just to be clear, and not that I'll go looking for confrontation, but if someone asks me a direct question about this issue, I will give them a direct answer." Done right, it is not a threat but a prediction, around which others can plan. It also can bring others to action by your example.

When to Walk Away

Even if you reframe the situation and follow the best practices for dealing with trust conflicts, there may be times you feel there is a pattern of no resolution. Some bosses and colleagues really do, for whatever reason, continue to behave in ways that are not trustworthy.

Knowing when and how to choose your battles is important.

The Harvard Negotiation Project popularized the notion of BATNA: the Best Alternative to a Negotiated Agreement. In other words, at which point would you prefer to walk away rather than abide by a negotiated deal? You can use the same concept here: At what point do you feel you would prefer to simply walk away from the firm rather than remain in an irresolvable trust conflict?

Here are four factors to help you consider whether walking away is the best option:

1. If everyone seems to be against you, there might be a good reason for it. You may be wrong. Go have a serious conversation with someone whose judgment you trust.
2. If this is the third disagreement about principles that you have had in six months, you may be wearing out your colleagues' patience with you. You may still be right, but being right alone isn't worth much—you also need to be judicious.
3. If your boss consistently behaves in untrustworthy ways, and you have tried unsuccessfully to address the issue (assuming your attempts were well done), seek the advice of other peers, either people who also report to your boss or people in parallel positions. Just check your motives first; the intention is to check your own sanity, not invite gossip.
4. If you have done all the above, then you need to determine where your personal ethical boundaries lie. Is this a big enough issue for you to walk away? What does walk mean? Lose the sale? Transfer departments? Leave the organization?

Be careful here: People overrate the incidence of truly unrecoverable situations. At the same time, it is also true that if you have no principles worth fighting for, you have none worth living for.

CASE STUDY

From the Front Lines: Walking Away from the Table

Anthony Iannarino, President and CEO of SOLUTIONS Staffing in Columbus, Ohio, tells about facing an accusation from a client.

"After going through two long Request for Proposal processes, I was finally presenting to the 14-person buying team for a dream client. One panel member I knew to be hostile asked a critical question. I knew he wouldn't like my answer, but I was truthful. He voted No—but I still won the job.

"At the contract signing, the 'No Vote' person read the conract and said: 'I see here you have failed to meet the commitment you made to us in your presentation.'

"I replied: 'I am sorry for any confusion, but I was very clear that I couldn't provide that service. I told you that doing so would destroy our ability to provide you with the whole package we proposed, including the price.'

"The No Vote said: 'You lied. You would have said anything in there just to get our business.'

"I got up and said: 'Then I am afraid I can't sign this contract. If you believe I lied to get your business, then I cannot take your business. I have never lied to get any business.' And I got up to walk out.

"At this point the main buyer intervened. He contradicted the 'No Vote' and upheld my account of the presentation. The contract was signed."

It was Anthony's willingness to put integrity ahead of the sale that, paradoxically, made the sale.

—*S. Anthony Iannarino (President and Chief Sales Officer, SOLUTIONS Staffing),*
As told to Charles Green

Worksheet: Constructive Confrontation

Bring to mind a relationship that seems untenable because there is something you cannot trust about your partner, yet you recognize constructive confrontation might help.

Evaluate the minuses and pluses of talking to him or her, and the probabilities of each outcome actually happening. Make the issue tangible, in a very simple way.

Talking: The Minuses	Probability (High/Med/Low)	Talking: The Pluses	Probability (High/Med/Low)

If your analysis still suggests you avoid the conversation, review it with a trusted friend or two.

Assuming you arrive at the conclusion to have the conversation, how might you approach your partner with a request for help and an honest willingness to listen? Script out the words you would say to open the conversation.

_____

_____

What do you notice as a result of this examination?

_____

_____

What actions do you intend to take?

_____

_____

_____

Trust-Based Negotiations

26
Chapter

Bringing trust to the negotiating table not only turns transactions into win-win opportunities, but also creates relationships out of transactional negotiations. With trust-building as a part of your negotiating approach, you will experience more rewarding and profitable outcomes and business relationships that stand the test of time. This chapter addresses the subtle pitfalls that lead to negotiation mediocrity and describes how to apply the trust principles to any negotiation for better results in the short term and the long term.

Negotiations 101: There is a parable about two monkeys that vividly illustrates the way negotiations usually play out. There once were two monkeys and one banana. Naturally, being monkeys, they both want the banana. They struggle briefly and the banana gets ripped in two. One proceeds to peel off his half of the banana and eat the skin, while the other throws away the peel of the banana and just eats the meat inside. One only wanted the peel, the other only the skin. Each gained just a portion of what they could have had if they had stopped grabbing and negotiated what each wanted.

While we all like to think of ourselves as higher-order beings, the fact is we often approach negotiations—efforts to create outcomes that satisfy various stakeholder interests—as a struggle to get our fair share. What gets left on the table, more often than not, are opportunities, potential, resources, and a boatload of trust. This is true whether you are negotiating a deal worth millions or a new job assignment.

> The key to trust-based negotiations is to live the trust principles, which means focusing as much (or more) on how you conduct yourself as you do on the near-term result you get.

Where Negotiations Go Wrong

Thanks to Roger Fisher and William Ury of the Harvard Negotiation Project, phrases like "focus on interests, not positions," "principled negotiation," and BATNA (Best Alternative to a Negotiated Agreement) have become part of the business lexicon.[2] But even if you're successful at focusing on win-win solutions and staying cool-headed by separating emotions

Insight: The Short-Term Performance Trap[1]

The Prisoner's Dilemma is a game that pits two players against each other in a blind negotiation. A prisoner goes free if he rats out the other prisoner while the other prisoner stays mum. If both rat out each other, they each get life in prison. If both stay mum, they each pay a much smaller penalty. When the game is played between strangers, for just one round, the most common result is the double-rat-out, yielding the worst possible result for both players. But if multiple rounds are played, the players quickly learn to cooperate, and the results improve.

The lesson for managers, sales managers, brokers, and so on, is clear: Every time you treat a customer transactionally, you are hurting your long-term profitability. But if you approach negotiations as collaboration, you can build trust with your customer over time, creating a stronger relationship and better results for both of you.

and positions, there are other impediments to successful negotiation. It's the subtle aspects of negotiations that can lead to mediocrity. For example:

- *Most negotiations are still viewed as more competitive than collaborative*, and more transactional than relational. The notion of win-win itself is a transactional concept. Many negotiations are in fact recurring, and the benefits of establishing relationships over time far outweigh those of a discrete series of win-win transactions.
- *Whether spoken or not, the imperative to follow conventional words of wisdom prevails*, such as, "Open high, scale back later," "See what they're willing to concede first," and "Control the agenda."

Read this list of typical negotiations pitfalls, and see how many you have encountered.

- Zero-sum thinking.
- Being afraid—of losing, of being treated unfairly, of looking foolish; letting the belief that tipping your hand is wrong determine your behaviors.
- Giving in to the temptation to hide or downplay any weaknesses or shortcomings on your side.
- Thinking in terms of sides to begin with.
- Playing it safe by not asking courageous questions, not saying what you really want, or how you really feel.
- Looking for common ground only at the surface level or in the short term.
- Giving in to the pressure of the negotiation at hand, rather than imagining this interaction as one of many interactions over time.
- Not doing enough preparation to clearly articulate why you want what you want.
- Thinking there is only one way to achieve the outcome you want.
- Spending most of your preparation time thinking, feeling, and deciding from *your* vantage point, rather than your partners'.
- Trying to maintain control—of the agenda, the conversation, the outcome.
- Getting stuck in the thinking that "no deal" is not an option.

Negotiating by the trust principles fundamentally changes the rules of the game.

These common traps are all in direct opposition to the mind-sets we talked about in Chapter 2, "Fundamental Attitudes": principles over processes, it's not about you, curiosity over knowing, we're all connected, and time works for us (not the other way around).

CASE STUDY

From the Front Lines: When the Client Doesn't Want to Hear It

Andy Lechter, of Studley Inc., tells about a big negotiation.

"I was working on a lease restructuring for a large law firm I've represented for years. The landlord was difficult, and my client was very smart and pretty emotional. Many times he asked me if he should just call the landlord or agent and tell them how upset and angry he was, and how he felt they weren't 'respecting his tenancy' (his firm was indeed one of the largest tenants in the building).

"But the landlord's representative was also pretty emotional. I felt he would have torpedoed the deal if we went around him by calling his boss or if we responded in an emotional way and pushed too hard. I stuck to the facts and focused on 'killing him with kindness'. (My client just wanted to kill him.) Rather than follow the 'customer is always right' rule or being subservient, I had to tell my client to bite his tongue in the interests of accomplishing his business objective. Each time after calming down, he always agreed that this was the best course of action, that I was telling him what he would tell his own clients. I knew that in recommending a different strategy than he wanted I was taking a risk and at least some of my credibility would be jeopardized— but that he might not be so forgiving if the landlord re-traded the deal or if we were unable to resolve matters. He made it clear to me the risk I was taking.

"We talked repeatedly. I always advised him to focus on reaching his longer-term objective. We stayed engaged, he did a lot of tongue-biting—and we finally got the lease he wanted."

There's a delicate balance between staying engaged with a client and telling them what they don't want to hear. Trust lets you walk that line.

—Andy Lechter (Studley Inc.)

Changing the Game by Working from Trust

Negotiating by the principles of trust fundamentally changes the rules of the game. Specifically:

- *Other Focus.* If you can approach the negotiation from the other's perspective first, then you lower your self-orientation, increase intimacy in the relationship, and generally improve the overall offering. Fairness looks differently when you are emotionally invested in the outcomes for all parties.

- *Medium- to Long-Term Perspective.* If you set your sights on the relationship, not the transaction, suddenly you have a large set of options for achieving fairness. You find it easier to agree to fairness over time than fairness in one instance. Conduct the first negotiation exactly as you would the 100th negotiation— with the same level of comfort and candor—and you will set a lasting and memorable tone.

> Conduct the first negotiation exactly as you would the 100th negotiation—with the same level of comfort and candor—and you will set a lasting and memorable tone.

- *Transparency.* You have reason to trust people if you believe that they will only tell you the truth and are willing to be examined about any aspect of it. If you trust them, you can tell them the truth as well—you can share what is at stake for you, you can be candid about your shortcomings, and you can bring everything that is being said elsewhere to the table.

The other party cannot help you achieve your objectives unless you share with them what those objectives are. It makes good strategic sense to share information, but on top of that, not sharing information decreases trust. The more you give away freely, the more you are likely to receive in return. This takes courage and a willing suspension of disbelief. That is why it's called trust.

- *Collaboration.* If you agree that a fair solution will be clear to each party, you will have a jointly driven measure of success for the negotiation. Think of your interests as intertwined with others' interests. Be unwavering in your commitment to create both joint goals and joint approaches to reaching them. Do the hard work required to get to the underlying drivers and motives, and then generate as many possible ways of satisfying them as possible—including no-deal. Be someone around whom others have the psychic freedom to choose what is best for them, and more often than not they will see you and your ideas as what is best for them.

Insight: 13 Ways to Negotiate from Trust

Try these 13 ways to negotiate from trust. Use it as a checklist for your next negotiation. How trustworthy are you willing to be?

1. Approach the negotiation from the other's perspective first.
2. Set your sights on the relationship, not the transaction.
3. Agree to fairness over time rather than fairness in one instance.
4. Conduct the first negotiation exactly as you would the 100th negotiation—with the same level of comfort and candor.
5. Share what is at stake for you.
6. Be candid about your shortcomings.
7. Bring everything that is being said elsewhere to the table.
8. Agree that if there is a fair solution, it will be clear to each party.
9. Think of your interests as intertwined with others' interests.
10. Be unwavering in your commitment to create joint goals and joint approaches.
11. Do the hard work required to get to the underlying drivers and motives, and then generate as many possible ways of satisfying them as possible.
12. Consider that no deal may be the best outcome for everyone.
13. Be someone around whom others have the psychic freedom to choose what is best for them.

To move from the monkey view of negotiation to a win-win model is a huge step indeed. But there is more. Adding the trust perspective to negotiations creates a richer emotional dimension of relationship. And all for the better.

From the Front Lines: Goodwill Payoff

Our colleague Stewart Hirsch tells a story about the value of goodwill.

"When I practiced law, I did hundreds of negotiations—deals, disputes, contracts. In one deal, where the other lawyer and I had built a particularly strong level of trust during the contract negotiations, he called me a few months after the agreement had been signed.

"He told me that there was a problem with the agreement. He thought there was a misunderstanding about which party was to pay certain charges. From my perspective, the agreement was clear: Those charges were his client's responsibility. Still, he asked if I would revisit the issue with my client.

"Because of the trust we'd built during the original negotiations, he felt comfortable asking me to do this. It turns out there was ambiguity in the original deal sheet. I discussed it with my client, and my client agreed to cover the charges.

"In the end, the trust relationship between the lawyers and between the clients allowed the situation to be resolved easily."

—*Stewart Hirsch (Trusted Advisor Associates)*

Worksheet: Negotiations: From Good to Great

Bring to mind a recent negotiation that you were involved in or observed. Consider the negotiating style, positioning, and approach taken by each of the participants. How were the trust principles absent or in evidence?

Other focus:

_____

_____

Transparency:

_____

_____

Medium- to long-term perspective:

_____

_____

Collaboration:

_____

_____

If the negotiation went well, what's made the biggest difference? If it fell short, what *would* have made the biggest difference?

_____

_____

What do you see as the prevailing mind-sets about negotiation in your environment in which you are working?

_____

_____

What can you apply during your next negotiation to build more trust in the process?

_____

_____

_____

Building Trust at a Distance

27

Chapter

Trust is critical for the effectiveness, creativity, and productivity of teams who collaborate from different locations. Leading with trust requires employing specific strategies to overcome the disadvantages of working in different locations. In this chapter, we discuss the top trust-building challenge for virtual teams, how intimacy and reliability can compensate for the downside of distance, how to use communication technologies strategically, and how to apply best practices for building trust at a distance.

How do you build trust when you never get a chance to look your team members in the eye and shake hands? Virtual teams face a unique challenge: compensating for the disadvantages of distance.

In co-located teams, physical proximity plays an important role in building trust. Contact is more frequent, visual and auditory cues enrich communication, and there are more opportunities for casual social interaction. The personal contact that comes from working in the same physical location creates a sense of connection. A sense of connection helps team members communicate and collaborate effectively.

> To build and maintain trust effectively, virtual teams need to strategically address the quality and quantity of interaction between team members.

Obviously problems arise when there is a low level of trust between team members in an in-house relationship. Those same problems are magnified even more in the case of distant relationships. Less-rich contact between members decreases the opportunities for building relationships and increases the opportunities for miscommunication that damages trust. Lack of trust affects both efficiency and effectiveness.

Virtual teams—which can include any form of non co-located working arrangements, multiple-site organizations, and geographically distributed or dispersed teams—need to

Insight: Trust First, Leadership Second

A study by OnPoint Consulting[1] ranked trust as one of the highest factors essential to virtual team success, second only to team leadership. Leading with trust may be even more important since the best virtual team leaders will get nowhere if their team doesn't trust them.

From the Front Lines: Asking the Right Question[2]

Juliana Slye manages remote employees as director of the government division at software maker Autodesk, based in San Rafael, California. She tells a story about checking in with remote team members.

"Remote employees are very conscious of managing your perception of them. They don't bring a problem to you until it has really escalated, because they don't want to burden you or take up your time."

"Without clues like a heavy sigh or a frustrated look on someone's face, it's hard to know when workers need support."

"You have to be disciplined as a manager to get out of the e-mail thread. You have to pick up the phone."

When she checks in with employees each week, Slye stays away from vague questions, like "How's it going?" and simply assumes that there are always some problems.

"I ask, 'What kind of challenges are you having?' Nine times out of 10 that's going to kick up something."

Rather than try to resolve the issue herself, she keeps employees focused on their own capacity to solve problems, asking, 'What would you like to see happening in a perfect world? Are any of those things achievable? How could you achieve them? What could you do *today*?'

—Juliana Slye (Autodesk, San Rafael, California)

compensate for this loss of contact and familiarity. To build and maintain trust effectively, virtual teams need to strategically address the quality and quantity of interaction between team members.

The Key to Building Trust at a Distance: Familiarity

The trust equation provides insights on how to improve the performance of remote and virtual teams by enhancing familiarity within the team. Familiarity is mainly connected to intimacy and reliability. If you feel connected to your team members (intimacy), and have constant and consistent experiences with them (reliability), then you will feel more familiar to each other and trust each other more.

> If you feel connected to your team members (intimacy), and have constant and consistent experiences with them (reliability), then you will feel more familiar to each other and trust each other more.

Intimacy

Intimacy expands the range of things you can talk about with others. If you can share personal emotions, difficult conversations, feelings, or doubts with someone else, then your intimacy level is high. Since distance constrains such topics of conversation, anything that can put them back into play is useful for increasing familiarity.

The tools for triggering familiarity based on intimacy include: making everyday small talk, talking about the personal not just the professional, and recognizing accomplishments. Much of this familiarity can be recreated for virtual teams.

High-tech communication tools can be especially helpful (see Figure 27.1).

- Include photos in internal directories and message systems.
- Work the room during meetings: Make a point to engage with team members on a personal as well as a professional basis on webinars, conference calls, and so on.
- Keep remote groups informed. Use cc on e-mail strategically.
- If you are asking something of someone after normal work hours in another location, acknowledge that fact and determine whether it is okay.

The bottom line: Make time building intimacy, and make it a priority.

Reliability

Promises made and kept, track records, and integrity are all part of reliability. Reliability also includes the familiarity established by repeated close interactions. Through everyday contact, like a request for information or a comment on the weather, you learn whether a colleague is terse or verbose, moody or upbeat, precise or general. Familiarity with your colleague's personality and character also translates into trust.

When you are silent or nonresponsive to communication (e-mail, voice mail, and the like) it can damage the way people perceive your reliability, as it leads them to misattribute explanations for this silence.[3] Take the initiative to communicate proactively about work issues that reflect reliability. For example, explain expected delays in response—let team members know when you will be available and unavailable.

- Set expectations up front and report on them regularly.
- Schedule regular meetings or check-ins.
- Make yourself available for communication.
- Respond to messages promptly.

Insight: Creating High Touch Environments[4]

Electronic technology has made virtual teaming possible, but it is not a perfect substitute for human interaction. One of the greatest performance barriers is the inability to replicate a "high-touch" environment in a virtual setting. While meeting face-to-face requires time and expense, virtual teams that invest in one or two such meetings per year perform better overall than those that do not.

There are several things that can be done to create a high-touch environment:

- Leverage synchronous tools (such as instant messaging) to increase spontaneous communication.
- Use tools such as electronic bulletin boards to create a sense of shared space.
- Carefully choose communication technologies that are most appropriate to the specific task. For instance, e-mail is good for simple information sharing, while conference calls are better suited for interactive sharing of ideas or plans.
- Make wider use of videoconferencing. Survey data suggests that teams that use video technology perform better in general than those that do not.

The lesson for remote teams is to increase the quality and quantity of contact to create familiarity and trust.

The Role of Technology in Communication

Because virtual teams have fewer opportunities for face-to-face communication, high tech communication becomes a most important method for creating trust and building relationships. The combination of richness and timeliness make a difference.

Media richness refers to the availability of visual and auditory cues. Richness positively affects team effectiveness, efficiency, amount of communication, and the relationships among team members.[5] Keep in mind that a phone call is more personal than voicemail, which in turn is a more direct connection than a letter or an e-mail.

Timeliness refers to the immediacy of feedback. Communication tools with high timeliness, such as video conferences, allow conversations in real time—participants are able to respond quickly or instantly. Low-timeliness tools, such as e-mail, are asynchronous—respondents need to check and reply to messages regularly, but can time-shift conversations at their convenience.

High timeliness and richness do not necessarily imply a tool is better, especially if it isn't used to its full capacity. Web and video conferences are all too often used in one-way broadcast mode. Webcasts have their place: the communication of important, standardized information. But most organizations spend too much effort on this.

> The less personal and immediate the method of contact, the more important it is to get your words right.

In contrast, low-timeliness, low-richness communication tools—such as e-mail, message boards, discussion groups, and online forums—make it possible to get everyone involved by relaxing the time dimension and powerfully improving familiarity for all participants. These time-shifting technologies have the added benefit of empowering otherwise introverted people to interact without the pressure of real-time performance.

The less personal and immediate the method of contact, the more important it is to get your words right. Written messages present a trade-off: they are good for conveying detailed information accurately, but less effective at conveying emotional nuances or a sense of personal connection. When written communication is your primary tool for building and maintaining trust, you are asking words to shoulder a big burden. It can be tempting to infer motivation and subtext. It is easy to accidentally create confusion and misconceptions. There is also greater risk of neglecting others' interests and misanticipating others' actions.

There is a risk that comes with a wide array of technological options—the risk of easily using low-level interactions when higher levels are required. There is no perfect way to guard against this, but here is a guideline: If you notice that you are glad you do not have to talk

Figure 27.1

Choosing the Right Communication Tool: Richness versus Timeliness

	E-mail	Instant messaging	SMS text messaging	Telephone conference	Web conference (with audio)	Video conference
Richness	Low	Low	Low	Medium	Medium	High
Timeliness	Low	High	Low to Medium	High	High	High

to someone personally—check your motives. You may be using technology as a socially acceptable form of avoidance.

Access to a range of rich communication options allows team members to benefit from much of the familiarity that co-located teams take for granted.

> If you notice that you are glad you do not have to talk to someone personally—check your motives. You may be using technology as a socially acceptable form of avoidance.

Ten Best Practices for Managing Virtual Teams

Combine high trust and good management to make the most of your virtual team:

1. *Make face time happen.* Bring new teams together for a kickoff meeting. If that is not possible, make more opportunities for team members to get to know each other early in the project. Then arrange to see team members at least a few times a year. Where feasible, bring them to the home office as well. You may have to do this through expense budgets, but recognize it is an investment.
2. *Use the right tools.* Set your team up with a range of appropriate communication tools. Plan ahead in your technology budget to keep these tools up to date.
3. *Increase team intimacy.* Plan extra time for activities that build relationships. Schedule virtual coffee breaks/happy hours. Allow for casual conversation in group calls.
4. *Make your work process consistent.* Schedule regular meetings (quarterly gatherings, weekly phone meetings, and such) to boost reliability, provide structure, and prevent gaps in communication.
5. *Set communication standards.* Establish protocols with the team on response times and message acknowledgement.
6. *Set goals and expectations.* Set them clearly, in writing, and revisit them often.
7. *Avoid over-communication and interruption.* Find out and respect optimal levels of communication and availability with your team.
8. *Be available.* Set reasonable guidelines for when and how team members in other time zones can contact you. Within those guidelines, make yourself as available and easy to reach as possible. When you absolutely cannot be reached, reply ASAP.
9. *Be explicit.* Encourage team members to be explicit in communicating what they are doing, thinking, and feeling.
10. *Model trust-based communication.* Share personal details about yourself. Communicate openly and honestly.

Worksheet: Trust in Virtual Teams

Consider the ten best practices for managing virtual teams outlined in this chapter. To what extent do you already apply these practices? What opportunities do you see to take your team(s) to the next level?

Best Practice for Managing Virtual Teams	Frequency	Opportunities
1. Make face time happen.	☐Y ☐N ☐Sometimes	
2. Use the right tools.	☐Y ☐N ☐Sometimes	
3. Increase team intimacy.	☐Y ☐N ☐Sometimes	
4. Make your work process consistent.	☐Y ☐N ☐Sometimes	
5. Set communication standards.	☐Y ☐N ☐Sometimes	
6. Set goals and expectations.	☐Y ☐N ☐Sometimes	
7. Avoid over-communication and interruption.	☐Y ☐N ☐Sometimes	
8. Be available.	☐Y ☐N ☐Sometimes	
9. Be explicit.	☐Y ☐N ☐Sometimes	
10. Model trust-based communication.	☐Y ☐N ☐Sometimes	

Building and Running a Trustworthy Organization

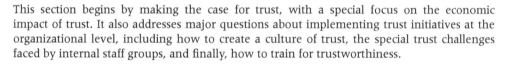

Trust is a core ingredient of an organization's success. Building and running a trustworthy organization is the result of an unwavering commitment to the four trust principles:

1. A focus on the other for the other's sake.
2. A collaborative approach to relationships.
3. A medium- to long-term relationship perspective.
4. A habit of being transparent in all your dealings.

Part

This section begins by making the case for trust, with a special focus on the economic impact of trust. It also addresses major questions about implementing trust initiatives at the organizational level, including how to create a culture of trust, the special trust challenges faced by internal staff groups, and finally, how to train for trustworthiness.

Making the Case for Trust

Building a trust-based organization frequently requires persuading others of the value of trust. The case for trust can be made on many dimensions. In this chapter we focus on those that are most likely to be of immediate interest to you and your organization: trust at the organizational level and its positive economic impact. We also explore the social and ethical benefits of trust.

You may find yourself making the case for greater degrees of trust in your organization or your business. We would like to make that job easier for you by describing the rewards and advantages of becoming an organization that leads with trust.

The main organizational benefits fall into three categories:

1. Economic benefits of trust
2. Social benefits of trust
3. Ethical benefits of trust

There are many other economic, social, and psychological benefits of trust that extend outside organizational boundaries and are therefore beyond the scope of this book. The interested reader might pursue Francis Fukuyama's book *Trust*,[1] which describes how differing national-cultural approaches to trust (for example, in China, Italy, and the Scandinavian countries) have created different models of business, commerce, and economics. Eric Uslaner's *Moral Foundations of Trust*[2] uses extensive data to explain why people come to place their trust in strangers and draws implications for social administrators and public policy. John Gottman's *Science of Trust*[3] explores interpersonal trust between couples through rigorously defining and measuring behavioral interactions.

Economic Benefits of Trust

The economic benefits of trust may be direct, such as lower costs, or indirect, such as increased innovation. While the most obvious examples of economic benefits may lie in the buyer-seller relationship, the financial impact of advisor relationships can be just as great.

Direct Economic Benefits of Trust

> While the most obvious examples of economic benefits may lie in the buyer-seller relationship, the financial impact of advisor relationships can be just as great.

Trust may either drive up revenue or drive down costs—and typically it does both.

Six Ways Trust Increases Revenue

1. *More and larger sales.* Trusted sellers consistently win more business and win bigger business.
2. *Repeat business.* Customer loyalty[4] is a massive driver of profitable sales, and nothing creates customer loyalty better than trust.
3. *More referrals.* Trusted partners naturally attract referrals from their customers.
4. *Faster time to market.* Trust-based organizations get products to market more quickly, resulting in earlier and higher-margin offerings.
5. *Faster decisions.* Decisive action is easier and accelerated when trust is present.
6. *Better decisions.* Decisions are based on more information and good intent, both of which lower risk.

Four Ways Trust Reduces Costs

> Trust may either drive up revenue or drive down costs—and typically it does both.

1. *Lower cost of sales.* Trusted sellers win more frequently, lowering the cost of sales and marketing.
2. *More sole-sourcing.* Buyers find less need to seek multiple bids, preferring to gain the speed and known quality of a trusted partner.
3. *Less double-checking and due diligence.* Expensive verifications can be eliminated or reduced when trust is present.
4. *Less performance tracking.* Trust-based relationships do not require the overhead of ongoing audits.

Note that most of the direct economic benefits are valid not only for the advisor/seller but for the client/buyer as well.

Indirect Economic Benefits of Trust

Not all trust effects show up immediately on your income statement or in your cost center. But indirect effects can benefit internal and external relationships, and eventually do make their way to the P&L.

Five Ways Trust Improves External Relationships

1. *Earlier involvement.* New business ideas are shared earlier as a result of greater confidence in capability and intent.
2. *More information-sharing.* Less restraint and more disclosure create deeper understanding of business issues.
3. *Improved communication.* A better grasp of each other's language and points of view leads to more productive communication overall.
4. *Greater influence.* Advice, information, and perspectives are more readily accepted.
5. *Increased commitment.* A genuine desire to help each other in many little ways has far-reaching impact.

Five Ways Trust Affects Internal Relationships

> Trust may be a soft skill, but its economic results are anything but soft.

1. *Greater employee loyalty.* A high-trust culture reduces attrition and increases commitment to the organization and to each other.

2. *Increased employee engagement.* A culture of trust boosts morale, productivity, and employee satisfaction.
3. *Increased accountability.* Employees who have the experience of being trusted feel a greater sense of ownership for results.
4. *Managerial agility.* Managers are more confident about delegating and can respond more flexibly when trust is present.
5. *Greater innovation.* More risk-taking ignites creativity and innovation.

Trust may be a soft skill, but its economic results are anything but soft.

CASE STUDY

From the Front Lines: A Trust-Based Business Unit

In 2005, Ross Smith became Director of an 85-person software test team within Microsoft. His team had great technical skills, passion, and excitement, but felt underutilized and unchallenged. Ross set out to improve innovation and productivity. Exploring options, they ran across a University of British Columbia study[5] by John F. Helliwell and Haifang Huang that equated the impact of high organizational trust to significant pay raises in terms of creating job satisfaction.

The team suddenly realized that innovation required freedom to fail, risk taking, building on others' ideas—all behaviors grounded in high trust. That cognitive snap, that a high-trust organization would address underutilization and latent talent, was the beginning of the solution.

In a high-trust organization, individuals could apply their skills, education, and experience at their own discretion. They could take risks and change processes themselves, because managers would trust them. The question was this: how to do it?

Ross asked the team to identify behaviors they felt influenced trust, positively or negatively. They realized that trust was subjective, situational, and very individual, and there was no single behavioral answer. As a result, the team put together a detailed playbook describing simple principles with discussion about how to implement.

They also modeled risk-taking and trust-building by using games to approach problems; everyone was allowed to play, experiment, and fail.

Microsoft is a heavy user of metrics, for Ross's team as well as throughout the company. The first noticeable difference was a higher-than-normal level of retention. After two and a half years, other things started to change dramatically—new test tools and new techniques were developed, and a high level of collaboration and partnership was working. Productivity numbers started to rise. As the project finished, the team was rated at or near the top across virtually every Microsoft productivity metric.

When Ross and several others from the original team moved to another division, they set out to introduce the trust-building ideas and practices which had worked so well before. Once again, they saw a high retention rate, a broader application of talent, and higher productivity numbers.

The metrics followed the changes in mind-set and behavior—not the other way around.

—Ross Smith (Microsoft), as told to Charles H. Green

Social Benefits of Trust

Trust strongly drives economic performance even at the level of national culture (for example, in France or China).[6] It shouldn't be surprising, then, that being trusting and trustworthy at the organizational level also affects the relationships between organizations and their stakeholders.

The Effect of Trust on Stakeholder Relationships

Trust-based organizations see benefits to their relationships not just with customers, but also with employees, suppliers, local communities, and shareholders.

All stakeholders benefit from the four factors of the trust equation:

1. *Credibility:* the ability to believe what an organization and its people say.
2. *Reliability:* the ability to reliably depend on an organization to do what it says it will do.
3. *Intimacy:* the ability to interact and share confidences with an organization's representatives.
4. *Low self-orientation:* the ability of the organization, through its people, to focus on and pay attention to the good of the stakeholders.

> The more instances of trust-building actions over time, and the longer the timeframe, the greater the link between trust and profitability.

Trust at the organization level helps stakeholders fulfill their various missions in rich ways, including helping them economically. Stakeholders who are treated in trust-based ways return the favor by providing support for the organization at key moments.

Shareholders are a particular case, benefiting most clearly from profits. It might seem obvious that a high-trust organization is a high-profit organization. But it is not obvious to all. Skeptics may believe that an organization can make more money through competition, market domination, and opportunism than through trust. And many feel that organizations have no choice in the matter.

The link between trust and profitability needs to be stated clearly: Not every instance of trust will produce profits. Not every trustworthy company will see quarterly income statements that are superior to all less trustworthy companies. Trust is not a guaranteed mechanical profit engine. But the more instances of trust-building actions over time, and the longer the timeframe, the greater the link between trust and profitability.[7]

Ethical Benefits of Trust

Because trust is about relationships between people, it inescapably has an ethical dimension, which in turn has an economic implication. We are not for a moment trying to justify ethics on economic grounds—but ethical behavior has consequences, among them economic.

> Because trust is about relationships between people, it inescapably has an ethical dimension, which in turn has an economic implication.

If you are like most people, you do not want to live in an organization where others see you solely as means to their ends. Indeed, if you thought the only reason people treated you well was to make money, you would not trust them. It is preferable to be in an organization where you are treated with some sense of dignity, you are trusted, and you can trust. And when you find yourself in those situations, you behave differently.

A trust-based organization is far more powerful than its trust-deprived counterparts because of this ethical dimension. This advantage shows up in two areas: relationships to people and to organizations.

The Effect of Trust-Based Ethics on Relationships to People

Leaders in a trust-based organization have ethical tools in their toolkit whereas leaders in trust-deprived organizations are limited to carrot-and-stick approaches. Which would you prefer?

Trust tools give a leader more flexibility in several respects:

- *Trust is simple.* To get a job done, a leader doesn't have to depend on complex organizational initiatives. Instead, she can appeal to commonly held trust principles.
- *Trust trumps incentives.* People in a trust-based organization will do the right thing, even in the face of contradictory incentives.
- *Trust gets stronger with use.* The more people behave in trust-based ways toward each other, the stronger their reciprocal ties to each other become.

The Effect of Trust-Based Ethics on Relationships to Organizations

Loyalty to an organization with shared values is much stronger than loyalty based just on mutually self-serving interests. Trust-based organizations have shared values:

- *Trust builds bridges.* Trust-based organizations easily find ways to bridge the gap between divisional or product islands.
- *Trust creates culture.* Common values make an organization develop distinctive language, ways of doing things, and reactions to similar events that you just cannot get through relying solely on processes, roles and responsibilities, and extrinsic incentives.

In making the case for trust, be sure to point out the large number of positive, sustainable side effects. When it comes to trust, you cannot help but do well by doing good.

> When it comes to trust, you cannot help but do well by doing good.

Worksheet: Your Custom Case

The case for trust can be made on many dimensions.
In what ways do you see the benefits of trust present in your organization today?

Economic:

_____

_____

_____

Social:

_____

_____

_____

Ethical:

_____

_____

_____

What opportunities exist to increase organizational effectiveness by increasing trust?

Economic:

_____

_____

_____

Social:

_____

_____

_____

Ethical:

_____

_____

_____

Creating a Culture of Trust

Compared to many change initiatives, creating a culture of trust requires a greater emphasis on personal change, and a lesser emphasis on traditional organizational tools like role definitions, processes, and incentives. The two primary tools for trust initiatives are values and virtues. In this chapter we describe these in detail, offer assessment tools for each, and suggest mechanisms by which to introduce them into an organization.

A high-trust organization is made up of people who are trustworthy, and appropriately trusting, working together in an environment that actively encourages those behaviors in employees as well as stakeholders. Creating a culture of trust requires a different emphasis than do most change initiatives—such as those designed to reduce accident rates, to increase customer-centricity, or to become compliant with the ISO-9000 family of standards. Trust by its nature is about interpersonal relations. For people to trust and be trusted by others, they must take personal risks and face personal fears in ways that cannot, by their nature, be planned and structured. That suggests a special emphasis: an initiative built around personal change.

You can compromise efforts to develop a culture of trust if you mistakenly apply methods and models of change built for other kinds of initiatives. For example, leading with trust requires stepping outside of self-interest as a matter of principle, whereas typical change programs often do the opposite and *engage* individuals' self-interest.

> For people to trust and be trusted by others, they must take personal risks and face personal fears in ways that cannot, by their nature, be planned and structured.

What it takes to create a trust-based organization is a complex topic. While this chapter is by no means comprehensive, it offers a concise view of some of the biggest levers to pull in your endeavor to create a culture of trust.

Figure 29.1 shows the difference in emphasis between typical change initiatives and trust initiatives.

Two Keys to Trust Culture Change: Virtues and Values

Central to creating a culture of trust are two basic dimensions of trust-based organizations: virtues and values. Virtues are the personal qualities that high-trust people embody, and

Figure 29.1

The Differences between Typical Change Initiatives and Building a Culture of Trust

Dimensions	Typical Change Initiatives	Trust Initiatives
1. Where it starts	At the executive level	Anywhere
2. Where the focus is	Business processes, structures, roles	Principles and personal attributes
3. What changes in people	Behaviors only	Mind-sets and behaviors
4. Who spreads it	Organizational leaders	Informal leaders
5. How it spreads	Systematically, through directives	Virally, through stories and examples
6. How it is implemented	Chain of command, followership	Personal accountability, responsibility, risk-taking
7. What motivates people	Incentives, mainly extrinsic	Aspirations, mainly intrinsic
8. How it is measured	Quantitative "smartly"	Qualitative wisely

---

CASE STUDY

From the Front Lines: Engineering a Turnaround[1]

Pediatric Services of America (PSA) Healthcare delivers home health care for medically fragile people, mostly children, which allows families to lead more normal lives under difficult conditions.

When Jim McCurry took over as CEO in 2009, PSA had been declining in revenue, market share, and profitability—proving that having a great mission alone isn't enough. By the end of McCurry's first year—at the tail end of a recession—the company had increased profitability, more than doubled total profits, and turned the market share decline into market share gain. Staff morale was up enormously. Expenses were down.

Here's what made the difference: the intentional use of principles to run the business.

Previous management was a classic top-down, measure-by-the-numbers team. Each month the bottom-performing offices were required to "justify" themselves on a conference call to the top management. At the annual meeting, office heads were required to double-up on hotel rooms. Orders were given, decisions had to be approved up the line, and the style was management by fear, intimidation, and numbers.

When Jim came on board, he told the staff: "From now on, this company is run for the customer. The area office managers work for the customer, and the rest of leadership works for them. Make your own decisions, and we'll help you make them. Don't wait for us to tell you what to do, you figure out what to do and do it—we trust you. No more intimidation, no more review boards. Our new mission has three parts: Action-oriented, Care-giving, and Trust-based—or ACT."

The PSA story is a vivid demonstration of collaboration, ethics, trust, openness, honesty, and integrity as anything but fuzzy phrases with "soft" outcomes. These are utterly workable principles that deliver bottom-line results.

—Jim McCurry (president and CEO, Pediatric Services of America), as told to Charles H. Green

values are what guide the organizations they work in. In trust-based organizations, virtues and values are consistent *and* mutually reinforcing.

We use these words very intentionally, because common language matters. Each deserves its own word and understanding, and both are required for trust culture change. In our experience, companies are likely to focus excessively on organizational values and give short shrift to personal virtues.

> Unless people take personal responsibility for their own behavior around trust, the organization will never be a trust-based organization.

The virtues *of trust are personal*, and involve your level of trustworthiness and your ability to trust. The virtues of trust are contained in the trust equation: credibility, reliability, intimacy, and self-orientation (see Chapter 4, "Three Trust Models"). It is virtuous for someone to tell the truth, to behave dependably, to keep confidences, and to be mindful of the needs of others. Unless people take personal responsibility for their own behavior around trust, the organization will never be a trust-based organization.

The values *of trust are institutional*, and drive the organization's external relationships, leadership, structure, rewards, and key processes. The values of a trust-based organization are reflected in the four trust principles: other-focus, collaboration, medium- to long-term perspective, and transparency. An organization that espouses these values treats others with respect, has an inclination to partner, has a bias toward a longer timeframe, and shares information.

> Trust-based organizations take values very seriously. If your organization has never fired someone for a values violation, then you've either been astoundingly successful in your hiring and development efforts, or you are not a values-driven organization.

Trust-based organizations take values very seriously. If your organization has never fired someone for a values violation, then you have either been astoundingly successful in your hiring and development efforts, or you are not a strongly values-driven organization.

Implementing Trust Initiatives

An organization does not always need to make big structural or operational changes to become more trust-based. It does not have to throw away the organization charts, abolish bonuses, redefine target markets, or change major business processes. Instead, implementing changes to increase trust should be focused on themes of language, leadership, and shared ethos.

Here are five tools for implementing a cultural shift toward trust:

1. Diagnostic assessment
2. Leading by example
3. The language of trust
4. Storytelling
5. Managing with wisdom, not metrics

Diagnostic Assessment

Building a culture of trust starts with a diagnostic assessment to determine the current state of affairs and to assess the gap between the as-is and the desired end state. For example, with clients we use the Trust Roadmap as a diagnostic at the organizational level and the Trust Quotient Assessment to collect individual and group data.

Benchmarking at the outset of a new trust initiative is a critical step:

- It defines the current state in ways that allow a future state to be described.

- It highlights priorities and levels of urgency.
- It sends a message about the concepts that are central to the trust initiative.

Diagnostics and benchmarking are critical enough that we explore them in greater detail in their own special "Spotlight on Trust Diagnostics" section at the end of this chapter.

Leading by Example

When it comes to changing personal attributes, there is no better teacher than a good example. Having people of influence act virtuously and have the courage to address untrustworthy behavior in the organization[2] speaks volumes. It also follows that the biggest trust destroyer in an organization is hypocrisy at the highest levels. Leaders whose actions violate critical attributes or violate principles tear down values and trust.

> When it comes to changing personal attributes, there is no better teacher than a good example.

Leading by example is not limited to people in formal leadership roles. Even if you have no organizational authority, you can commit yourself to thinking, speaking, doing, and *being* in ways that reflect how you want others to think, speak, do, and be. It requires demonstrating the attributes you want others to emulate, and living by the organization's principles.

Someone who leads by example to create a culture of trust will:

- Trust others inside and outside the organization.
- Be willing to go first.
- Own up to his mistakes.
- Be willing to forgive others for their honest, well-intentioned mistakes.
- Hold *himself* accountable when he doesn't see the behaviors he wants to see in others.
- Take opportunities to provide both positive and corrective coaching in the moment.
- Solicit feedback on his performance—really listen to it, publish it, and act on it.[3]

The Language of Trust

Language is, fundamentally, a way in which the world is organized—memorable phrases, mnemonic devices, and word associations can help you recall and make sense of things. Language is critical when dealing with a topic as complex and situational as building a culture of trust. Vocabulary is the handmaiden of virtues and values.

People working to create trust-based organizations use language to:

- Consistently convey a few simple messages in repeated, memorable phrases.
- Reinforce their commitment to working from principles, not processes.
- Express the shared ideology of the organization (values), and what it explicitly means in terms of personal behavior (virtues).

As you endeavor to influence your organization, you can introduce others to the trust principles, the trust equation, and other concepts you've acquired in the course of reading this book so you all have a common language about trust.

Storytelling

Stories trump PowerPoint decks when it comes to mobilizing culture change. The business world is not short on resources for improving the technology to deliver your storytelling.

CASE STUDY

From the Front Lines: High-Trust Culture[4]

"Our CEO, Jim Conlon, repeatedly reminds our associates and our clients that the only reason we exist is that the people, businesses, and organizations in our markets have chosen to do business with us. If you do the right things for the right reasons, good outcomes will ensue."

Jim is reinforcing the importance of principled behavior, first and foremost, and using language as a tool to do it. For years, the leadership team at the bank has been repeating this simple message: it is about customer experience, believe in trust, people matter, and behaviors start with attitudes. Their meetings, conversations, relationships, and decisions are all anchored in these themes.

The staff of Bangor Savings is passionate, engaged, and making a difference in their own lives and those of their communities. The key to their success boils down to one thing: the consistent application of a core set of trust principles to all the bank's affairs.

— *John Edwards (Executive Vice President of Bangor Savings Bank) as told to Charles H. Green*

What it is short on is leaders who actually use stories as a tool for change. When was the last time you attended—or led—an important group meeting that used stories rather than decks as the primary tool to inspire, motivate, and inform?

Here are nine reasons that well-told stories make a difference when building a culture of trust:

1. *Stories have wide appeal*, and therefore address the challenge of mobilizing a diverse audience.[5]
2. *Stories create meaning.* They allow people to make sense of things, to establish an order or relationship, and to put events in a context.
3. *Stories teach lessons* in an engaging way.
4. *Stories make data memorable*, so learning sticks.[6]
5. *Stories are a form of metaphor*, and metaphors help people make connections in ways that linear, rational minds won't allow.[7]
6. *Stories create emotional connection.* They appeal to the heart as well as the head, inviting laughter, tears, discomfort, and appreciation.[8]
7. *Stories lower emotional resistance.* People are more willing to accept ideas when they hear stories, especially when those stories resonate with previously held beliefs.[9]
8. *Stories offer insight* into the character, beliefs, and vulnerability of the storyteller.
9. *Stories inspire action.* They give us intellectual insight into specific behaviors to adopt, and the emotional motivation to do so.

Managing with Wisdom, Not Metrics

Metrics are traditionally used as a tool for managing operations and monitoring change efforts. Unfortunately, many of the measures that leaders focus on in today's business world may be considered *smart*, though they are not *wise* when it comes to trust initiatives. Too often leaders:

From the Front Lines: Leading with Trust[10]

A few years ago, I (Charlie) watched Bill Green, then-Chairman and CEO of Accenture, as he addressed a very senior leadership group at the end of a two-day offsite meeting. Relaxed, he sat on a stage chair on a small platform and took questions from the 75–80 people in the room.

About halfway in, someone asked about a recently announced organizational shift.

"Bill," the person asked, "how do we know that the incentives are rightly aligned with the new global roles; that if I ask my colleague in Eastern Europe or Australia for help, they'll be incented to do the right thing?"

Green quickly stood up, visibly tensing at the question.

"Let me ... well ... ," he sputtered, "Okay, I guess I'm glad you asked that question. Because I want to tell you—I don't want to hear that question again.

"Here's what I mean. And I expect everyone in this room to get this; moreover, I expect everyone in this room to make sure you teach everyone back in your offices too.

"Here's the thing. When there's a conflict between the incentives and the right thing: you do the right thing, and then fix the incentives later. Understand? This is critical.

"We must be a values-driven organization before we are an incentives-driven organization. You design incentives to reinforce and reward behavior—you don't design them to drive behavior. Values are what we need to drive behavior. If there's a mismatch, you fix the incentives. After you do the right thing.

"And just to be clear: the right thing is almost always defined in terms of the client—not in terms of our internal P&L."

—Charles H. Green

- Focus primarily on transactions and processes.
- Emphasize quantitative over qualitative measures.
- Refuse to invest without a precise ROI justification.
- Rely on extrinsic incentives for compliance with organizational values.

Here's the problem: Managing only through traditional metrics doesn't further the goal of creating a culture of trust. For the values and virtues of a trust-based organization to be effective, people must adopt and act from higher-order mind-sets.

Imagine telling your spouse you want to be a better partner. To get there, you suggest weekly measurements of spousal performance, using a scale of 1 to 10, along with rewards for achieving and exceeding those metrics. Imagine the reaction! A clinical focus applied to something as complex as a long-term personal partnership seems obviously inappropriate. Why should it be any less inappropriate when applied to a trust initiative in an organization?

The alternatives to metrics are to:

- Look for evidence of values and virtues being lived on a daily basis. Do people hold each other accountable for trustworthy behavior?
- Listen for changes in the language over time. Do employees talk about the organization as we or they? Do people speak about customers with appreciation and respect?

- Seek qualitative feedback. Interview clients, talk to vendors, and make it safe for employees to be candid about their experience of the organization.
- Invest in doing the right thing. Evaluate opportunities in terms of the big picture, not just the quarterly return. Make decisions that align with your company's values—period.
- Focus on intrinsic rewards. Provide employees with autonomy, opportunities for mastery, and a sense of purpose.[11]

A different kind of culture—a culture of trust—requires a different kind of scorecard.

Spotlight on Trust Diagnostics

A successful trust initiative begins with a two-part diagnostic process: an organizational effectiveness assessment, which looks at trust system-wide, and a personal trustworthiness assessment, which looks at trust at the individual and work group levels.

Organizational Effectiveness Assessment

The objective of an organizational effectiveness assessment is to diagnose the current status of the organization and to clearly identify priorities for a trust initiative. In our work with clients, we have developed the Trust Roadmap. Inspired by tried-and-true frameworks for thinking about organizational effectiveness, such as Marvin Weisbord's Six-Box Model[12] and the McKinsey 7-S Framework,[13] the Trust Roadmap includes five aspects of organizational effectiveness to consider when evaluating and designing a culture of trust:

1. *External Relationships:* how your organization relates to other organizations.
2. *Leadership*: how your leaders behave, both within and outside the organization.
3. *Structure*: how your organization is set up to get work done.
4. *Reward:* how virtues and values are positively reinforced.
5. *Processes*: how work actually gets done.

We map these five aspects of organizational effectiveness to the four trust principles (see Chapter 4, "Three Trust Models"). The result is a Trust Roadmap that shows specific ways that the principles manifest, or not, at the organizational level. The Trust Roadmap identifies key areas for concern and action.

Figure 29.2, The Trust Roadmap, provides a framework for assessing your organization, with sample indicators for each cell.

Once your organization has taken the assessment, some questions for analysis and discussion may include:

- How well does your organization score?
- What are the critical areas for improvement?
- Where does your organization currently excel?
- Which areas could use reinforcement and support?

Personal Trustworthiness Assessment

The objective of a personal trustworthiness assessment is to diagnosis the current levels of trustworthiness in individuals and work groups. We use the Trust Quotient Assessment, which is to personal attributes what the Trust Roadmap is to organizational attributes. The

Figure 29.2

The Trust Roadmap

		A	B	C	D
			Medium- to Long- Term Perspective		
		Collaboration		Transparency	Other Focus
1	External Relationships	You work together with customers, suppliers, and others to respond innovatively to opportunities and problems.	You consider past, present, and future when negotiating a current deal with people outside of the organization.	Your organization is open and honest in its dealings with people outside of it.	In working with customers, suppliers, and clients you put their needs first, not yours.
2	Leadership	Your leaders seek opinions and work together with employees at all levels as part of the decision-making process.	Your leaders are willing to sacrifice short-term gains for the long-term benefit of the organization.	Employees understand your leadership's rationale for making decisions.	Your leaders set the right examples by putting others first, even at the expense of short-term gain.
3	Structure	It's clear your teams/groups/divisions coordinate their efforts.	There's an effective handoff between the people who sell the work and the people who do the work.	Employees understand who does what at your organization.	Others know whom to contact within the organization to get what they need.
4	Rewards	Your organization encourages collaboration.	Your organization acknowledges people for doing the right thing from a long-term perspective.	Your employees feel fairly dealt with regarding money, advancement, and recognition.	You ensure that your rewards and incentives don't get in the way of employees' doing the right thing.
5	Processes	There is no need to go around the system to get things done at your organization.	Your internal business processes encourage long-term thinking (for example, strategic planning, project planning).	The way things get done at your organization is clear to employees.	Your planning and reporting processes (for example, account planning, management reporting) encourage a focus on your customers.

20-question diagnostic test is based on the four variables of the trust equation: credibility, reliability, intimacy, and self-orientation. Your score, or TQ, is based on answers to the questions.

You may take a short form of the Trust Quotient Assessment for free at http://HowTrustworthyAmI.com.

The table below describes each of the six Trust Temperament types:

Trust Temperament	Highest Ranked Attributes	Motto
The Expert	Credibility, Reliability	"Lead, follow, or get out of the way." —Anonymous
The Doer	Reliability, Intimacy	"As for accomplishments, I just did what I had to do as things came along."—Eleanor Roosevelt
The Catalyst	Credibility, Intimacy	"A genuine leader is not a searcher for consensus but a molder of consensus." —Martin Luther King, Jr.
The Professor	Credibility, (low) Self-orientation	"The important thing is not to stop questioning. Curiosity has its own reason for existing." —Albert Einstein
The Steward	Reliability, (low) Self-orientation	"My goal wasn't to make a ton of money. It was to build good computers." —Steve Wozniak
The Connector	Intimacy, (low) Self-orientation	"It's not what you know, it's who you know." —Anonymous

Having gauged your trustworthiness using the four variables of the trust equation, here are some questions for analysis and discussion. These questions may be applied to individuals or teams:

* Do the results feel intuitively accurate to you?
* How can you better leverage your strengths?
* What can you do to improve your trustworthiness?
* What have you learned about trust-based relationships as a result of this assessment?

Worksheet: Your Trust Roadmap

The Trust Roadmap shows specific ways that the trust principles manifest, or not, at the organizational level. It identifies key areas for concern and action. Use it to diagnose the current status of your organization and to clearly identify priorities for a trust initiative.

Using the framework below, and the examples in this chapter, create your own custom Trust Roadmap. Design it with at least one entry per cell.

		A	B	C	D
		Collaboration	Medium- to Long-Term Perspective	Transparency	Other Focus
1	**External Relationships.** How your organization relates to other organizations.				
2	**Leadership.** How your leaders behave, both within and outside the organization.				
3	**Structure.** How your organization is set up to get work done.				
4	**Rewards.** How virtues and values are positively reinforced.				
5	**Processes.** How work actually gets done.				

Use surveys, focus groups, interviews, or a combination to determine how well your organization scores.

What are your organization's strengths?

_____

What are the critical areas for improvement?

_____

What actions will you take as a result?

_____

_____

Trust in Internal Staff Functions

30
Chapter

In the world of professional services, the term *trusted advisor* conjures up images of subject matter experts working with external clients. But there is another group for whom the term is equally relevant: those in internal roles who provide the same kind of specialized expertise within their organization. This chapter is specifically written for people in internal staff functions such as Legal, Human Resources (HR), Information Technology (IT), and Finance. It examines the external misconceptions that impede building trust, and identifies specific ways for specialists on the inside to increase the levels of trust and influence with internal clients.

"Trust me, I'm from HR/IT/Legal/Finance." Does this phrase make you want to take a bow of deep respect, or to chuckle? For many organizations, it depends. Stereotypes, cross-cultural clashes, and internal tensions abound when it comes to shared services organizations. The great challenge for you if you serve in one of these internal staff functions is to maintain objectivity and collegiality at the same time, while rising above any negative labels that exist.

In one sense, internal staff face exactly the same uphill battle as their colleagues on the outside—to successfully influence others over whom they have no direct authority. But internal staff have unique additional challenges:

> The great challenge of these internal staff functions is to maintain objectivity and collegiality at the same time.

1. *Overfamiliarity*. Because internal staff eat in the same lunchroom as their clients and are readily known by their first names, they tend to not receive the same respect as outside experts.
2. *Inseparability*. An internal consultant cannot fire her client. They are joined at the hip, like a married couple, for better or worse.
3. *Poorly defined boundaries*. The contractual relationships between internal functions staff and their clientele are generally murkier, which causes trust issues to be murkier as well.

The good news is that internal staff can build trust and make progress by bringing trust perspectives to their functions' unique challenges.

> In one sense, internal staff face exactly the same uphill battle as their colleagues on the outside—to successfully influence others over whom they have no direct authority.

The Top Trust Barriers by Function

While internal staff may collectively share a client base, the job in fact varies considerably by the reputation and image of the profession in question. Consider the vastly different perception of HR compared to Finance, or how differently people view lawyers from information technology specialists. While those differences can be caricatured as casual stereotypes within an organization, those stereotypes present unique challenges for each group.

- *The IT challenge.* Ask many line employees about their company's IT group, and you will hear, "The problem with IT is they use too much jargon and don't deliver on time or on budget." Strip out the value-laden words, and what we hear is that IT has a reputation for being non-user-friendly, and that its big trust opportunity may lie in *improving reliability*.
- *The HR challenge.* In contrast to their IT colleagues, HR suffers from speaking the same language as everyone else, which means everyone else feels equal to them in expertise. HR folks are often the first to claim they don't get the respect they deserve, and the more they ask for respect, they less they get. HR's big trust opportunity starts with *improving credibility*.
- *The Legal challenge.* Managers often complain: "The trouble with lawyers is they always tell me what I can't do, and don't help me with what I *can* do." Lawyers are caught between avoiding doing the wrong thing at the cost of not doing the right thing. The legal team can lead with trust by *taking a more holistic perspective on risk*.
- *The Finance challenge.* Finance tends to be known for speaking clearly, meeting deadlines, and being very sober about risk—very sober about pretty much everything in fact. Internal clients fear that Finance people will relentlessly grind them down on budgets, financial analyses, plans, and forecasts. Finance people, it is generally believed, are uncompromisingly right. Finance can improve trust by *increasing intimacy*.

Each of these groups has an opportunity to improve their own working conditions as well as the outcomes for their internal clients by improving their clients' level of trust.

Five Trust-Enhancing Opportunities for Internal Staff

The trust equation provides a framework for focusing on the greatest trust opportunities for each function. While your organization may vary, in general, the areas of opportunity shown in Figure 30.1 are typical.

Below are targeted suggestions for each area of opportunity.

- *Increase credibility (HR).* To improve credibility, try to apply your knowledge to a specific client situation—in their language. Instead of letting the client know that you have seen the latest, greatest research on teaching Emotional Intelligence, use Emotional Intelligence yourself to help identify, and identify yourself with, client issues. For example, "Joe, do you find your people are as involved in work as you'd like them to be? Where do you see that playing out? And how big an issue is it for you? In what terms?" Then do an outstanding job of truly listening to the answer.
- *Improve reliability (IT).* Reliability is an issue that often affects IT more than the other staff functions, and it is one of the easiest trustworthiness variables to improve. Simple awareness is a good place to begin. Reliability lends itself far more easily to measurement than do the other components of trust. Figure out good measures of reliability and track them. Try increasing the number of promises you make, even small ones—then make sure to meet them.

Area of Opportunity	Function			
	HR	**IT**	**Legal**	**Finance**
1. Credibility	√			
2. Reliability		√		
3. Intimacy: Empathy		√	√	√
4. Intimacy: Risk-taking			√	√
5. Self-orientation	√	√	√	

Figure 30.1

Five Trust-Enhancing Areas of Opportunity

- *Strengthen intimacy via empathy (IT, Legal, Finance).* Intimacy is the variable that makes an advisor client-friendly. Empathy in particular—relating easily to others, and making yourself easy to relate to—leads a client of IT, Legal, or Finance to feel comfortable sharing information with you. You do not have to resort to commenting on kids' pictures, college degrees, or the latest sports scores to establish Intimacy. Make a point to learn things about your clients' business lives—then ask them for help in understanding things that you genuinely do not understand about them.

- *Strengthen intimacy via risk-taking (Legal, Finance).* Both Finance and Legal get tarred with the brush of being too averse to risk. The charge may seem unfair; part of the job is to manage downside risk. But no matter how right you think you are, if your perceptions of risk management differ from those of your clients, you are misaligned and this is a problem.

   Organizations that adopt an adversarial relationship—for example, where Legal represents the downside and Management argues for the upside—create vast areas of unnecessary cost, mistrust, and confusion. It is far better to create collaborative relationships where issues can be sorted out mutually. The burden falls on staff people to state the terms at the outset: "We are here to collaborate with you in jointly determining the right amount of business risk to take on, consistent with legal, regulatory, and market-based risk. We all work for the same organization, and we are committed to working with you."

   There is risk-taking inherent in choosing a collaborative approach over a custodial one and that is precisely the point. This is your opportunity to expand your level of risk-tolerance in a way that serves your client relationships without compromising your professional edicts.[1]

Insight: The Difference between Personal and Private[2]

In thinking about intimacy, it is useful to distinguish between the private and the personal. By private we mean knowing the names of your clients' children, tracking your clients' outside interests, perhaps playing a sport together. We have no strong feelings either way about your need to be intimate on the private issues. That is completely dependent on you and your client and what works for both of you.

   At the same time, we are adamant about the need for you to be personal when it comes to work life. All the ups and downs and emotional issues are on full display in organizational life, and you ignore them at your peril. Your effectiveness and even professionalism are dependent on your ability to relate to your client as a human being, and not just as a rational, calculating professional.

- *Reduce self-orientation (HR, IT, Legal).* Nearly everyone can improve her trustworthiness by lowering her self-orientation. Of the four internal staff functions, this is particularly useful for HR, IT, and Legal. Too many employees see HR as needy, lawyers as overbearing, and IT people as mechanistic, all of which are forms of overly developed self-orientation. Whether true or not, these perceptions must be overcome. If the perception is wrong, then better yet—you get extra credit for getting your client to recognize that you are not the stereotype they thought you were.

  While the self-orientation solution is harder than for the other issues, it is well within reach. Simply be very, very sure to see issues from the client's vantage point—not just from yours. No one is asking you to abdicate your professional perspectives, just to see it from the other side of the table as well.

  If a client says to you, "We want to do X, how can we do it?" start by confirming his perspective. For example, say something such as, "Interesting idea. Let me make sure I understand what this means to you. Tell me more about what you could do with this, how it would make you more successful. I want to make sure I know where you're coming from, first and foremost." This approach will go a long way toward demonstrating your commitment to being of service.

  You will find additional suggestions for improving each trustworthiness variable in Chapter 4, "Three Trust Models," and Chapter 21, "Accelerating Trust."

Don't Confuse Your Metrics with Your Mission

With external professional organizations like law firms and consulting firms, economic relationships are pretty clear—for X amount of money you will get Y results and/or effort. It is usually easy for external professionals to align their economic relationships with their mission, and so it is relatively easy to define metrics to track performance.

With internal staff functions, the economic relationships are often less clear—and thus the alignment between metrics and mission can be more challenging. At one extreme, there is a central organization where all functions report to a C-level executive, are separately budgeted, and managed as cost centers with business units charged general overhead. At the other extreme, internal units compete with external professionals, and business units choose the provider they prefer. And in the middle of the continuum lies a myriad of hybrid options: blends of charge-backs, value-pricing, policies for when and when not to use internal resources, budgeting for services, and so forth.

Insight: Five Ways Internal Staff Can Enhance Trust

1. *To improve credibility,* apply your knowledge to a specific client situation—in the client's language.
2. *To improve reliability,* try increasing the number of promises you make, even small ones. Then make sure to meet them.
3. *To improve intimacy via empathy,* make a point to learn things about your clients' business lives. Then ask them for help in understanding things that you genuinely don't understand.
4. *To improve intimacy via risk-taking,* choose a collaborative approach over a custodial one.
5. *To reduce self-orientation,* see and express issues from your client's vantage point.

Given the range of options, most companies end up with a blended approach that is less clear than either extreme in terms of the economics, obligations of the parties to each other, and metrics. That means the mission-metric link is not firmly established, and the need for trust is elevated.

There are good business reasons for choosing one or another approach, all beyond the reach of this book. Regardless of your metrics or business unit goals, your first mission should always be to serve your total organization by *doing the right thing*. Sometimes that mission won't align with your unit's performance metrics. When there is a conflict, it is your job to first do what is right, and then correct the misalignment.

> Regardless of your metrics or business unit goals, your first mission should always be to serve your total organization by doing the right thing.

This kind of situation can be lonely and hard to address. Take heart in knowing that if you are ever faced with such a conflict, you are addressing important organizational issues with far-reaching impact.

Worksheet: Perception Is Reality

Understanding and accepting how you are perceived in your internal staff function is the first step in building trust within your organization.

Consider the following questions. This is an excellent team exercise.

How is your staff function perceived by the organization as a whole? Be honest in your responses; not wishful. Consider key stakeholder groups when you do your analysis, and what relationship strengths and weaknesses they see in you.

What do they say about you? In what ways do they (or don't they) involve you in strategic conversations or projects? How would you characterize the majority of your relationships with members of that group?

Stakeholder Group	Relationship Strengths (Their Perception)	Relationship Weaknesses (Their Perception)
1.		
2.		
3.		
4.		
5.		

Envision the *desired future state:* How do you want to be perceived? Involved? Related to? Write a vivid description.

_____

_____

How might your function *collectively build trust* within the organization as a whole?

_____

_____

In what ways can you *personally build trust* with your stakeholders?

_____

_____

Tip: Share your assessment and ideas with your stakeholders, and get their feedback.

_____

_____

Training for Trustworthiness

Can people learn how to be trustworthy? The short answer is yes. This chapter looks at what is required to teach the mind-sets and skills of trustworthy people. It explores specific training strategies to inspire aha moments and make their lessons stick. It also provides you with tactics for creating a supportive learning environment and strategically involving key stakeholders.

There are at least two very real challenges when it comes to training for trustworthiness:[1]

1. *You cannot learn trustworthiness from a textbook.* Learning to be trustworthy requires high-touch experiences combined with practice over time to become habitual. Even the book you are reading right now is only as good as the extent to which you do apply it consistently in your own business dealings. You cannot just cognitively understand your way into leading with trust. It takes time and practice to become natural.
2. *If your underlying mind-set is not right, trustworthiness skills will be ineffective.* It is not enough for you to follow a behavioral checklist. Attitudes and ways of thinking drive decisions and actions. You may have exceptional interpersonal skills that would be thwarted, either temporarily or consistently, by a limiting mind-set.

The answer to these challenges lies in a creative, dynamic, and sometimes unconventional approach to trustworthiness training.

> You cannot just cognitively understand your way into leading with trust. It takes time and practice to become natural.

The One-Two Punch for Trustworthiness Training

In boxing, a one-two punch is a powerful combination of moves that are especially effective in delivering a blow. The two actions together deliver better results than either does alone. It is the same for trustworthiness training. Here the one-two punch consists of (1) experiencing the aha moment and (2) making it stick. Both are required to train for trustworthiness in a way that has sustainable impact.

1. *Experience the aha.* The aha moment is the epiphany about how trust works. It is when you get it. It happens when you gain a clear and often sudden understanding of the complex

dynamics of trust. It is like a little opening of the psyche: through it, you see something you never saw before—an enabling way of being, a specific skill gap, or an opportunity to take action. Experiencing the aha directly challenges the underlying mind-sets that have been holding you back.

> An aha engages the brain and the heart: You understand something in a new way and feel compelled to do something about it at the same time.

An aha goes beyond intellectual understanding. For example, you might read Chapter 3, "The Dynamics of Influence," and come to recognize listening as the key to being influential. But it is not until you receive specific feedback during an exercise that you see precisely where your listening skills fall short, even though you felt pretty good at listening in the first place.

To get an aha moment, it is not enough to follow a behavioral checklist. Attitudes and ways of thinking drive decisions and actions. An aha engages the brain and the heart: You understand something in a new way and at the same time you feel compelled to act on that new understanding.

2. *Make it stick.* Practice over time forms habits, develops muscle memory, and reduces the trepidation that interferes with your motivation to apply what you have learned. For example, it is a lot easier to consistently put hard truths on the table when you have done it successfully three times in the past week. Making it stick addresses the need for time and practice to have it become natural.

CASE STUDY

From the Front Lines: Making It Stick

One global accounting firm has found a way to bridge the gap between learning and real life; they bring account teams working on strategic accounts together in a learning lab—a dedicated physical space—to solve real problems.

A lab leader helps the client teams think through the challenges they want to address before the participants arrive at the lab. Then they come together face-to-face to spend a day together—often from a variety of locations. Everyone on the team must be present. Sometimes clients join in.

Each lab is completely modular and moveable, and equipped with rolling whiteboards, tear sheets, and props to promote focus and levity—such as paddles with images of elephants that are raised to flag elephant-in-the-room issues. There are no power strips for connecting laptops, no projectors, and few tables. Together, teammates play out different scenarios, examine their own behavior from the clients' perspective, and identify pivotal moments—moments from the past or moments they want to create—that will make a difference in their work. A facilitator helps draw out the conversation and reframe issues. A lab advisor, a senior partner who is deliberately assigned from another project, asks tough questions and keeps the team honest.

A team's lab time ends with a list of specific action items, documented by lab assistants and executed by the teams themselves. Many teams come back later to advance their learning and assess their progress.

The take-away: Giving team members a dedicated space and dedicated time to experience learning, with real problems from their own work, takes client excellence to a whole new level.

—As told to Andrea P. Howe

On an organizational level, the repetitive application by a critical mass of people helps make the individual aha a collective one, and embeds a consistent way of being into the culture.

How to Set Off the Aha: A Nine-Point Checklist

Here are nine best practices for setting off the aha. Use them as a checklist. Large-scale training programs—those that run several days for a large number of people—will ideally use all of them.

1. *Use simple frameworks.* Break trustworthiness into bite-sized, digestible pieces that are easy to remember. We recommend using the three trust models: the trust equation, the trust creation process, and the trust principles. (See Chapter 4, "Three Trust Models.")
2. *Provide out-of-character experiences.* Challenge existing mind-sets and allow something new and really different to emerge from role-playing exercises, simulations, and other experiential learning events. Make these 80 percent of your design, not 20 percent. Stretch participants outside their comfort zones into a place where existing assumptions, paradigms, and beliefs are temporarily suspended. Note that very few people actually like these until after they have experienced them, and some never like them. Don't let that stop you.
3. *Fail forward.* The brain actually works better when making mistakes. In *How We Decide*, Jonah Lehrer reports that a computer programmed to play chess by measuring what it got "wrong" ended up beating the reigning chess champion.[2] In the case of trustworthiness training, design role-playing exercises that allow participants to make mistakes safely— when participants see how they went wrong, they can learn indelible lessons while simultaneously conquering their fears.[3]
4. *Tell stories.* Stories convey the paradoxes of trustworthiness better than any rigorous intellectual model. They are an especially powerful tool for shifting mind-sets. Stories motivate, persuade, inform, and inspire by engaging intellect and emotions. Stories also provide a vivid example of what success looks and feels like, painting a clear picture of how changes in thought, action, and ways of being have led to greater success.

   > Stories convey the paradoxes of trustworthiness better than any rigorous intellectual model.

5. *Encourage the tough conversations.* There is no trust without risk, and there is no learning about trustworthiness without risk either. It's vital to discuss thought-provoking concepts, teach tough lessons, and engage in candid conversations. Welcome and validate honesty, authenticity, and vulnerability.
6. *Link in real-life situations.* There is no substitute for learning how to apply trust lessons within a specific business context—that is what the real world demands, after all. Bridge the gap between theory and application. Use custom-developed group cases as well as individual participants' scenarios ("I've got a stakeholder who …") so that learning can be applied right away.
7. *Incorporate personal feedback.* Highly personalized learning can be life-changing. Individual feedback from self-assessment instruments, stakeholder interviews, and 360° reviews often reveals blind spots, limiting beliefs, and skill gaps in a compelling way. Ideally, this feedback is gathered both before and after a learning program so that shifts can be tracked and celebrated.
8. *Make time for reflection.* Reflection is a critical part of the adult learning process.[4] Through reflection, you will find patterns and meaning in an experience, which in turn bring

clarity to situations. Do this as an individual and as a group. For example, at the individual level, private learning journals written without self-consciousness or inhibition can help articulate new insights and what to do next.[5]

9. *Mix up learning groups.* Create regular opportunities for wide cross-sections of staff to work together. A max-mix, or maximum mixture, represents diversity in terms of seniority, specialization, geographical location, and more. These can spark aha moments better than more homogeneous groups.

Eleven Ways to Make It Stick

The mantra of trustworthiness training is "Practice, practice, practice." To make the lessons of trustworthiness training stick, keep the conversation alive, encourage practical application, and celebrate successes over time.

Following are 11 specific methods for sustaining aha moments,[6] in order of least to greatest investment. Lead them from within, or hire experts to help you. Choose a combination that aligns with your strategy and culture, as well as your time, budget, and resource constraints. Keep in mind: The more experiential and interactive, the more effective and long-lasting your training results will be.

1. *Set up action learning groups[7] or learning labs.* Convene teams (intact or max-mix) on a regular basis for short periods to work real issues and role play, using the lenses of the three trust models. Groups can convene either in person or virtually, and be either self-led or facilitator-led.

2. *Arrange check-in calls and office hours.* Regularly scheduled times for learners to check in are a low-cost way to keep them focused on applying what they are learning. Participants share stories of trust successes and failures, report progress on real business issues, and define next steps toward achieving a specific result.

3. *Schedule teach-back assignments.* Participants convey key lessons to colleagues outside the original training group. For example, a short lecture at an all-hands meeting on the trust equation and how to apply it. Teaching new lessons to others requires and inspires a higher level of mastery. In addition, there is a pollinating effect when learning is shared with a larger group.

4. *Create online learning communities.* Use your web resources for members to share knowledge, experiences, and insights. Stories can be conveyed within cohort learning groups and/or a broader audience.

5. *Continue learning with book clubs.* Champions assign discussion topics from relevant reading material on trust-based relationships.

6. *Present 60- to 90-minute webinars to refresh and advance lessons.* An interactive mix of discussion and new learning delivered via webinar technology keeps the conversation alive and provides opportunities to learn about advanced trust topics.

7. *Set up peer coaching.* Peer coaching is similar to action learning groups, only done one-to-one. These buddy relationships can be established within a learning program or in conjunction with an existing mentoring program.

8. *Arrange professional coaching.* Coaching is a targeted, high-impact way to accelerate learning for select individuals and teams. Focus on key accounts or strategic initiatives. Just-in-time coaching focuses on applying the three trust models to a specific issue at hand, at the time a need arises.

9. *Repeat personal assessments.* Have participants benchmark and compare results 9 to 12 months after participating in a program.

10. *Provide mastery programs for select leaders.* Make advanced learning opportunities available to a select group who are then tasked with being internal role models and champions.
11. *Train-the-coach/train-the-trainer.* Expand your capacity to teach trustworthiness by developing people as in-house coaches and trainers.

Create the Right Learning Environment

Training for trustworthiness will prove most effective if you create a learning environment that keeps motivation and interest high and encourages risk-taking.

How to Keep Motivation and Interest High

1. *Give the "why."* Tell why it is important, why it is exciting, why it is worth the time to be involved. If participants are energized, they will seek out new learning on their own.[8]
2. *Insist that people be fully present and focused.* Set the tone that this is a different kind of learning experience. Some ways to do this:
   - Design exercises to be realistic and challenging to keep people on their toes.
   - Hold face-to-face programs offsite whenever possible.
   - Be firm about electronic distractions, like laptops and smart phones.
3. *Make it fun.* Learning and play go hand-in-hand. Play stimulates the imagination and arouses curiosity, which leads to discovery and creativity. If you are going to have to practice over and over and over again to be masterful, you might as well enjoy yourself in the process.

Insight: Six Troubleshooting Tips for Trust Training

Training for trust requires a particular kind of approach that can be subtly different from other kinds of training. Here are six common pitfalls that will limit your success when training for trust.

As you set up and deliver your trust training program, make sure you avoid:

1. *A purely linear, logical design.* Trustworthiness is paradoxical and highly personal. It is best served by nonlinear learning.
2. *A complex competency model.* The tenets and behaviors of trustworthiness are simple, just not easy to implement. An overly sophisticated behavioral model can be a distraction. Keep it simple.
3. *An overambitious agenda.* Soak time, breathing room, and ample opportunities for reflection are nice to have in more traditional training—in trustworthiness training they are all critical.
4. *Intellectualizing.* Talking about trust can be a convenient way to avoid experiential exercises like role-playing. Make time for discussion while keeping the focus on practice.
5. *Underestimating.* Beware your own limiting mind-set about what participants are willing to try ("Oh, they'll never do …" or "We couldn't ask them to do …"). People are remarkably willing to step up given the right combination of motivation, challenge, and safety.
6. *Focusing on traditional metrics.* The results of trustworthiness training may not show up right away or may show up in unexpected ways. Adapt your scorecard accordingly.

From the Front Lines: Role-Playing Pays Off

"The value of role-playing couldn't be highlighted any better than the example that one of our course participants experienced in real time at one of my (Charlie's) sessions. The exercise asked a group of business leaders to play the role of one of their most challenging clients while a colleague held a typical meet-and-greet.

"One male partner chose a woman who was then a presidential appointee at one of Washington's largest government agencies. The partner was flummoxed by two aspects of the relationship. One, a number of her direct reports were using the services of his organization, so he had to be careful of jumping the chain of command. Two, she kept asking for feedback, and what others inside and outside the organization were saying about her, a question he didn't feel he could answer without jeopardizing the firm's relationship.

"The exercise got off to a good start, but then the 'client' asked over and over: 'How are we doing?'

"The other executive in the role play finally said: 'Why do you keep asking that?'

"The 'client,' the senior partner, answered quickly: 'I'm just looking for information.'

"A light bulb went off: She hadn't been asking about how her staff felt about her; she was looking for information outside her own glass bubble as a senior official.

"The senior partner immediately shot off an e-mail asking his client to have coffee and catch up. She answered right away with: 'I'll buy.'"

— *Charles H. Green, about Greg Pellegrino (Global Industry Leader for the Public Sector Industry, Deloitte)*

How to Encourage Risk-Taking

Risk-taking is critical in trustworthiness training. Without risk there is no trust, and if that conceptual point is not reflected in the training itself, it will remain an abstraction. People need to practice taking risks to learn how to take risks. Create a safe space where people can trust each other, and they will make quantum leaps in return. Some examples:

- Do not forgo the getting to know you part of a program.
- Design activities that level the playing field.
- Be very acknowledging of the people who participate in role plays.

Worksheet: Design for Success

Consider the design of your organization's existing or planned trustworthiness training. Which best practices for setting off the aha are included?

☐ Use simple frameworks.
☐ Provide out-of-character experiences.
☐ Fail forward.
☐ Tell stories.
☐ Encourage the tough conversations.
☐ Link in real-life situations.
☐ Incorporate personal feedback.
☐ Make time for reflection.
☐ Mix up learning groups.

For the best practices that you have checked, what's working well? Why?

_____

_____

What might you consider revising or adding?

_____

_____

In what ways does your design make provisions for sustaining aha moments?

☐ Set up action learning groups or learning labs.
☐ Arrange check-in calls and office hours.
☐ Schedule teach-back assignments.
☐ Create online learning communities.
☐ Continue learning with book clubs.
☐ Present 60- to 90-minute webinars to refresh and advance lessons.
☐ Set up peer coaching.
☐ Arrange professional coaching.
☐ Repeat personal assessments.
☐ Provide mastery programs for select leaders.
☐ Train-the-coach/train-the-trainer.

Consider your organizational strategy and culture, along with time, budget, and resource constraints. In what ways is the mix you have selected well-positioned to support your efforts?

_____

_____

What might you consider adding or revising?

List of Lists

Chapter 1 Fundamental Truths

Ten Fundamental Truths

Fundamental Truth 1: Trust Requires Trusting and Being Trusted
Fundamental Truth 2: Trust Is Personal
Fundamental Truth 3: Trust Is about Relationships
Fundamental Truth 4: Trust Is Created in Interactions
Fundamental Truth 5: There Is No Trust without Risk
Fundamental Truth 6: Trust Is Paradoxical
Fundamental Truth 7: Listening Drives Trust and Influence
Fundamental Truth 8: Trust Does Not Take Time
Fundamental Truth 9: Trust Is Strong and Durable, Not Fragile
Fundamental Truth 10: You Get What You Give

The Three Ps of Trust

1. Trust is Personal.
2. Trust is Paradoxical.
3. Trust is Positively correlated to risk.

Chapter 2 Fundamental Attitudes

Five Fundamental Attitudes

Fundamental Attitude 1: Principles over Processes
Fundamental Attitude 2: You Are More Connected than You Think
Fundamental Attitude 3: It's Not about You
Fundamental Attitude 4: Curiosity Trumps Knowing
Fundamental Attitude 5: Time Works for You

Chapter 3 The Dynamics of Influence

Three Steps to Being More Influential

1. Change the way you think about how people think.
2. Understand an important driver of influence: reciprocity.
3. Do a better job of listening, not a better job of making your case.

Five-Point Checklist for Being More Influential in Meetings

1. Before you enter the meeting, take one minute to prepare your mind.
2. When you state your point of view during a meeting, state it crisply and simply.
3. Spend the majority of your time listening.
4. When you get the cue that it is your turn to be listened to, be sure to build on what has been said.
5. When the conversation begins to conclude, summarize the outcome with your partner.

How to Prepare Your Mind
1.   Quietly detach from the outcome.
2.   Remind yourself that the ultimate objective of the meeting is to improve your partner's situation, as well as the relationship between you. Period.
3.   Be willing to be influenced in the process.

Chapter 4 Three Trust Models

Three Trust Models for Being Personally and Organizationally Trustworthy
1.   *The trust equation* lays out the four components of trustworthiness.
2.   *The trust creation process* shows how to build trust in conversations.
3.   *The trust principles* provide a set of values to guide organizational decisions and individual actions.

Obvious Ways to Boost Your Credibility
•   Develop deep expertise in your industry.
•   Stay current with industry trends and business news.
•   Offer your point of view when you have one.

Unexpected Ways to Increase Your Credibility
•   Be willing to say "I don't know," when "I don't know" is the honest answer.
•   Express passion for your subject.
•   Communicate with self-assurance: a firm handshake, direct eye contact (when culturally appropriate), and a confident (not arrogant) air.

Ways to Boost Your Reliability
•   State expectations up front and report on them regularly.
•   Make lots of small promises and consistently follow through on them.
•   Be on time (as culturally appropriate).
•   Communicate if you fall behind and take responsibility for it.
•   Use others' language, templates, dress code, and so on, respecting their norms and environment.

Ways to Promote Intimacy in a Relationship
•   Listening beyond another's words by tuning in to the music of her communications such as tone, emotion, and mood, and then acknowledge those elements out loud.
•   Telling someone what you really appreciate about him, rather than keeping it to yourself.
•   Using a person's name.
•   Sharing something personal about yourself—it makes you human and far more interesting.

Subtle Ways High Self-Orientation Sneaks Into Interactions
•   Rushing to a solution.
•   Hoarding information, resources, and ideas.
•   Talking a lot.
•   Subtly competing for attention and recognition.

Strategies to Lower Your Self-Orientation
•   Take the time to find the best solution.
•   Share time, resources, and ideas.
•   Ask lots of questions from a place of curiosity to figure out what success for your partner really looks like.
•   Negotiate for a true win-win.
•   Listen even when it is uncomfortable to be silent.
•   Speak hard truths, even when it feels awkward to do so.
•   Give your partner the credit.

The Trust Creation Process
•   Engage (E)—offer something of value in an open discussion about issues key to the other.
•   Listen (L)—hear what is important and real to the other and earn the right to offer solutions.

- Frame (F)—state the root issue in terms acceptable to both, using caveats, problem statements, and hypotheses; take personal risks to explore sensitive issues in depth; articulate a point of view.
- Envision (E)—define an alternate reality or to-be state of affairs, including win-win descriptions of outcomes and results along with emotional and political states.
- Commit (C)—jointly articulate actionable next steps that imply commitment and movement on the part of each party.

Examples of Using ELFEC in a Sales Context
- Engage: "I hear X may be an issue for you. Is that right?"
- Listen: "Gee, that's interesting. Tell me more: what's behind that?"
- Frame: "It sounds like what you may have here is a case of Y."
- Envision: "How will things look three years from now if we fix this?"
- Commit: "What if we were to do Z?"

The Trust Principles
- A focus on the other for the other's sake, not just as a means to your own ends.
- A collaborative approach to relationships.
- A medium- to long-term relationship perspective, not a short-term transactional focus.
- A habit of being transparent in all your dealings.

Actions That Will Not Build Trust
- You claim you are customer-focused and yet you …
  - o Define problem statements that overtly or covertly blame the other party for the problem.
  - o Get tentative about suggesting additional work you could do.
  - o Set a goal to double revenue in an account.
- You claim you are collaborative and yet you …
  - o Don't present your ideas until they are fully formed and polished.
  - o Secretly love to win arguments.
  - o Practice sales techniques like Always Be Closing.
- You claim you think in the long-term and yet you …
  - o Set up projects and relationships in ways that are not sustainable.
  - o Make a bad first deal just to get in the door.
  - o Hoard work for yourself when if you were really honest you would admit that a competitor could do a better job.
- You claim you are transparent and yet you …
  - o Say things to yourself or to each other that you don't/won't say to your clients.
  - o Avoid delivering bad news.
  - o Cover up or downplay mistakes so as not to make others uneasy.

Chapter 5 Five Trust Skills

Characteristics of the Five Trust Skills
- They can appear elementary.
- You can practice them, and you should, over and over.
- They are linked.
- Their effect increases when combined with attitudes.

Characteristics of Someone Who Partners Well
- Maintains a mind-set of collaboration, not competition.
- Works from a position of equal status.
- Is willing and able to both lead and follow.
- Balances assertiveness and cooperation.
- Deals with disagreements and missteps productively and gracefully.
- Demonstrates a commitment to sharing responsibility for achieving a goal.
- Takes responsibility for her role in the partnership's successes and failures.

When You Take Risks You:
- Act proactively to reduce ambiguity.
- Acknowledge uncomfortable situations out loud.
- Deliver hard news promptly and concisely.
- Take responsibility for mistakes.
- Are willing to express emotions.
- Share something personal.

Self-Knowledge Blind Spots that Interfere with Building Trust
- You don't realize the full extent of your need to be liked, which interferes with your willingness to say something unpopular, which, in turn, lowers your credibility.
- You are unaware of your strong internal drive to achieve, moving too quickly from listening to commitment, thus rushing the process of trust-building.
- You don't grasp your fear of appearing unprepared, which prevents you from engaging in the messiness that the best collaborations usually require.

Chapter 6 Listen

Four Barriers to Paying Attention
1. A habit of talking
2. Everyday distractions
3. A fear of intimacy
4. The little internal voice

Three Steps for Rational Listening
1. Listening for data
2. Putting it in context
3. Offering acknowledgment

Listening to Build Intimacy
- Listening for nonrational data
- Putting it in context
- Offering nonrational acknowledgment

Nine Ways to Express Empathy
1. "That makes sense."
2. "That's a valid concern/problem."
3. "It sounds like [restate what you heard—words and music]."
4. "If I understand you correctly, _____."
5. "In other words, _____."
6. "So from your perspective, _____."
7. "I can appreciate how [challenging/frustrating/disappointing/unnerving/irritating/lonely/exciting/motivating] that would be."
8. "If I were in your shoes, I would probably be [concerned/upset/angry/disappointed/ disheartened/ready to throw in the towel/happy/relieved/encouraged/psyched], too."
9. "I'm [disappointed/concerned/disheartened/sorry/happy/excited/relieved/encouraged] to hear that."

How to Acknowledge Another When You Don't Agree
- "*I see* you're concerned about investing a lot of money and time without being sure of the return. That makes sense."
- "Sounds like it's imperative for you to have the right executive sponsor in place before we move forward. That makes sense."
- "It makes sense to *consider all the options before you decide which firm you want to hire.*"

How to Acknowledge Groups
- "It sounds like we're 95 percent there in terms of agreeing on XYZ."
- "I'm hearing real concern expressed by at least half the group about ABC."

Seven Listening Best Practices
1. Really care.
2. Tune in.
3. Acknowledge early and often.
4. Express yourself nonverbally.
5. Keep it about them—not you.
6. Get a little Zen.
7. Think out loud.

Three Reasons to Use Empathy in Your Daily Encounters
1. The stakes are low.
2. The environment is target-rich.
3. You will make a big difference for someone.

Chapter 7 Partner

How to Be a Good Partner
- Maintain a mind-set of collaboration, not competition.
- Work from a position of equal status.
- Lead and follow.
- Balance assertiveness and cooperation in the face of conflict.
- Deal with disagreements and missteps productively and gracefully.
- Demonstrate a commitment to sharing responsibility for achieving a goal.
- Take responsibility for your part in the partnership's successes and failures.

Ten Common Partnering Barriers
1. A narrow view of relationships.
2. A win/lose mind-set.
3. Undermanaged self-orientation.
4. Lack of confidence.
5. An overdeveloped ability to criticize.
6. A tendency to either lead or follow.
7. A need for immediate gratification.
8. Intolerance of ambiguity.
9. Discomfort with conflict.
10. Limited view of problems and opportunities.

Chapter 8 Improvise

Techniques You Can Learn from Improv Performers
- Being quick to respond instead of over-thinking.
- Providing "Yes, and ..." responses where they build on what has already been said, instead of contradicting or denying what someone else has offered.
- Subordinating their own egos to support what the collective is creating instead of stealing a scene by hogging the spotlight.
- Giving up being clever and witty and funny and instead getting real.

Four Key Skills of Improv
1. Being open to new ideas
2. Listening
3. Being in the moment
4. Underthinking

Red Alert Role-Play Scenarios for Two or More People
- "I'm very disappointed in your work product."
- "We'd like to find someone else to lead the workshop for us. There are concerns about your style."
- "What experience do you have in XYZ industry?"
- "Why are you so much more expensive?"
- "I'm not sure I really see the point, this is all just common sense."
- "We're giving the account to someone else."

Two Advantages of Thinking Out Loud
- Frees you up to be a better listener.
- Trains you to be collaborative.

Chapter 9 Risk

Four Dynamics between Trust and Risk
1. Trust and risk go hand-in-hand.
2. The relationship between trust and risk is paradoxical.
3. Reasons not to risk are usually personal.
4. Risk-taking is transformative.

Six Ways to Practice Risk-Taking
1. Be proactive about reducing ambiguity.
2. Acknowledge uncomfortable situations out loud.
3. Deliver hard news promptly and concisely.
4. Take responsibility for mistakes.
5. Be willing to express your own emotions.
6. Share something personal.

Where People Go Wrong with Risk Assessment
- Underestimate the value of forthrightness even when the truth being told is unpleasant to hear.
- Overestimate the cost of disapproval.
- Overestimate the probability of a situation righting itself.

To Tell or Not to Tell: The Three-Question Transparency Test
1. Is your reason for not telling for your benefit or for theirs?
2. If you don't tell and he finds out later, will he feel misled?
3. Would you tell her if she were your friend?

When to Name It and Claim It
- When you want to raise a topic that you might otherwise be tempted to avoid.
- Situations that require a metaconversation to break an ineffective pattern.

Topics You May be Tempted to Avoid
- Staffing/team issues
- Pricing
- Scope creep
- Sensitive behavioral topics
- Wrong project or client
- Situations that require a metaconversation
- Aloofness
- Resistance or combativeness
- No communication

Four Steps to Name It and Claim It
1. Define the issue.
2. List all your concerns about speaking the issue.
3. Turn your concerns into one or more caveats.
4. Put it all together.

Four Ways Caveats Can Improve Intimacy
- Warns your partner that something is coming.
- Demonstrates humility.
- Expresses your own emotion and vulnerability, which evokes empathy from another.
- Preemptively defuses a conflict. If they are thinking it and you are stating it, the conflict loses power and the relationship gains power.

Examples of "At the risk of" Caveats
- "At the risk of embarrassing myself …"
- "At the risk of causing some momentary awkwardness …"
- "At the risk of overstepping my bounds …"

Other Effective Caveats
- "Since bad news doesn't get better with age …"
- "I pride myself in my subject matter expertise, and I may be on the verge of looking stupid here …"
- "This is awkward, and there's just no way around it …"
- "I just can't think of a better way to say this …"

Chapter 10 Know Yourself

How Self-Knowledge Blind Spots Impede Trust-Building
- You don't realize the full extent of your need to be liked, and therefore you don't see how it keeps you from saying something unpopular.
- You are not aware of the intensity of your internal drive to achieve.
- You don't fully grasp your discomfort with feeling unprepared.

Three Approaches to Expand Your Self-Knowledge
1. Look inward.
2. Turn blind spots into insights.
3. Experiment regularly.

How to Use Self-Knowledge to Increase Trust
- When you realize the full extent of your need to be liked, you see the importance of developing comfort and skill with saying unpopular things.
- When you are aware of the intensity of your internal drive to achieve, you see the negative impact this has on your ability to be a masterful listener.
- When you fully grasp your discomfort with feeling unprepared, you see how this degrades your ability to improvise and partner.

Chapter 11 Trust-Based Marketing and Business Development

Four Ways to Apply the Four Trust Principles to Sales and Business Development
1. A focus on the other for the other's sake, not just as a means to your own ends.
2. A collaborative approach to relationships.
3. A medium- to long-term perspective, not a short-term transactional focus.
4. A habit of being transparent in all your dealings.

Four Ways to Focus on Your Customer
1. Share ideas.
2. Give away free samples.
3. Tell your prospects why they don't need you.
4. Make cross-selling about your client.

Client Focus in Action

- You're an accounting firm. It's tax season. Everyone thinks you're busy. Surprise them with a two- to three-hour clinic for your clients' kids, who are now college graduates, on how to do their own taxes.
- You're a restaurant owner. You know who your good customers are. Surprise them next visit by picking up the tab. Quietly.
- You're a doctor. When you have good test results for a nervous patient, don't wait for the next visit. Call and celebrate together.
- You're a development director for a charitable organization. Your donors are your customers. Instead of asking them for money, turn the tables—ask how a particular donor is affected by the economy. How can you add value to his life? Who can you put him in touch with?
- Go drop coins in someone's parking meter or pay the toll for the guy behind you. It's cheap behavioral training for client focus. And it makes two people feel good.

Three Ways to Use a Collaborative Approach to Drive New Business

1. Collaborate internally first.
2. Approach networking collaboratively.
3. Collaborate your way into referrals.

Collaboration in Action

- You're a speaker or trainer. Put together a speaking tour or a combined webinar of like-minded people—including those you used to think of as competitors.
- You're a business-to-business (B2B) manufacturing salesperson. Call a key customer. Suggest the two firms sit down together offsite for a day and discuss what you could do better together to make things cheaper, faster, or more profitable for both of you. Be prepared to share your manufacturing process, costs, and profit margins, so you can figure it out together.
- You're in an internal staff group of a large company (HR, Legal, Finance, IT, and so on). Identify three or four of the same departments in other large companies in your geographic area. Create a collaborative work group across the companies that meets (within bounds of legal agendas) to share best practices and work opportunities.
- You're a professional services firm with underemployed staff. Offer to swap similarly underemployed staff with a client. Both will gain valuable perspective and experience without being taken off critical work. The employees involved will feel grateful and challenged. And the linkages between the firms will be strengthened. None of which would easily happen in good economic times.
- You're in a business where sales are large and take time. At the next sales presentation meeting, have a client co-present with you. And make a point of it, saying, "Working collaboratively with you is what we believe in."

Focus on Relationships, Not Transactions

- Build relationships with those you've screened out.
- Promote relationships.

Long-Term Focus in Action

- Pick your top three clients and strategize internally on how you can strengthen your relationship for the long run.
- Help everyone you know who has been laid off.
- If you're a consulting organization, establish your alumni network.
- If a key customer is in the middle of an important job with you and they can't afford for you to finish it, talk it over with them and offer to defer payment until such time as the customer can pay.

How to Be Transparent with Prospects and Clients

- Share your business model.
- Share information.

Transparency in Action

- Share your cost structure with your customers. This will eliminate any suspicions they have about your pricing. They will also appreciate your candor and come to trust you more.
- In sales conversations, compare your product or service to others. Include all relevant information—the good, the bad, and the ugly—to help your customers make informed choices. Some buyers will go with your competitors as a result of what you've shared. Even so, you will still end up with more and better business in the end.
- Tell the truth about your own emotional reality. You are far more likely to get the straight scoop from your client about her reality, which puts you in a much better position to be of service.
- Share information about your backlog, prospective orders, or plans as they affect vendors and suppliers. Having advance, non-binding discussions about the future is invaluable to those who sell to you. Help them, and they will help you.

- Share your product development plans with your customers before the products are ready for prime time. The software industry figured out long ago that users are more likely to buy what they've had a hand in developing, if you give them the chance. If you're in professional services, sharing the early version of a new service with potential clients will give you invaluable insight, help educate your buyers, and increases trust.

Chapter 12 Trust-Based Networking

Benefits of Trust-Based Networking
- Personal commitments to other networkers.
- Greater responsiveness to you in times of need.
- Richer and more positive responses when you request a reference.
- Calls returned faster when you need a favor.
- A genuine sense of well-being that comes from helping others you care about without strings attached.

Ten Best Practices for Trust-Based Networking
1. Be present.
2. Recognize others' contributions.
3. Collaborate.
4. Talk about yourself less and your partner more.
5. Add value.
6. Diversify your network.
7. Research.
8. Make introductions.
9. Take better notes.
10. Keep making contact.

Five Pitfalls of Online Networking
1. Getting down to business too soon.
2. Promoting yourself too much or too aggressively.
3. Faking sincerity.
4. Indiscriminate connection.
5. Confusing party lines with private lines.

Ten Best Practices for Trust-Based Networking Online
1. Engage.
2. Return comments.
3. ABC: Always Be Crediting.
4. Collaborate.
5. Increase your other:self ratio.
6. Set knowledge free.
7. Diversify your online network.
8. Connect within networks.
9. Automate your research.
10. Keep making contact.

Chapter 13 Delivering the Pitch

Nine Rules for Delivering Your Winning Pitch
1. Sometimes the best pitch is no pitch.
2. Don't skip the pre-pitch warm-up.
3. Make it interactive.
4. Have a point of view.
5. Take the preoccupation out of price.
6. With PowerPoint, less is more.
7. Stop selling your qualifications.

8. Do not denigrate the competition.
9. Be willing to ditch the pitch.

How to Make Your Pitch Interactive

- Tell the client ahead of time you would like to ask for reactions.
- Build "And what about you?" questions into your pitch.
- Offer data about similar situations and ask for comment.
- Ask the client if they would consider a first-meeting approach: Instead of a standard pitch, offer to treat the pitch like a first meeting as if you had already been hired.
- If you have had prior pitch conversations, refer to them during your time with the client. It shows you paid attention.

How to Use PowerPoint Effectively

- Most presentations are lengthy leave-behinds in disguise. Build your pitch on the presentation, not the leave-behind.
- Less is more: Limit yourself to six bullets per slide, six words per bullet.
- Do not read aloud what is written: Use stories and metaphors to make your points instead.
- Visuals are great, great, great—use photos, not clipart.
- Except for the title page, lose the logos and fancy backgrounds.

Chapter 14 Handling Objections

Four Common Manipulative Sales Tactics

1. *The Boomerang.* "Sure it costs a lot, but doesn't your wife deserve the best?"
2. *The Feel-Felt-Found Model.* "I sure understand how you feel about that. You're not alone; others have felt that same way. And what we have found is that...."
3. *The Conditional Close.* "So you like the metallic blue color. If I can find one from another store, will you take it today?"
4. *The Deflection.* "Yes, I see what you mean ... hmm ... well, let me show you the range of colors you can have...."

Two Kinds of Wrong-Thinking

1. The win-lose mind-set.
2. Taking it personally.

Three Good Ways to Think about Objections

1. Objections are invitations.
2. Objections are concerns.
3. Objections are opportunities.

Three Ways to Improve the Quality of Your Conversations

1. Change your language.
2. Actively pursue concerns.
3. Meet emotion with emotion.

Sales Conversations: Deadwood Phrases to Ditch

- Are there any objections left?
- If I could X, would you Y?
- Which address should I send that to?

Sales Conversations: Power Phrases to Add

- If I were in your shoes ...
- I sense you have some concerns ...
- Tell me how you feel about that ...

How to Actively Pursue Customer Concerns

- Maintain an ongoing list of customer concerns.
- Review your list of concerns together.

Questions to Keep Current with Clients
- How are we coming along here?
- Is this process helping the decision?
- Are we meeting your time schedule?
- Since we last talked, are there any concerns that have emerged to add to the list?

Chapter 15 Talking Price

Common Pricing Fears
- "I don't want to mention price too early. Because if we lead with a high price to give ourselves bargaining room, they'll reject us before they understand the total picture. And they'll go with someone else."
- "We lost that deal on price. That's the third time this month. The salespeople are right—it's a very price-competitive market out there, and we are pricing ourselves right out of business."
- "I can't believe they objected to our price. We bent over backwards to make it a good price. They are just price-buyers. Either that or the competition is really out to get us."

The Best-Kept Secrets about Talking Price
- You *can* talk about price right up front.
- Price talk is rarely about the price.
- There's a logical way to handle price concerns that keeps your emotions under control.

Two Psychological Issues Driving Sticker Shock
1. The customer's desire to know the price now.
2. The customer's tension about whether his price expectations are reasonable.

How You Increase Price Anxiety When You Avoid Talking Price
1. The longer the wait between price question and answer, the more tension the customer feels.
2. The customer feels responsible and guilty for having been so far off in his initial estimate of the cost.

The Simple Solution to Price Anxiety
- First, talk about price early in the sales conversation.
- Second, make it safe for your customer to have inaccurate initial estimates about price.

Two Sample Statements That Reduce Price Anxiety
1. "At the risk of raising price before we've talked about design or context or value, let me just make sure neither of us— mainly me!—is potentially embarrassed here. I'm guessing that this is going to be something like a low five-digit number. Is that different by a digit or two from what you're expecting? I just want to make sure we're all working in the same region on the likely cost here."
2. "You know, people have a hard time telling pricing apart on these services— they can cost a lot, or a little. They can range from $22,000 to $222,000, depending on a number of factors. We can hone in on what's right for you—I just wanted to let you know there's a big range."

The Three Primary Drivers of Price Concerns
1. Fear of being taken advantage of.
2. Miscommunication about the project or process.
3. Misunderstanding of quality needed.

How to Discuss a Competitor's Bid
- Commit to resolution. Make sure you spend enough time understanding and empathizing with the client's concerns.
- Suggest a series of price drivers. Commit to exploring each in turn.
  a. Start with scope and design issues.
  b. Move on to quality issues.
  c. If the issue is not yet settled, put your business model on the table.

Chapter 16 Closing the Deal

Six Reasons to Avoid Always Be Closing
1. Closing closes down the conversation.
2. Closing is usually attempted prematurely.
3. Closing is seller-centric.
4. Closing objectifies the buyer.
5. Closing is transactional.
6. Closing leads to fewer sales.

Five Practices to Stop Closing and Start Helping
1. Let go of the sale itself.
2. Understand your buyer's motives.
3. Envision a positive future.
4. Keep your personal needs out of it.
5. Replace closing language with action language.

Chapter 17 Developing New Business with Existing Clients

Three Ways to Develop New Business by Expanding Existing Relationships
1. Move *upstream* in the organization.
2. Cross-sell *within* the organization.
3. Seek referrals *outside* the organization.

Seven Questions to Help You Sell Upstream
1. What is the need?
2. What is the want?
3. What is the business case?
4. Who are the key stakeholders?
5. If your existing client has not already raised the issue, why is that?
6. What's in it for your existing client?
7. How will you enlist the support of your existing client?

Cross-Selling: What Clients Need From You
- Someone who can be relied on to do due diligence.
- Someone who understands her business.
- Someone who is on her side.
- Someone who knows when to call another expert on the team.

Three Strategies for Successful Cross-Selling
1. Talk to your client about the new offering.
2. Talk to your colleague about your existing client.
3. Chair their first meeting.

Seven Tips for Requesting Referrals
1. Be direct.
2. Less is more.
3. Make it easy.
4. Be whole-hearted about it.
5. Give your client a gracious way out.
6. Build referral requests into your sales process.
7. Close the loop at the end of a project.

Chapter 18 Selling to the C-Suite

Mental Preparation for Effective C-Suite Selling
- Manage your motives: Think about when *not* to sell to the C-suite.
- Manage your role: Are you presenting yourself as a salesperson—or a sounding board?
- Manage your emotions: Are your own personal reactions in check?

Three Bad Reasons for Targeting the C-Suite
1. You have not succeeded at the lower levels of the organization.
2. You think the C-suite is the only place "real" work gets done.
3. You want the badge of honor.

How Trusted Advisors Can Act as a C-Suite Sounding Board
- Facilitate a collaborative discussion.
- Explore strategic options from his point of view and yours.
- Listen with curiosity and interest.
- Come as close as you can to feeling what it must be like to be *this* CXO facing *these* issues or opportunities.
- Identify ways you can help him make a decision that is right for his organization.
- Speak the truth in a direct, respectful, and unvarnished way.
- Demonstrate a willingness to see things through.
- Recommend or support that no decision be made if choosing to do nothing is the best decision.

How High Self-Orientation Sabotages C-Suite Sales
- You fall back into patterns or habits that are comfortable, but not necessarily effective—like the march of a thousand slides, or being overly aggressive.
- You fail to make an emotional connection with the CXO because you are preoccupied with your own concerns and interests.
- You allow the pressures of time to dominate, attempting to get all of your credentials, your service's benefits, and the reasons for buying out on the table in the first 10 minutes of your meeting.
- You overpromise out of anxiety, and therefore sell something you cannot deliver.

Nine Best Practices for Successful C-Suite Meetings
1. Bring the right mind-set.
2. Prepare, then adapt.
3. Make connecting a priority.
4. Bring five slides (if any), not 50.
5. Listen with empathy.
6. Speak plainly and honestly.
7. Master the 30-second answer.
8. Do your thinking out loud.
9. Watch the CXO's watch, not yours.

Chapter 19 Reviving Stalled Relationships

Stalled Relationship Situations
- You want to get into an account, and you are getting politely brushed off.
- You are at some point in the business development process, and the buyer stops returning your calls.
- You have requested an initial meeting. Despite your best attempts at engaging, you are not getting a reply back.
- You are nearing the end of an assignment and have requested a conversation about follow-on work. You are getting polite, late, or evasive messages, but no meetings.
- You know your buyer is working with a competitor. You have a feeling this has something to do with your buyer's nonresponsiveness, although you do not have proof.

A Thousand Factors for a Communication Breakdown

1. Your original message got lost in transmission.
2. Your buyer is in a new job and does not want to feel bound by past decisions.
3. A decision was reversed by his manager, resulting in embarrassment.
4. The budget got cut.
5. Your buyer just realized she does not have authority to make that decision.
6. Your buyer is overworked and simply has not been able to get back to you.

    …

    …

    …

    1000. You have horribly offended your buyer.

Identify the Problem: What Are You Trying to Do?

- Assuage your own guilt?
- Apologize to the client?
- Get an apology from the client?
- Justify your own actions?
- Engage in an argument against a concern you imagine the client has?
- Get a reaction from the client because you feel disrespected?

Two Basic Strategies to Revive Stalled Relationships

1. Acknowledge the communication barrier.
2. Up the ante.

Three Cases When It's Right to Walk Away

1. There's a competitor on the scene, and she is a trusted advisor to your buyer.
2. Your buyer is simply not interested.
3. You've made an unrecoverable error.

Chapter 20 Starting Off Right

Three Ways Kickoffs Go Wrong

1. Putting tasks before relationships.
2. Putting the present before the past.
3. Putting the plan before the culture.

Four Key Ingredients for a Successful Kickoff

1. Put the agenda on the agenda.
2. Get to know the team.
3. Envision a successful result.
4. Articulate the Rules of Engagement.

Three Ways to Overcome Skepticism

1. If *you* are skeptical, get the opinions of two other seasoned and highly successful project managers from your organization or others.
2. If *your team* is skeptical, then share this chapter with them and hold a meeting to discuss the issue.
3. If *your partner* is skeptical, hold a separate meeting with her to discuss the merits of the more personal dimensions of a successful kickoff.

Chapter 21 Accelerating Trust

Three Steps for Creating Trust Quickly

1. Mind your mind-set.
2. Set your intentions.
3. Demonstrate trustworthiness.

Six Fast Payback Actions to Create Credibility
1. Show you've done your homework.
2. Have and state a point of view.
3. Speak the truth, always.
4. Answer direct questions with direct answers.
5. Express your passion.
6. Convey confidence.

Four Fast Payback Actions to Ratchet Up Reliability
1. Make lots of small promises.
2. Be on time.
3. Use others' terminology.
4. Dress appropriately.

Four Fast Payback Actions to Increase Intimacy
1. Name the proverbial elephant in the room.
2. Listen with empathy.
3. Tell your partner something you appreciate about him.
4. Be yourself.

Seven Fast Payback Actions to Shrink Self-Orientation
1. Give ideas away.
2. Build a shared agenda.
3. Don't solve problems prematurely.
4. Ask open-ended questions.
5. Ask questions that may seem out of scope.
6. Relax your mind.
7. Practice thinking out loud.

Chapter 22 Navigating Politics

Typical Political Challenges
- Dealing with multiple agendas, opinions, priorities, goals.
- People who seek public acknowledgment.
- Corporate cultures that avoid blame or bad press.
- Leaders who avoid risk-taking or directive decision-making.
- Lack of transparency among others.
- More than one person who sees herself as your primary client.
- Getting stuck in the middle of an issue.

Seven Best Practices for Dealing with Organizational Politics
1. See the organization as your client.
2. Put politics on the table.
3. Stay neutral.
4. Frame the issue.
5. Be a guide, not a decision-maker.
6. Envision a positive future.
7. Proceed with respect.

Questions about Navigating Client Politics
- What if you have a strong point of view about what's right?
- How can you protect your own interests while being of service at the same time?
- How do you remain professional and effective?

Temptations When Dealing with Client Politics
- Avoiding conflicts at all costs, taking sides only if forced to take a position.
- Jumping in when you know something about the issue, and/or when the situation has the potential to affect your own business interests.

A Five-Step Model for Navigating Client Politics
- Step 1: Notice political flash-fires.
- Step 2: Reframe the issue.
- Step 3: Determine key players.
- Step 4: Develop your own point of view on the best solutions.
- Step 5: Align your actions.

Five Things to Do When Asked to Share Your Point of View
1. Frame your reply in terms of the root business issue.
2. When the invitation is genuine, respond directly, and without a lengthy supporting argument.
3. When the intent is hostile, decline politely.
4. When you feel forced to respond to an either/or question, refuse politely but firmly.
5. If you are invited to be a part of a conversation about the issue, jump at the chance to facilitate the discussion.

Chapter 23: Shifting from Tactics to Strategy

Four Key Questions to Shift the Conversation from Tactics to Strategy
1. How are you part of the problem?
2. What barriers are preventing your partner from thinking strategically?
3. What really matters to your partner?
4. How can you help clear the path for what matters to your partner?

How You Might Be Part of the Problem
- Your credibility is low—you have yet to establish yourself as a go-to person for strategic matters.
- You are not being transparent about your concerns and frustrations and therefore are not proactively elevating the conversation.
- You are not delivering your message in a way that is easy for your partner to hear it.
- You are spending too much time trying to convince your partner to adopt your ideas, forgetting the power of reciprocity and the value of empathetic listening.
- The majority of your time is spent being responsive to your partner's tactical requests, thereby reinforcing the tactical as what matters most.
- You are making assumptions about your partner's capabilities based on your observations, and sticking her in a box as a result.
- You are focused on your own agenda and therefore not really listening to what matters to your partner.

How to Determine What Barriers Are Preventing Your Partner from Thinking Strategically
- How does the world look from here?
- What are the demands on my time?
- What distractions/challenges/pressures am I dealing with that make it difficult to focus on strategic issues?
- How does it feel to be in my seat?

How to Determine What Really Matters to Your Partner
- What's important to me professionally? What's behind that?
- What's important to me personally? What's behind that?
- How does my tactical orientation serve me?
- Would a strategic orientation help me? If so, in what ways?

How to Clear the Path for What Matters to Your Partner
- What are the connections between what matters to me and what matters to my partner?
- What, if anything, about those connections are compelling from her vantage point?
- Where are the disconnects?

- Does it make sense to proceed? With whom?
- How could I open the conversation in a way that is both respectful and compelling?

Chapter 24 My Client Is a Jerk: Transforming Relationships Gone Bad

Three Reasons Why Saying "My Client Is a Jerk" Is Ineffective
1. It is highly subjective.
2. It is unverifiable.
3. The object of the statements—your client—is not likely to agree.

Three Steps to Transform Difficult Relationships
1. Reframe your thinking.
2. Reframe the problem.
3. Listen masterfully.

How to Reframe Your Thinking
- Are you attached to a particular outcome? Let go.
- Are you attached to winning? Check your ego at the door.
- Are you attached to being justified? Be curious instead.

How to Reframe the Problem
- State the true, root issue in terms acceptable to both parties, using problem statements, caveats, and hypotheses.
- Take personal risks to explore sensitive issues in depth.
- Articulate a point of view.

Characteristics of a Good Problem Statement
- It is a rigorous statement of fact, devoid of blame.
- It reflects a *we* approach, which means it has *you* in it.
- It reflects a longer-term, relationship-based perspective.
- It resonates emotionally as well as rationally.
- It imputes good motives.

Reframing: Five Steps to a Better Problem Statement
1. Write down the problem statement as authentically as you can state it.
2. Take the (exclusive) focus off your partner.
3. Remove any version of the verb "to be."
4. Revisit the subject of your problem statement and make sure your "we" includes both parties.
5. Imagine showing it (or speaking it) to your partner.

Words of Caution (for Creating an Effective Problem Statement)
1. Reframing the problem statement to include both parties is often the hardest step.
2. If you are dissatisfied with the final problem statement, you don't quite have it yet.
3. There are times when a difficult issue needs to be put on the table and the best way to do that is to Name It and Claim It, not reframe the problem.

Chapter 25 Dealing with Untrustworthy People

The Two Most Corrosive Qualities Found in Organizations
1. A tendency to blame others.
2. An inability to constructively confront issues.

Things to Know When You Disagree with the Boss
- You are not the boss of your boss. Your boss is the boss of you. So if the issue ever comes down to who wields the most power, you might want to remember that.

- You will rarely convince anyone that you are right, particularly your boss, as long as that equates to convincing her that she is wrong. If your objective involves being right, then you may have an ego problem.
- You have to earn the right to be right. Your boss won't listen to you until you listen to and understand her.

Increasing Organizational Trust: Why You Need to Lead the Change
- Trust requires truth-telling.
- Trust requires relationship.

Three-Step Approach to Constructive Confrontation
1. Assess the risks.
2. Make a sincere attempt at understanding the other party.
3. Make a decision.

How to Assess the Risks on Paper
- Draw two columns. Start with the negative because it is uppermost on your mind—it will preoccupy you if you put it off.
- Write down the worst-case result.
- Move on to the pluses of taking action. Assign probabilities.
- Then move on to the pluses and minuses of not taking action. Assign probabilities.

What to Do When You Can't Confront
- Assume responsibility.
- Clarify boundaries.
- Articulate your intentions.

Is Walking Away the Best Option?—Four Factors to Consider
1. If everyone seems to be against you, there might be a good reason for it.
2. If this is the third disagreement about principles that you have had in six months, you may be wearing out your colleagues' patience with you.
3. If your boss consistently behaves in untrustworthy ways, seek the advice of others.
4. If you have done all the above, then you need to determine where your personal ethical boundaries lie.

Chapter 26 Trust-Based Negotiations

Common Negotiation Pitfalls
- Zero-sum thinking.
- Being afraid—of losing, of being treated unfairly, of looking foolish; letting the belief that tipping your hand is wrong determine your behaviors.
- Giving in to the temptation to hide or downplay any weaknesses or shortcomings on your side.
- Thinking in terms of sides to begin with.
- Playing it safe by not asking courageous questions, not saying what you really want, or how you really feel.
- Looking for common ground only at the surface level or in the short term.
- Giving in to the pressure of the negotiation at hand, rather than imagining this interaction as one of many interactions over time.
- Not doing enough preparation to clearly articulate why you want what you want.
- Thinking there is only one way to achieve the outcome you want.
- Spending most of your preparation time thinking, feeling, and deciding from *your* vantage point, rather than your partners'.
- Trying to maintain control—of the agenda, the conversation, the outcome.
- Getting stuck in the thinking that "no deal" is not an option.

How Negotiating by the Principles of Trust Fundamentally Changes the Rules of the Game
- *Other Focus.* If you can approach the negotiation from the other's perspective first, then you lower your self-orientation, increase intimacy in the relationship, and generally improve the overall offering.
- *Medium- to Long-Term Perspective.* If you set your sights on the relationship, not the transaction, suddenly you have a large set of options for achieving fairness.
- *Transparency.* You have reason to trust people if you believe that they will only tell you the truth and are willing to be examined about any aspect of it.

- *Collaboration.* If you agree that a fair solution will be clear to each party, you will have a jointly driven measure of success for the negotiation.

13 Ways to Negotiate from Trust

1. Approach the negotiation from the other's perspective first.
2. Set your sights on the relationship, not the transaction.
3. Agree to fairness over time rather than fairness in one instance.
4. Conduct the first negotiation exactly as you would the 100th negotiation—with the same level of comfort and candor.
5. Share what is at stake for you.
6. Be candid about your shortcomings.
7. Bring everything that is being said elsewhere to the table.
8. Agree that if there is a fair solution, it will be clear to each party.
9. Think of your interests as intertwined with others' interests.
10. Be unwavering in your commitment to create joint goals and joint approaches.
11. Do the hard work required to get to the underlying drivers and motives, and then generate as many possible ways of satisfying them as possible.
12. Consider that no deal may be the best outcome for everyone.
13. Be someone around whom others have the psychic freedom to choose what is best for them.

Chapter 27 Building Trust at a Distance

How to Build Intimacy with High-Tech Communication Tools
- Include photos in internal directories and message systems.
- Work the room during meetings: Make a point to engage with team members on a personal as well as a professional basis on webinars, conference calls, and so on.
- Keep remote groups informed. Use cc on e-mail strategically.
- If you are asking something of someone after normal work hours in another location, acknowledge that fact and determine whether it is okay.

How to Raise Reliability in Remote Teams
- Set expectations up front and report on them regularly.
- Schedule regular meetings or check-ins.
- Make yourself available for communication.
- Respond to messages promptly.

How to Create High Touch Environments
- Leverage synchronous tools (such as instant messaging) to increase spontaneous communication.
- Use tools such as electronic bulletin boards to create a sense of shared space.
- Carefully choose communication technologies that are most appropriate to the specific task.
- Make wider use of videoconferencing.

Ten Best Practices for Managing Virtual Teams
1. Make face time happen.
2. Use the right tools.
3. Increase team intimacy.
4. Make your work process consistent.
5. Set communication standards.
6. Set goals and expectations.
7. Avoid over-communication and interruption.
8. Be available.
9. Be explicit.
10. Model trust-based communication.

Chapter 28 Making the Case for Trust

The Main Organizational Benefits of Trust
- Economic benefits of trust
- Social benefits of trust
- Ethical benefits of trust

Six Ways Trust Increases Revenue
1. More and larger sales
2. Repeat business
3. More referrals
4. Faster time to market
4. Faster decisions
6. Better decisions

Four Ways Trust Reduces Costs
1. Lower cost of sales
2. More sole-sourcing
3. Less double-checking and due diligence
4. Less performance tracking

Five Ways Trust Improves External Relationships
1. Earlier involvement
2. More information-sharing
3. Improved communication
4. Greater influence
5. Increased commitment

Five Ways Trust Affects Internal Relationships
1. Greater employee loyalty
2. Increased employee engagement
3. Increased accountability
4. Managerial agility
5. Greater innovation

Stakeholder Benefits from the Trust Equation
- *Credibility*: the ability to believe what an organization and its people say.
- *Reliability*: the ability to reliably depend on an organization to do what it says it will do.
- *Intimacy*: the ability to interact and share confidences with an organization's representatives.
- *Low self-orientation*: the ability of the organization, through its people, to focus on and pay attention to the good of the stakeholders.

Trust Tools Give Leaders More Flexibility
- Trust is simple.
- Trust trumps incentives.
- Trust gets stronger with use.

Why Trust-Based Organizations Have Shared Values
- Trust builds bridges.
- Trust creates culture.

Chapter 29 Creating a Culture of Trust

Five Tools for Implementing a Cultural Shift toward Trust
1. Diagnostic assessment
2. Leading by example

3. The language of trust
4. Storytelling
5. Managing with wisdom, not metrics

Why Benchmarking at the Outset of a New Trust Initiative Is a Critical Step

- It defines the current state in ways that allow a future state to be described.
- It highlights priorities and levels of urgency.
- It sends a message about the concepts that are central to the trust initiative.

Someone Who Leads by Example to Create a Culture of Trust Will

- Trust others inside and outside the organization.
- Be willing to go first.
- Own up to his mistakes.
- Be willing to forgive others for their honest, well-intentioned mistakes.
- Hold *himself* accountable when he doesn't see the behaviors he wants to see in others.
- Take opportunities to provide both positive and corrective coaching in the moment.
- Solicit feedback on his performance—really listen to it, publish it, and act on it.

How People Working to Create Trust-Based Organizations Use Language

- Consistently convey a few simple messages in repeated, memorable phrases.
- Reinforce their commitment to working from principles, not processes.
- Express the shared ideology of the organization (values), and what it explicitly means in terms of personal behavior (virtues).

Nine Reasons That Well-Told Stories Make a Difference When Building a Culture of Trust

1. *Stories have wide appeal*, and therefore address the challenge of mobilizing a diverse audience.
2. *Stories create meaning*: They allow people to make sense of things, to establish an order or relationship, or to put events in a context.
3. *Stories teach lessons* in an engaging way.
4. *Stories make data memorable*, so learning sticks.
5. *Stories are a form of metaphor*, and metaphors help people make connections in ways that our linear, rational minds never allow.
6. *Stories create emotional connection*; they appeal to the heart as well as the head, inviting laughter, tears, discomfort, and appreciation.
7. *Stories lower emotional resistance*. People are more willing to accept ideas when they hear stories, especially when those stories resonate with previously held beliefs.
8. *Stories offer insight* into the character, beliefs, and vulnerability of the storyteller.
9. *Stories inspire action*; they give us intellectual insight into specific behaviors to adopt, and the emotional motivation to do so.

Common Ways that Leaders Focus on the Wrong Measures

- Focus primarily on transactions and processes.
- Emphasize quantitative over qualitative measures.
- Refuse to invest without a precise ROI justification.
- Rely on extrinsic incentives for compliance with organizational values.

Alternatives to Metrics for Trust Initiatives

- Look for evidence of values and virtues being lived on a daily basis. Do people hold each other accountable for trustworthy behavior?
- Listen for changes in the language over time. Do employees talk about the organization as we or they? Do people speak about customers with appreciation and respect?
- Seek qualitative feedback. Interview clients, talk to vendors, and make it safe for employees to be candid about their experience of the organization.
- Invest in doing the right thing. Evaluate opportunities in terms of the big picture, not just the quarterly return. Make decisions that align with your company's values—period.
- Focus on intrinsic rewards. Provide employees with autonomy, opportunities for mastery, and a sense of purpose.

The Trust Roadmap's Five Aspects of Organizational Effectiveness
1. *External Relationships*: how your organization relates to other organizations.
2. *Leadership*: how your leaders behave, both within and outside the organization.
3. *Structure*: how your organization is set up to get work done.
4. *Rewards*: how virtues and values are positively reinforced.
5. *Processes*: how work actually gets done.

Chapter 30 Trust in Internal Staff Functions

Unique Challenges of Dealing with Internal Staff
*   Overfamiliarity
*   Inseparability
*   Poorly defined boundaries

The Top Trust Barriers by Function
*   The IT challenge: improving reliability.
*   The HR challenge: improving credibility.
*   The Legal challenge: realigning around risk profiles.
*   The Finance challenge: increasing intimacy.

Targeted Suggestions for Each Challenge
*   Increase credibility (HR). Improve reliability (IT). Strengthen intimacy via empathy (IT, Legal, Finance). Strengthen intimacy via risk-taking (Legal, Finance). Reduce self-orientation (HR, IT, Legal).

Five Ways Internal Staff Can Enhance Trust
1. To improve credibility, apply your knowledge to a specific client situation—in the client's language.
2. To improve reliability, try increasing the number of promises you make, even small ones. Then make sure to meet them.
3. To improve intimacy via empathy, make a point to learn things about your clients' business lives. Then ask them for help in understanding things that you genuinely don't understand.
4. To improve intimacy via risk-taking, choose a collaborative approach over a custodial one.
5. To reduce self-orientation, see and express issues from your client's vantage point.

Chapter 31 Training for Trustworthiness

Two Challenges to Training for Trustworthiness
1. You cannot learn trustworthiness from a textbook.
2. If your underlying mind-set is not right, trustworthiness skills will be ineffective.

The One-Two Punch for Trustworthiness Training
*   *Experience the aha.* The aha moment is the epiphany about how trust works.
*   *Make it stick.* Practice over time forms habits, develops muscle memory, and reduces the trepidation that interferes with your motivation to apply what you have learned.

How to Set Off the Aha: A Nine-Point Checklist
1. Use simple frameworks.
2. Provide out-of-character experiences.
3. Fail forward.
4. Tell stories.
5. Encourage the tough conversations.
6. Link in real-life situations.
7. Incorporate personal feedback.
8. Make time for reflection.
9. Mix up learning groups.

Eleven Ways to Make It Stick
1. Set up action learning groups or learning labs.
2. Arrange check-in calls and office hours.
3. Schedule teach-back assignments.
4. Create online learning communities.
5. Continue learning with book clubs.
6. Present 60- to 90-minute webinars to refresh and advance lessons.
7. Set up peer coaching.
8. Arrange professional coaching.
9. Repeat personal assessments.
10. Provide mastery programs for select leaders.
11. Train-the-coach/train-the-trainer.

Six Troubleshooting Tips for Trust Training

Avoid these pitfalls:
1. A linear, logical design.
2. A complex competency model.
3. An overambitious agenda.
4. Intellectualizing.
5. Underestimating.
6. Focusing on traditional metrics.

How to Keep Motivation and Interest High
- Give the "why."
- Insist that people be fully present and focused.
  - Design exercises to be realistic and challenging to keep people on their toes.
  - Hold face-to-face programs offsite whenever possible.
  - Be firm about electronic distractions, like laptops and smart phones.
- Make it fun.

How to Encourage Risk-Taking
- Do not forgo the getting to know you part of a program.
- Design activities that level the playing field.
- Be very acknowledging of the people who participate in role plays.

Notes

Chapter 1 Fundamental Truths

1. Source: Charles H. Green, "Do You Trust the Taxi-Driver? Or Not?" *Trust Matters* (blog), March 8, 2010, http://trustedadvisor.com/trustmatters/do-you-trust-the-taxi-driver-or-not.
2. Robert B. Cialdini, *Influence: The Psychology of Persuasion* (New York: Quill, 1984).

Chapter 2 Fundamental Attitudes

1. Mahan Khalsa, interviewed by Charles H. Green. *Trust Matters* (blog), March 23, 2011, http://trustedadvisor.com/trustmatters/trust-sales-and-getting-real-interview-with-author-mahan-khalsa/.
2. Source: Hazel Thompson, "The Surprising Reason You Lost That Last Sale," *Trust Matters* (blog), February 9, 2011, http://trustedadvisor.com/trustmatters/how-your-fear-of-intimacy-lost-you-the-sale.
3. Source: Stewart Hirsch, "Building Trust By Design," *Trust Matters* (blog), June 9, 2011, http://trustedadvisor.com/trustmatters/building-trust-by-design/.

Chapter 3 The Dynamics of Influence

1. Source: Charles H. Green, *Trust-Based Selling* (New York: McGraw-Hill, 2005), 81.
2. Robert B. Cialdini, *Influence: The Psychology of Persuasion* (New York: Quill, 1984).
3. John Gottman and Nan Silver, *Seven Principles for Making Marriage Work* (New York: Crown Publishers, 1999).
4. Source: Andrea Howe, "Everyday Empathy," *Trust Matters* (blog), July 22, 2010, http://trustedadvisor.com/trustmatters/everyday-empathy/.

Chapter 4 Three Trust Models

1. Source: Andrea Howe, "Impeccability vs. Perfection: Who's Got Your Back?" *Trust Matters* (blog), March 4, 2010, http://trustedadvisor.com/trustmatters/Impeccability-vs-Perfection-Whoand8217s-Got-Your-Back/.
2. Source: Andrea Howe, "Old Faithful and Reliability," *Trust Matters* (blog), April 20, 2010, http://trustedadvisor.com/trustmatters/old-faithful-and-reliability/.
3. Ruben Vardanian, interviewed by Michael Useem and Valery Yakubovich, "Russia's Best-Known Investment Banker, Ruben Vardanian, on Building Trust in a Fast-Moving World," *Knowledge@Wharton* (blog), June 11, 2008, http://knowledge.wharton.upenn.edu/article.cfm?articleid=1977.
4. The other could be a client, customer, internal coworker, boss, partner, or subordinate.
5. Ava J. Abramowitz interviewed by Charles H. Green, "Ava J. Abramowitz on Essentials of Negotiation (Trust Quotes #15)," *Trust Matters* (blog), November 3, 2010, http://trustedadvisor.com/trustmatters/ava-j-abramowitz-on-essentials-of-negotiation-trust-quotes-15/.
6. Keith Ferrazzi, *Never Eat Alone: And Other Secrets to Success, One Relationship at a Time* (New York: Crown Business, 2005).

Chapter 5 Five Trust Skills

1. Source: Sandy Styer, "Apollo 13: A Love Song to Collaboration," *Trust Matters* (blog), April 1, 2010, http://trustedadvisor.com/trustmatters/apollo-13-a-love-song-to-collaboration/.
2. Mahan Khalsa, interviewed by Charles H. Green. *Trust Matters* (blog), March 23, 2011, http://trustedadvisor.com/trustmatters/trust-sales-and-getting-real-interview-with-author-mahan-khalsa/.

Chapter 6 Listen

1. Thomas Friedman, Commencement Address, May 18, 2009, Grinnell College. (Archived transcript available at www.grinnell.edu/offices/confops/commencement/archive/2009/friedman.)
2. Source: Charles H. Green, "A Marketing Company That Gets It on Trust," *Trust Matters* (blog), June 20, 2008, http://trustedadvisor.com/trustmatters/a-marketing-company-that-gets-it-on-trust/.
3. Spoken empathy is only one part of empathy; the whole range of nonverbal communication is equally powerful, and must be in sync with the spoken word. In other words, you cannot fake your way into empathy.

Chapter 7 Partner

1. Thomas-Kilmann Conflict Mode Instrument (TKI).
2. Robert Porter Lynch, interviewed by Charles H. Green, "Robert Porter Lynch on Trust, Innovation and Performance (Trust Quotes #2)," *Trust Matters* (blog), March 3, 2010, http://trustedadvisor.com/trustmatters/robert-porter-lynch-on-trust-innovation-and-performance-trust-quotes-2.
3. Source: Sandy Styer, "At the Corner of Assertiveness & Cooperation: Collaboration," *Trust Matters* (blog), April 8, 2010, http://trustedadvisor.com/trustmatters/at-the-corner-of-assertiveness-and-cooperation-collaboration/.
4. Jill Jusko, "How to Build a Better Supplier Partnership," *Industry Week*, May 18, 2011, http://www.industryweek.com/articles/how_to_build_a_better_supplier_partnership_24607.aspx?ShowAll=1/.
5. Daniel Goleman, "Free Won't: The Marshmallow Test Revisited," DanielGoleman.com (blog), August 4, 2007, http://danielgoleman.info/2007/08/24/free-wont-the-marshmallow-test-revisited/.

Chapter 8 Improvise

1. Chip Grizzard, interviewed by Andrea Howe, "Real People, Real Trust: A CEO You Should Know," *Trust Matters* (blog), April 27, 2011, http://trustedadvisor.com/trustmatters/real-people-real-trust-a-ceo-you-should-know/.
2. Cary Paul, "Laughter Is the Best Corporate Medicine," *BossaBlog*, July 14, 2010, http://bossanovaconsulting.com/bossablog/2010/07/14/laughter-is-the-best-corporate-medicine/.
3. Shawn Westfall, "The Fastest Way to Trust: Laughter," *BossaBlog*, May 4, 2011, http://bossanovaconsulting.com/bossablog/2011/05/04/the-fastest-way-to-trust-laughter/.

Chapter 9 Risk

1. Source: Charles H. Green & Andrea P. Howe, "Truth, Lies & Unicorns: The Cost of Dishonesty in Business," *Rain Today*, February 2007, http://www.raintoday.com/pages/2172_truth_lies_unicorns_the_cost_of_dishonesty_in_business.cfm/.

Chapter 10 Know Yourself

1. Daniel Goleman, *Emotional Intelligence: Why It Can Matter More than IQ* (New York: Bantam, 1995).
2. L. J. Rittenhouse, interviewed by Charles H. Green, "L.J. Rittenhouse on Trust and Candor (Trust Quotes #8)," *Trust Matters* (blog), April 14, 2009, http://trustedadvisor.com/trustmatters/lj-rittenhouse-on-trust-and-candor-trust-quotes-8/.
3. Daniel Goleman, *Working with Emotional Intelligence* (New York: Bantam, 2000).

Chapter 11 Trust-Based Marketing and Business Development

1. Richard Branson, "Richard Branson on Winning Customers' Trust," *BNET Owners Only* (blog), March 4, 2011, http://www.bnet.com/blog/smb/richard-branson-on-winning-customers-trust/3872.
2. Source: Charles H. Green, "Day 2 of 5: Trust-based Business Development in a Recession: Principle 1, Client Focus," *Trust Matters* (blog), February 10, 2009, http://trustedadvisor.com/trustmatters/day-2-of-5-trust-based-business-development-in-a-recession-principle-1-client-focus/.
3. Source: Charles H. Green, "Day 3 of 5: Trust-based Business Development in a Recession: Principle 2, Collaboration," *Trust Matters* (blog), February 11, 2009, http://trustedadvisor.com/trustmatters/day-3-of-5-trust-based-business-development-in-a-recession-principle-2-collaboration/.

4. Joe Girard and Stanley H. Brown, *How to Sell Anything to Anybody* (Fireside, 2006), 38.

5. Source: Charles H. Green, "Day 4 of 5: Trust-Based Business Development in a Recession: Principle 3, Long-Term and Relationship Focus," *Trust Matters* (blog), February 12, 2009, http://trustedadvisor.com/trustmatters/day-4-of-5-trust-based-business-development-in-a-recession-principle-3-long-term-and-relationship-focus/.

6. Source: Hazel Thompson, "The Surprising Reason You Lost That Last Sale," *Trust Matters* (blog), February 9, 2011, http://trustedadvisor.com/trustmatters/how-your-fear-of-intimacy-lost-you-the-sale.

7. Stewart Hirsch, comment on Andrea Howe, "Trust and Golf: How Neither Makes Sense," *Trust Matters* (blog), October 9, 2009, http://trustedadvisor.com/trustmatters/trust-and-golf-how-neither-makes-sense/.

8. Source: Charles H. Green, "Day 5 of 5: Trust-based Business Development in a Recession: Principle 4, Transparency," *Trust Matters* (blog), February 13, 2009, http://trustedadvisor.com/trustmatters/day-5-of-5-trust-based-business-development-in-a-recession-principle-4-transparency.

Chapter 12 Delivering the Pitch

1. Michelle Peluso, interviewed by Daisy Wademan Dowling, "The Best Advice I Ever Got: Michelle Peluso, President and Chief Executive Officer, Travelocity," *Harvard Business Review*, October 2008, http://hbr.org/2008/10/the-best-advice-i-ever-got-michelle-peluso-president-and-chief-executive-officer-travelocity/ar/1/.

Chapter 13 Delivering the Pitch

1. Source: Andrea Howe, "Trust and Golf: How Neither Makes Sense," *Trust Matters* (blog), October 9, 2009, http://trustedadvisor.com/trustmatters/trust-and-golf-how-neither-makes-sense/.

2. Source: Charles H. Green, "The Point of Listening Is Not What You Hear, But the Hearing Itself," *Trust Matters* (blog), October 26, 2007, http://trustedadvisor.com/trustmatters/the-point-of-listening-is-not-what-you-hear-but-the-hearing-itself/.

3. Source: Craig Leach, interviewed by Charles H. Green, "Best B2B Sale of the Month: Selling by Doing, Not Selling by Telling," *Trust Matters* (blog), December 3, 2009, http://trustedadvisor.com/trustmatters/best-b2b-sale-of-the-month-selling-by-doing-not-selling-by-telling.

Chapter 14 Handling Objections

1. Neil Rackham, interview by Charles H. Green, "Neil Rackham on Trust in Professional Selling (Trust Quotes #5)," *Trust Matters* (blog), March 24, 2010, http://trustedadvisor.com/trustmatters/neil-rackham-on-trust-in-professional-selling-trust-quotes-5/.

Chapter 16 Closing the Deal

1. See, for example, William T. Brooks and Thomas M. Travisano, *You're Working Too Hard to Make the Sale* (New York: McGraw-Hill, 1995). See also interview with Neil Rackham, author of SPIN Selling (*Trust Matters* [blog], March 24, 2010, http://trustedadvisor.com/trustmatters/neil-rackham-on-trust-in-professional-selling-trust-quotes-5).

2. Neil Rackham, *SPIN Selling* (New York: McGraw Hill, 1988).

3. See interview with Neil Rackham about his research for *SPIN Selling* (Trust Matters [blog], March 24, 2010, http://trustedadvisor.com/trustmatters/neil-rackham-on-trust-in-professional-selling-trust-quotes-5).

4. Note that for low-priced goods, sellers who were trained in closing techniques had slightly shorter sale times and a slightly increased rate of sale (76 percent vs. 72 percent). In other words, closing techniques increased sales only slightly.

Chapter 17 Developing New Business with Existing Clients

1. See Frederick Reichheld, *The Loyalty Effect: The Hidden Force Behind Growth, Profits and Lasting Value* (Harvard Business School Press, 1996).

2. Sally Foley Lewis, comment on Charles H. Green, "Tell Your Customers Why They Don't Need You," *Trust Matters* (blog), January 5, 2011, http://trustedadvisor.com/trustmatters/tell-your-customers-why-they-dont-need-you/.

3. A particular case of selling upstream—selling to the C-Suite—is addressed in Chapter 18.

Chapter 21 Accelerating Trust

1. Source: Charles H. Green, "Top Trust Myths: 1 of 2: Trust Takes Time," *Trust Matters* (blog), July 14, 2010, http://trustedadvisor.com/trustmatters/top-trust-myths-1-of-2-trust-takes-time/.
2. Thomas Baumgartner, Markus Heinrichs, Aline Volanthen, Urs Fischbacher, and Ernst Ferhr, "Oxytocin Shapes the Neural Circuitry of Trust and Trust Adaptation in Humans," *Neuron* 58, no. 4 (2008): 639–650.
3. Peter A. Boss, David Terburg, and Jack van Honk, "Testosterone Decreases Trust in Socially Naïve Humans," *PNAS* 107, no. 22 (2010): 9991–9995.

Chapter 25 Dealing with Untrustworthy People

1. These strategies do not apply to cases involving legal violations.
2. Source: Charles H. Green, "How to Convince Your Boss You're Right," *Trust Matters* (blog), October 18, 2010, http://trustedadvisor.com/trustmatters/how-to-convince-your-boss-youre-right/.

Chapter 26 Trust-Based Negotiations

1. Source: Charles H. Green, "Negotiation and the Short Term Performance Trap," *Trust Matters* (blog), July 23, 2007, http://trustedadvisor.com/trustmatters/negotiation-and-the-short-term-performance-trap/.
2. Roger Fisher, William Ury, and Bruce Patton, *Getting to Yes: Negotiating Agreement Without Giving In* (New York: Houghton Mifflin Harcourt, 1991).

Chapter 27 Building Trust at a Distance

1. Darleen DeRosa, "Virtual Success: The Keys to Effectiveness in Leading from a Distance," *LIA* 28, no. 26 (2009): 9–11.
2. Kelly Pate Dwyer, "How to Manage Employees in Remote Locations," CNET, CBS, September 27, 2007, http://www.bnet.com/article/how-to-manage-employees-in-remote-locations/165147/.
3. Pearn Kandola, "The Psychology of Effective Business Communications in Geographically Dispersed Teams" (CISCO Whitepaper Executive Summary, September 2006), http://newsroom.cisco.com/dlls/2006/eKits/psychology_business_comm.pdf/.
4. Darleen DeRosa and Richard Lepsinger, *Virtual Team Success: A Practical Guide for Working and Leading from a Distance* (San Francisco: John Wiley & Sons, 2010).
5. Pearn Kandola, "The Psychology of Effective Business Communications in Geographically Dispersed Teams" (CISCO Whitepaper Executive Summary, September 2006), http://newsroom.cisco.com/dlls/2006/eKits/psychology_business_comm.pdf/.

Chapter 28 Making the Case for Trust

1. Francis Fukuyama, *Trust: The Social Virtues and the Creation of Prosperity* (New York: Simon & Schuster, 1995).
2. Eric M. Unslauer, *The Moral Foundations of Trust.* (Cambridge: Cambridge University Press, 2002).
3. John Gottman, *The Science of Trust: Emotional Attunement for Couples.* (New York: W. W. Norton & Company, 2011).
4. See Frederick Reichheld, *The Loyalty Effect: The Hidden Force Behind Growth, Profits and Lasting Value* (Boston: Harvard Business School Press, 1996).
5. See, for example, Francis Fukuyama, *Trust: The Social Virtues and the Creation of Prosperity* (New York: Simon & Schuster, 1995).
6. John Helliwell and Haifang Huang, "Well-Being and Trust in the Workplace," *Journal of Happiness Studies* (October 24, 2010): 1–21.
7. Interested readers may want to look at the research of Trust Across America (www.trustacrossamerica.com), who have created and back-tested a model of stock market performance by highly trustworthy companies, showing a powerful correlation.

Chapter 29 Creating a Culture of Trust

1. Source: Charles H. Green, "What a Trust-Based Company Looks Like," *Trust Matters* (blog), March 2, 2010, http://trustedadvisor.com/trustmatters/what-a-trust-based-company-looks-like/.
2. David Maister, "Creating a High-Trust Organization," *Passion, People, and Principles* (blog), May 24, 2006, http://davidmaister.com/blog/97/Creating-a-High-Trust-Organization.
3. David Maister, "Accountability: Effective Managers Go First," *Strategy and the Fat Smoker Podcast* (podcast), http://davidmaister.com/podcasts/7/115/.
4. Source: Charles H. Green,"A Trust-Based Organization: Bangor Savings Bank," *Trust Matters* (blog), May 26, 2010, http://trustedadvisor.com/trustmatters/a-trust-based-organization-bangor-savings-bank/.
5. Sims Wyeth, "Public Speaking: Split Shot Audience," *High Stakes Presentations* (blog), Syms Wyeth & Co., www.simswyeth.com/tag/story-telling-and-speaking/.
6. According to Michael Margolis, author of *Believe Me: The Art of Business Storytelling* (New York: Get Storied Press, 2009), anthropologists contend that 70 percent of everything we learn—even as adults—is through stories.
7. Anne Miller has written a book on precisely this subject, called *Make What You Say Pay* (Chiron Associates, 2010). In chapters organized by application, Miller gives numerous examples of metaphors: to explain new concepts, to simplify a complex pitch, to shift a paradigm, to close a deal, and more.
8. Sean Kavanagh, "Storytelling Tips and the Irish Tradition," *The Ariel Group InterAct Blog* (blog), http://blog.arielgroup.com/blog-1/bid/22001/Storytelling-Tips-The-Irish-Tradition/.
9. Sims Wyeth, "Public Speaking."
10. Source: Charles H. Green, "Accenture CEO Bill Green: What Leading from Principle Sounds Like," *Trust Matters* (blog), June 21, 2010, http://trustedadvisor.com/trustmatters/accenture-ceo-bill-green-what-leading-from-principle-sounds-like/.
11. Daniel Pink, *Drive* (New York: Riverhead Books, 2009).
12. Marvin Weisbord, *Productive Workplaces: Organizing and Managing for Dignity, Meaning and Community* (San Francisco: Jossey Bass, 1987).
13. McKinsey 7S Framework, www.mindtools.com/pages/article/newSTR_91.htm/.

Chapter 30 Trust in Internal Staff Functions

1. We recognize there are some specific exceptions to this rule; cases where institutional opposition should intentionally be built in. Examples include the ombudsman role, internal audit, and certain financial risk managers.
2. Source: Charles H. Green, "Negotiation and the Short Term Performance Trap," *Trust Matters* (blog), July 23, 2007, http://trustedadvisor.com/trustmatters/negotiation-and-the-short-term-performance-trap/.

Chapter 31 Training for Trustworthiness

1. BossaNova Consulting, "Learning that STICks" (BossaNova Consulting Whitepaper, November 2008), www.bossanovaconsulting.com/resources/learningthatSTICks.pdf/.
2. Jonah Lehrer, *How We Decide* (New York: Houghton Mifflin, 2009), 50.
3. This parallels William James's descriptions in *Varieties of Religious Experience* (New York: Library of America, 1988) of the "once-born" and the "twice-born." The once-born come into the world religiously, live religious lives of peace and happiness, and die at peace with their God and their religion. The twice-born, by contrast, have been to hell and back—and know the difference. Their religion is constantly informed by a sense of grace, because they know how thin is the line that separates sanity and insanity, rich and poor, lucky and unlucky.
4. Kolb Learning Model.
5. Sandra Kerka, "Journal Writing and Adult Learning," *ERIC Digest*, no. 174 (1996).
6. BossaNova Consulting, "Learning that STICks" (BossaNova Consulting Whitepaper, November 2008), www.bossanovaconsulting.com/resources/learningthatSTICks.pdf/.
7. A form of action learning came into the public eye with Jack Welch's well-known "Work-Outs": large groups of employees, aided by facilitators, working together to find solutions to ongoing problems within the business. See Thomas A. Stewart, "GE Keeps Those Ideas Coming," *Fortune* 12, no. 4 (August 12, 1991): 40–45.
8. David Maister, "Why Most Training Is Useless," http://davidmaister.com/articles/1/96/.

Selected Bibliography

Abramowitz, Ava J. *Architect's Essentials of Negotiation*. Hoboken, NJ: John Wiley & Sons, 2009.

Brooks, William T., and Thomas M. Travisano. *You're Working Too Hard to Make the Sale*. New York: McGraw-Hill, 1995.

Cialdini, Robert B. *Influence: The Psychology of Persuasion*. New York: Quill, 1984.

Covey, Stephen R. *The 7 Habits of Highly Effective People*. New York: Free Press, 2004.

DeRosa, Darleen, and Richard Lepsinger. *Virtual Team Success: A Practical Guide for Working and Leading from a Distance*. Hoboken, NJ: John Wiley & Sons, 2010.

Ferrazzi, Keith. *Never Eat Alone: And Other Secrets to Success, One Relationship at a Time*. New York: Crown Business, 2005.

Firestein, Peter. *Crisis of Character: Building Corporate Reputation in the Age of Skepticism*. New York: Union Square Press, 2009.

Fisher, Roger, William Ury, and Bruce Patton. *Getting to Yes: Negotiating Agreement Without Giving In*. New York: Houghton Mifflin Harcourt, 1991.

Fukuyama, Francis. *Trust: The Social Virtues and the Creation of Prosperity*. New York: Simon & Schuster, 1995.

Galford, Robert M., Charles H. Green, and David H. Maister. *The Trusted Advisor*. New York: Free Press, 2001.

Girard, Joe, and Stanley H. Brown. *How to Sell Anything to Anybody*. New York: Fireside, 2006.

Goleman, Daniel. *Emotional Intelligence: Why It Can Matter More than IQ*. New York: Bantam, 1995.

Goleman, Daniel. *Working with Emotional Intelligence*. New York: Bantam, 2000.

Gottman, John. *The Science of Trust: Emotional Attunement for Couples*. New York: W. W. Norton & Company, 2011.

Gottman, John, and Nan Silver. *Seven Principles for Making Marriage Work*. New York: Crown Publishers, 1999.

Green, Charles H. *Trust-Based Selling*. New York: Free Press, 2001.

Illig, Randy, and Mahan Khalsa. *Let's Get Real or Let's Not Play: Transforming the Buyer/Seller Relationship*. New York: Portfolio Hardcover, 2008.

Lehrer, Jonah. *How We Decide*. Boston: Houghton Mifflin, 2009.

Margolis, Michael. *Believe Me: The Art of Business Storytelling*. New York: Get Storied Press, 2009.

Pink, Daniel. *Drive*. New York: Riverhead Books, 2009.

Rackham, Neil. *SPIN Selling*. New York: McGraw-Hill, 1988.

Reichheld, Frederick. *The Loyalty Effect: The Hidden Force behind Growth, Profits and Lasting Value*. Boston: Harvard Business School Press, 1996.

Rittenhouse, L. J. *Buffett's Bites*. New York: McGraw-Hill, 2010.

Rittenhouse, L. J. *Do Business with People You Can Trust: Balancing Profits and Principles*. New York: andBEYOND Communications, 2007.

Unslauer, Eric M. *The Moral Foundations of Trust*. Cambridge: Cambridge University Press, 2002.

Weisbord, Martin. *Productive Workplaces: Organizing and Managing for Dignity, Meaning and Community*. San Francisco: Jossey-Bass, 1987.

About the Authors

Charles H. Green

Charles H. Green is author of *Trust-Based Selling* (2005), and coauthor of the bestselling business book *The Trusted Advisor* (with David H. Maister and Robert M. Galford, 2000), ranked a Top 25 Business Book by *Inc.* magazine and 800-CEO-Read.

As founder and CEO of Trusted Advisor Associates, Green has been researching, teaching, and coaching the building of trust in business settings for 15 years, working with global firms from Boston to Beijing to Barcelona. He previously worked with the MAC Group and its successor, Gemini Consulting, for 20 years, where his roles included strategy consulting, VP Planning, and other leadership positions.

Focusing on trust in business relationships, Green works with complex organizations to improve trust in sales, internal trust between organizations, and trusted advisor relationships with external clients and customers. His focus is on trust as it affects human relationships, including trust in ethics, social relationships, politics, and psychology.

In addition to his books, Green has written a number of articles in leading business journals, including *Harvard Business Review*, *Directorship Magazine*, *American Lawyer*, the *CPA Journal*, and *Commercial Lending Review*. He is also a contributing editor at RainToday.com, and writes at the highly respected business blog Trust Matters (www.trustedadvisor.com/trustmatters).

He holds a degree in philosophy from Columbia University (1972) and an MBA from Harvard Business School (1976).

Andrea P. Howe

Andrea P. Howe is the founder and President of BossaNova Consulting Group and Director of Learning Programs for Trusted Advisor Associates. In 20 years of consulting, she has designed and delivered hundreds of off-sites, workshops, presentations, and learning programs in interpersonal skills and mind-sets. She previously worked for the technology consulting firm American Management Systems (AMS), where her roles included project manager, client relationship manager, and Director of Leadership Development.

A skilled seminar leader serving top global firms in accounting, consulting, and other professional services, her areas of focus include building trusted advisors, trust-based selling, and trust coaching.

A returning guest lecturer for MBA students at American University and George Washington University, Howe holds an MS in Organization Development from the American University/NTL program (2002), a BBA in Computer Information Systems from Texas A&M (1992), and certifications in team development, collaborative problem-solving, and action learning.

She writes at the highly respected business blog Trust Matters (www.trustedadvisor.com/trustmatters).

Index